HOW TO WRITE WINNING
PROPOSALS FOR YOUR
COMPANY OR CLIENT

HOW TO WRITE WINNING PROPOSALS FOR YOUR COMPANY OR CLIENT

Ron Tepper

WILEY

JOHN WILEY & SONS

New York • Chichester • Brisbane • Toronto • Singapore

This publication is designed to provide accurate and
authoritative information in regard to the subject
matter covered. It is sold with the understanding that
the publisher is not engaged in rendering legal, accounting,
or other professional service. If legal advice or other
expert assistance is required, the services of a competent
professional person should be sought. *From a Declaration
of Principles jointly adopted by a Committee of the
American Bar Association and a Committee of Publishers.*

Library of Congress Cataloging in Publication Data:

Tepper, Ron, 1937–
    How to write winning proposals for your company or
client / Ron Tepper.
        p.   cm.
    Bibliography: p.
    ISBN 0-471-60932-3—ISBN 0-471-52948-6 (pbk.)
    1. Proposal writing in business.   I. Title.
HF5718.5.T46   1988
658.1'5224—dc19   88-17217
                                                    CIP

Printed in the United States of America

10 9 8 7 6 5 4 3 2 1

Contributors

Don Kracke: An advertising and marketing executive with more than 30 years experience. A decade ago, he founded the Design Center, a company that has revolutionized licensing and design in housewares and other related fields. His proposals to companies in a wide variety of industries have resulted in contracts with companies ranging from Sears to Coca Cola. Mr. Kracke, an author himself (*How to Turn Your Ideas into a $Million*), is outspoken about how proposals should be written, and the facts he has gathered to back up his opinions are impressive.

John Hamond: For nearly 20 years, Mr. Hamond has been writing internal and external research and development proposals for one of the major aerospace and defense firms in the country. His job is to sell his management, as well as executives in other companies, on investing in the future. Without any formal training, his proposals have had more than an 80 percent success ratio. The format he has devised for Request for Proposal (RFP) writing, as well as for his internal approaches, are detailed within this book.

Carol Geisbauer: There are few proposal areas more challenging or difficult than that of grants. Ms. Geisbauer has been answering RFPs for her nonprofit organization (Helpline) for eight years. Her track record is impressive: On the average she gets 20 out of 25 grants funded each year. Her expertise is such that she is utilized by many agencies as a professional RFP reader. In that capacity,

v

she reads and grades an average of 450 proposals a year. She has definite ideas as to what makes a proposal a winner—or a loser.

Gary Minor: Mr. Minor has spent his entire aerospace engineering career submitting RFPs to government agencies. His company, TRW, is one of the most profitable and successful contractors in the country, and last year his division accounted for nearly $250 million worth of business. Minor maintains that "not all RFPs are as they appear to be. There are 'general' and 'specific' ones that all vendors should be aware of before they go to the trouble of submitting a proposal."

Pat Unangst: Ms. Unangst has been evaluating RFPs and other proposals for the past ten years. She points out why RFPs have changed, and the surprising new elements that vendors will find in the proposals of the future. She spends a good deal of her time formulating and writing RFPs and evaluating submissions. There are ways for vendors to obtain valuable information before they submit any proposal, but few take advantage of the outlets available to them.

Sam Schauerman: One of the most distinguished educators in the country. President of El Camino College, Dr. Schauerman has been in the grant/proposal field for more than three decades. He provides insight into the approach both private foundations and others are looking for when they read proposals. He also provides some intriguing thoughts on the procedures that internal proposals should follow.

Jim Baxter: One of the most important elements in any proposal is "proposalmanship," which this aerospace/engineering veteran explains in depth. Mr. Baxter, who has two decades of experience in both external and internal proposal writing, has become an authority on "proposal areas of the future."

Dan McClain: President of one of the largest chamber of commerce organizations in the country, Mr. McClain has not only written proposals for funding, but has spent time on the other side of the fence where he saw and evaluated numerous proposals that were submitted to governmental organizations. He has done a thorough analysis of what differentiates a "good" from a "bad" proposal, and the important part that research plays in both, whether it be in-house or external.

Ed Pearson: An engineer, Mr. Pearson deals with one of the most volatile type of proposals imaginable—proposals to local governments and politicians. The last ten years have led to significant changes that Mr. Pearson outlines. The proposal of two decades ago would have little chance of passing today.

Jay Abraham: A marketing consultant and multimillionaire, Mr. Abraham's writing style is unique to proposal writing. He is one of the few consultants who specializes in the "letter/proposal," a difficult document to write and one that differs dramatically from the typical written proposal. Nevertheless, with an unorthodox approach that he maintains others can imitate, he has built a thriving young company, with the bulk of his business coming from cold calls that he closes with his letter/proposal.

Bob Ritchie: A former vice president of one of the largest aluminum manufacturers in the country, Mr. Ritchie is noted for his expertise in the area of internal proposals and his analysis of the politics that comes into play when any in-house proposal is presented. Today, Mr. Ritchie, who spent nearly 20 years as a company employee, runs his own communications firm, and makes almost as many external proposals as he did internal while a corporate executive.

Raelene M. Arrington: Ms. Arrington is marketing director of one of the "Big 8" accounting firms—a company that is extremely active in proposal writing. Accounting firms no longer just present proposals to prospective clients for annual reports and audits; they are writing prospective companies' proposals on everything from computer integration to mergers and acquisitions.

Joe Izzo: CEO of an aggressive, profitable data processing firm that makes proposals to some of the largest companies in the country. Mr. Izzo stresses the importance of research when making any proposal, whether it is internal or external. He explains that having a majority in favor of your proposal does not always guarantee a contract—and he tells why.

Paul Hackett: Mr. Hackett is a principal in three different companies and has been researching and writing proposals (both internal and external) in the private sector for close to 20 years. In his opinion, proposal writing for companies in the private sector has changed dramatically and will continue to do so in the future because of a number of governmental factors and new laws that potential clients are facing.

Larry Schmidt: Mr. Schmidt has dealt with governmental agencies for the past 20 years. He maintains there is a growing sophistication among agencies and consumers that has made proposal writing and presentations more complex and difficult than ever. "Oftentimes," he says, "it is not the decision-makers but their supporting staff that makes the decision." And it is important to recognize the true decision-makers with any proposal.

Bill Johnson: Mr. Johnson is CEO of his own firm, and cautions all those making proposals to be aware of "the changing ethics" they are going to find within companies and potential clients in the private sector. Mr. Johnson is unusual in his field in that his proposals are all paid for by the prospective clients.

Ed Velton: A consultant who operates Positioning to Win, Inc., a nationwide proposal consulting firm that specializes in aiding companies answering RFPs and helping them win big dollar government contracts. Mr. Velton volunteers some provocative ideas on proposal writing today and how companies can improve their "batting average."

Tom Kaplin: A partner in Techmedia, a Philadelphia-based consulting firm that has carved a reputation in the defense industry with its expertise in RFPs, Mr. Kaplin offers some surprising thoughts as to why companies and subcontractors are having problems with government agencies.

Sam Brownell: Mr. Brownell works for one of the top defense contractors in the country. His division is responsible for all the proposals submitted for his firm, and last year it brought in nearly $100 million worth of business. His experience dates back nearly two decades.

Acknowledgments

In addition to the many consultants in both the private and public sectors who gave their time for this book, I would like to extend a special thanks to John Wiley & Sons editor Michael Hamilton, who contributed many of the ideas and the approach for this book.

RON TEPPER

Contents

CONTENTS

Introduction

Merriam-Webster and Don Kracke have a difference of opinion. Webster defines a proposal as a document "put forward for consideration." While Kracke would not necessarily disagree with that definition, he feels those words leave out the real purpose of a proposal—proposals are "vehicles aimed at getting someone to part with their money. And," adds Kracke, "anytime you go after the purse strings you had better have a convincing argument."

In other words, proposals are not just requests, they are persuasive, logical propositions loaded with solid, factual support and backup in order to sell someone, some company, or some agency.

They are also documents that are not difficult to write. Kracke should know. He has been writing them for more than 30 years, and has sold more than 200 major ideas to clients via proposals. He is also one of eight private industry executives who contributed their confidential thoughts and expertise to this book. These eight executives from the private sector are joined by nine from the government and public area, as well as two consulting specialists who present a unique insight into RFPs (Request for Proposal) and RFQs (Request for Quotation), the two most common proposals submitted to government agencies.

Together, these 19 professionals have more than 400 years' experience in proposal writing. In the private sector, Kracke has been successful with more than 70 percent of his proposals. On the government and public sector side, a developmental engineer has been writing proposals for 19 years with an 80 percent success ratio. His approach to proposals and his skill in the area is the envy of many in the defense and aerospace field.

There is advice from the executive director of a small, community-based organization who has a track record of succeeding more than 80 percent of the time when she goes after a grant or RFP, plus the insight of Dr. Sam Schauerman, a college president who competes for foundation funds.

The contributors to this book have researched and encountered every internal and external proposal situation imaginable. Their successes range from innovative external proposals for SDI (or "Star Wars") and Coca Cola® to selling internal management on new corporate structures, engineering developments, and research and development (R&D) projects.

Throughout the book, they carefully detail the steps involved in successful proposal writing. In addition, the contributors:

- Analyze the language and "true" meaning behind the RFPs and RFQs that are issued by the government
- Show how the successful proposer finds out about RFPs and influences them long before they are written
- Detail how to get to the decision-makers and avoid wasting time with proposals that will never fly
- Detail the steps to making successful internal presentations, and explain why a majority in favor of your proposal does not always ensure victory
- Discuss graphics, format, style, language, psychology, and the verbal proposal, which is a critical part of the internal presentation
- Dissect proposal writing and show the key elements involved in putting together an effective, saleable "pitch"
- Punch holes in long-held theories about how proposals should be written and presented
- Include some of their most successful proposals so readers can get a first-hand look at what a winning proposal should look like

In addition, the 19 contributors also spend time projecting what areas, both internal and external, will comprise the hottest proposals of the future.

Most important, their advice and case histories are all presented in practical, how-to terms. There is no theory involved. Everything is based upon past successes . . . or failures from which valuable lessons can be learned.

Despite the variety of occupations and the multitude of different types of proposals these 19 individuals submit, there are a number of opinions and techniques they share. For example, all stress the need for research—whether it is an RFP or a consultant making a pitch to a private company—before a word is ever placed on paper, or an internal proposal is ever presented at a meeting. They all emphasize the critical role a verbal presentation plays when making an internal proposal.

A portion of the information supplied by engineers and management in the governmental/aerospace/public sector was confidential, although certainly not secret nor in violation of any government security clearances. However, in order to protect the privacy of certain individuals in the engineering and high technology sector, we have changed their names and those of their companies.

Suffice to say, the engineering contribution relating to both external and internal proposal writing for aerospace and other high tech companies, came from senior management and widely recognized leaders in the field. It could not have been utilized without confidentiality.

Equally revealing were the comments from those in the private sector. For the most part, their names or affiliations have not been changed.

CHAPTER 1

Proposals—
They Have Changed

The more things seem to change,
the more they remain the same.

That adage may be accurate for some things, but it is far from the truth when it comes to proposal writing. Few things have changed more than the art of proposal writing.

Generally, proposals fall into the following categories:

1. *Internal Proposals.* Where engineers and others vie for R&D funds as well as money for new product (and idea) development, new plants, and reorganization within a firm. These proposals must be decided upon by top management. It takes a selling job within your own company.

2. *Private Industry Proposals.* Where service and other companies compete for business with each other. Their prospective clients range from small, entrepreneurial firms to large, Fortune 500 companies. Private industry proposals encompass everything from consultants to companies trying to sell products.

3. *RFPs (Request for Proposals) and RFQs (Request for Quotation) and Grants.* Where competition for government agency and foundation dollars is intense. To answer an RFP (Request for Proposal) requires the most research and paperwork. It is the government's (or a public agency's) way of asking for a

1

proposal. An RFQ (Request for Quotation) differs slightly. RFQs are either the government's or a public agency's way of asking for a "quote" for a particular product or service. In other words, it is a matter of the proposer supplying a product and pricing it. RFQs are simpler and quicker to submit. Grants are the same as an RFP; they usually follow the same format. Generally, grants come from a foundation or an agency that has funds to give.

All successful proposals, whether they be private industry, public sector, or internal, do one thing: They answer needs. They do not sell the services of a company, but they show how that company (or a consultant from that company) can help another firm meet its goals or answer its needs. Or, as in the case of internal proposals, they show how a company can increase profits, production, or solve a problem.

In the last decade, the proposal business has become more sophisticated and competitive. Some of the changes are due to new laws, others because of computers, and still others because of new approaches to advertising, a change in ethics, or the scrutiny of the media.

For example, a number of states and federal agencies now set aside a percentage of all contracts for minority vendors. In many cases, women fall into that minority category. Large defense contractors actively search for smaller companies that may help them live up to new laws and guidelines set down by the government. That means there is opportunity for smaller companies to obtain contracts from the government, either as a prime or a subcontractor.

OPPORTUNITIES FOR SMALLER COMPANIES

A prime contractor refers to the company and/or individual who contracts directly with the government or a public agency. For instance, Boeing may have a contract with the U.S. government to supply a certain type of aircraft. They are the prime contractor. Within that airplane, however, there may be parts (i.e., a radio) that Boeing does not make. Therefore, Boeing has to sign a contract with a subcontractor. The subcontractor usually fills out an RFQ that Boeing has issued.

Aside from the demand for the involvement of more minorities in government contracts, computers have changed proposals dramatically. They have enabled companies with limited budgets to compete graphically and to turn out presentations that are among the finest ever produced. Today, with computers and letter quality printing every proposal can be equal (at least cosmetically) to any other.

In the private sector, professions that once were loathe to advertise (i.e., attorneys, accountants, and so on) go by new rules. Where once most professionals found clientele via referral, they are now in heated competition. Advertising, direct mail, and promotion have become a recognized technique by these professions. They use all three to attract potential clients and open the door for a proposal.

Scrutiny of the media and the economy have had a dramatic effect on those who submit RFPs. In the mid-to-late sixties, so-called community-based organizations (CBO), which provided nonprofit services on a local level to consumers within a community, found it easy to extract funds from the government through such programs as President Johnson's "War on Poverty." The grants (or RFPs) they submitted sailed through with little opposition and virtually no scrutiny. Seldom was there even an audit.

The CBOs specialized in using government funds to find jobs for the unemployed, feed the homeless, or provide job training for local residents.

Today, there are still CBOs but their numbers have diminished and the proposals that were once funded without question are tossed in the wastebasket without a second thought. In order for a CBO to obtain funding it not only has to submit a perfect, well-researched document with back-up, but it may need political clout or friends in high places as well.

IMPACT OF MISMANAGEMENT

Mismanagement and waste has had an impact on obtaining funding in this area. "Technically poor proposals were funded all the time," recalls Carol Geisbauer, Executive Director of Helpline, a

CBO in Southern California that operates with a yearly budget of $500,000, all raised from foundation (or other) grants, and monies from RFPs.

"The proposals," continued Geisbauer, "might not have been correct but the politicians were willing to take a stand. They would back an organization and support its request for funding. Then the roof caved in."

The roof was in the form of organizations such as CETA, a job-training service funded by the government. In its rush to put people to work, the government failed to audit where the money was going. As a result money slipped through the cracks and into a lot of pockets.

The media jumped on that story (in addition to numerous other abuses in which federal money was misused) and the climate changed. Starting with President Nixon's tenure, the controls mounted and the funds began to shrink.

Today, few politicians will come out in favor of a CBO's request for funds. They are not interested in taking the heat if something goes wrong. They may give lip service to a project or cause, but there is no way a politician is going to take a stand and be embarrassed by the mistakes of a local organization.

IMPORTANCE OF CONNECTIONS

Because of the reticence, CBOs have diminished in numbers. Those that remain have a proven record. "New CBOs have little chance of succeeding," says Geisbauer. "No one wants to go out on a limb and give them funds. They'd prefer to stick with the old reliable. It is going to be quite difficult for anyone who has a newly organized group to obtain funding . . . unless they have connections."

Connections are of particular importance to CBOs. With budget constraints there is a limited pool of money. "Out of 500 proposals, only 50 will be funded," says Geisbauer. "Those 50 are the CBOs that are established and have accomplished things." Still, there is ample funding available—even for the new organizations. It is a matter of research, doing the proper work first, then preparing the right proposal.

Connections have made a significant impact in the aerospace and defense industry. The company that waits for a defense industry RFP to be issued before they prepare an answer is "going to be out in the cold," says Tom Kaplin, a consultant with 22 years of RFP writing experience.

The complexities of answering a major multimillion dollar RFP are such that it is not possible for a major contractor to put everything together in 30–90 days, the usual period that it takes to answer a request from an agency once news of it is published in the *Commerce Business Daily.*

(The exception is the RFQ, Request for Quotation. Usually, RFQs only require a company to submit a proposal based upon price for a particular product. Companies that bid on RFQs already have the technology or the product exists. They can answer in 30 days or less.)

Astute companies that are after government contracts make contact with the agencies (Department of Defense, Navy, Army, Air Force, Marines, and so on) on a regular basis. They have marketing representatives "making the rounds" all the time. They learn what is being planned for the future, and they match their company's technology and products to those plans. If they have a "fit," they get ready for the RFP that they know will be coming.

When the proposed SDI (Strategic Defense Initiative), otherwise known as Star Wars, program began to get attention from the media, a number of contractors began to take a close look at the project in order to see how their company might get involved. Representatives from every major defense firm were talking to the Department of Defense, in order to try and find out what the administration was planning. What kind of system did it envision? What kinds of products would it be willing to invest in? What kind of RFP would it issue?

Before an RFP was issued, every major company that thought it had the technology was ready to answer. Interestingly, Hughes Aircraft Company, which had not been noted for its ability in the area, wound up with two contracts when it successfully answered a pair of RFPs. It was an example of preparation. Hughes knew what was coming and it was ready to answer the RFP when it was issued. Today, marketing is everything in the defense industry.

"INSIDE" MARKETING

In the government sector, marketing does not mean selling, but rather it refers to the many representatives a contractor can put in the field so they know what's coming. If large contractors do not have a force of marketing specialists making the rounds of various agencies, they will never know what is going on. The best marketing specialists usually have a technical background. This enables them to visit the labs and scientists and talk the same language.

Subcontractors are plagued with the same time problem. If they wait for the *Commerce Business Daily* to see which RFPs may interest a prime contractor, they are missing out. (Subcontractors are usually given contracts from prime contractors. The prime contractor is the winner of the RFP.) Subcontractors must have their ears to the ground as well. They must approach the prime and submit their bids long before the RFP is published and becomes common knowledge. The prime cannot formulate his plans and costs without the sub's prices in hand. Thus the subs who are successful are those who contact prime contractors early in the game. They, too, have their marketing ears to the ground, not only at the prime's place of business but they also read newspapers, watch what Congress is doing, and some even approach agencies so they know the magnitude of contracts that will be coming.

The increased marketing has changed the grading of proposals that are submitted to the government. Obviously, a proposal that gives X amount of points for each section is meant to be scored objectively, but there is an inside track. The company with the connections, and the upfront awareness that a proposal is going to be asked for, is usually going to be the winner. With marketing activities, a company can join the winning crowd.

Connections mean a great deal in the grant field as well. (Grants are no different than RFPs although some may come from private foundations as well as government agencies. They usually have the same strict written requirements.) Colleges and universities have discovered that. Grants from private foundations and the government have become intensely competitive. So much so that many educational institutions are hiring professional grant writers to submit their bids.

"Years ago," explains Dr. Sam Schauerman, President of El

Camino College, "grants were written by inexperienced people. In fact, I wrote a number of them. Today, however, things have become much more competitive. When a non-pro is involved, I would say the success ratio is no more than one in 15. With a grant writer, your percentage jumps to 50 percent."

THE "PRO" GRANT WRITER

The professional grant writer knows people in the field. He has the connections. If he is writing for funding to Kellogg (a large foundation that specializes in funding educational grants) and he is a professional, chances are he has talked to the decision-makers previously. He can pick up the telephone and obtain insight into some of the grant questions that a non-pro might have difficulty finding out.

The grant writer knows what the reader of the grant proposals are looking for. He knows how to state the case or need. He knows how to tie it in with the most important points.

That does not mean universities have to hire professional grant writers. "People can be trained to be professional grant writers, but it takes time," says Dr. Schauerman. The problem some universities have encountered in attempting to train grant writers is that many faculty members do not want the extra duties. They already have their hands full with classes, exams, and other activities.

Dr. Schauerman sees this as a problem, but one that is not insurmountable. In the future, he foresees the day when faculty members are compensated for writing grants and, if they write a winning proposal, they are given additional funds. Some day we may see the "commissioned professor."

Carol Geisbauer can certainly be classified a professional when it comes to grant writing, although she has had no training other than what she put herself through. Geisbauer learned the art of proposal writing by researching other proposals that were on file and doing her homework. Before she ever put a word on paper, she knew exactly what was required.

She says anyone can be a "pro grant writer" if they follow the rules. About 80 percent of her proposals have been funded. To fund her organization's $500,000 a year budget, she submits anywhere from 20–25 proposals per year. That means her average proposal is for $25,000.

To Carol Geisbauer, competing against professionals is not as disturbing as some of the other changes that have come about. The biggest headache is the emergence of the abnormal amount of reporting and auditing in the governmental proposal/grant writing sector. Because of the excess paperwork, she will seldom go after a grant that is for less than $10,000. The sum may be appealing, but the paperwork it creates can diminish the profit.

"In the CETA days, there was no auditing. Today, I might be audited by as many as five different accountants, all sent from the same agency that supplied the funds," says Geisbauer, "and the five will all come at different times. It can be maddening."

The checking and double-checking is all part of the politicians' desire to protect themselves. "They are all afraid," Carol says, "that there might be one loose nut out there. One nut out of 100 can ruin a political career."

CHANGES IN ATTITUDE

Close scrutiny by the media, and a growing interest in the environment and no or slow growth, has turned the building and development field into an industry under a microscope. The builder has become the "bad guy." As a result, the building proposal that would have been filed and passed with ease a decade ago would not even be considered today.

"If you want to build 150 units, file for 200," maintains Larry Schmidt, a long-time developer who has wrestled with many local government agencies. "In many cases, politicians want to demonstrate to their constituents that they are listening. If you file for 200, you automatically lose 50. That's standard operating procedure."

Connections have come to mean a great deal in the industry. Knowing staff members who make recommendations to politicians or other superiors is a must, although it does not guarantee the builder his proposal will be approved. It does ensure the builder will know almost immediately—long before he prepares a proposal—that his plan will not fly. Proposals that once sailed through in three to four months can now take two years.

"Proposals are not as simple as they once were," says Ed Pearson, an engineer who deals extensively with private and public agencies. "There is more sophistication and greater numbers of people on staff for the proposer to deal with. And no one wants to stick their neck out."

UTILIZING CONNECTIONS

The awareness and hesitation mean one thing to the proposal writer—before turning in a written document homework must be done. Homework includes more than researching facts and figures. It means talking to the decision-makers or those within the agency or company. It means utilizing connections.

Fifteen years ago, an incomplete proposal to a government agency would have been returned with a friendly note regarding the problem. The note might have said fix it and get it back to us as soon as possible. Today, with the consumer advocate organizations and watchdog agencies, that would not happen. There would be no friendly note, only an unfriendly rejection.

Despite the complexities, RFPs are becoming readable and the instructions that come with them understandable. Companies dealing with the federal government are beginning to find things being simplified as more and more governmental agencies begin to see the difficulties involved with the paperwork.

Although complete simplification is not here as yet, it appears that it is on the way. RFPs that were once too difficult to comprehend come with explanatory booklets. Although it is not yet a trend, proposers are hopeful the simplicity will continue.

Complexity of RFPs that are issued at the local and regional level remains. In fact, many of the requirements have become stiffer and the paperwork more lengthy. Pat Unangst, an administrator of an agency that accepts and reads hundreds of RFP answers each year, says it will continue.

"There isn't enough time to review the hundreds of bids many government agencies get for each RFP, so a number of agencies have made the requirements tougher. They make the vendor supply more information than he or she ever has. In effect, the agency is making the vendor do the agency's homework."

For those submitting RFPs, the added requirements are a night-mare of research and paperwork. To some in the private sector, the added load is not worth the contract. Joe Izzo, who heads JIA Management, a data processing firm that specializes in making proposals to the private sector, says the RFPs "are ridiculous. They are evaluated by how much they weigh, not what they say."

On the other hand, there are those who feel that although the increased requirements may be exacting they should not discour-age anyone. "Much of the information requested may seem super-fluous, and it probably is. But you suddenly find that something you had to dig out for one proposal is asked for in another. So all the time is not a waste. The critical thing is to make sure you answer all the questions that are posed. Too many vendors get knocked out of the box because they say 'oh, no one really cares about that.' They do," says Carol Geisbauer.

CHANGES IN PRIVATE SECTOR PROPOSALS

The government is not the only sector that has made its proposal requirements more exacting. Private firms have gone through an equal amount of changes. There are few chief executives who want to tell their fellow managers or board members they picked "Joe Blow's firm because he seemed like he knew what he was saying." They want backup with a formal proposal. Consultants and others are finding they can no longer obtain the business with a contract and a handshake. Many CEOs also prefer a proposal from more than one firm so they can compare services, price, and justify deci-sions to their directors.

The desire for formal presentations has opened the door for com-petition in the private sector. The accounting field is a good exam-ple of how heated the battle for business has become. For years, CPA firms were forbidden to advertise their services, and seldom did one CPA firm find itself in competition with another if it was making a proposal. Proposals meant little when there was nothing for the prospect to make comparisons to. With the advent of ads, customers became cognizant of other firms and the services they promised.

In addition, the emphasis on the economy and the many tax changes that have come and gone have given accounting a high priority in the corporation. Companies are more conscious of cost cutting and profit margins. They want the best deal for their dollars, and they are willing to shop and look around at more than one proposal.

"Although we are reticent to advertise we see the need to become more proactive than reactive," says Raelene Arrington, Director of Marketing for Coopers & Lybrand, one of the Big 8 accounting firms. What Arrington means is that Coopers and other firms cannot sit around and wait for the business to come in the door.

"I do not mean going out and spending money in a magazine for an institutional ad because that is hard to measure. I believe that direct mail is certainly more measurable and effective for a firm like ours and it could be the wave of the future."

Direct mail would serve as a lead generating device for Coopers and other service firms. Postage-paid cards that were returned could ultimately result in a proposal. The amount of returned cards could be tallied, and the conversions to clients added up. The cost of the ad could be compared to the number of clients generated and the potential income.

With intense competition, private sector proposals are scrutinized before they ever are submitted to a client. This is in sharp contrast to the days when only a one-page letter detailing fees and services would be given to the client.

"Proposals have become an important part of the process of getting new business, and they better make sense," says Arrington. "There is no room for broad generalizations."

PROPOSAL PRICING

Bill Johnson, who heads an accounting firm that specializes in "management troubleshooting," says that pricing has undergone sharp revisions. It used to be possible to charge a flat fee for many services but that is no longer the case.

"In our industry and many others, tax laws have had dramatic impact. There is more work and it is tougher to estimate. We've changed to time (hourly) and charges (expenses) billing."

The hourly rates, depending upon who is doing the work, is spelled out in the proposal. "Time (hourly rates of the individual who is doing the work) and charges (expenses incurred while doing the job) requires an explanation in the proposal. Certain verbiage is needed so the prospective client understands he or she is going to be paying an hourly rate for the person who is doing the work, as well as expenses."

This approach is more effective than the old flat rate or fixed fee. Clients were often quoted a flat rate or fixed fee, then when the bill arrived, they found additional charges. The added charges were usually inserted when the firm discovered it was not making money because the job was more extensive than it first estimated. In trying to make up for the mistake, fees (charges) were fabricated. This type of approach did nothing but alienate customers and lose clientele.

In industries such as accounting, where new laws change almost yearly, flat fees are too much of a risk to quote. Wise companies in these fields stay away from flat fees, and if a client insists, the most they will do is give them a price range as to what they expect the services to cost.

Pricing is important, but it is not the deciding factor (unless a company's fee is way out of line) in the private sector. Paul Hackett, who runs three companies in a competitive industry, says that "when we are called, management has already decided they are going to spend the money. Unless the fee is exorbitant, it will not make a difference in the decision-making process."

LOW BID DOES NOT ALWAYS WIN

The attitude towards the low bid has changed significantly among government contractors as well. In the past, it was always assumed when submitting a proposal, especially to a governmental agency, that the lowest bid got the job. "The joke in the industry used to be that when the component blew up or broke down, 'it was obvious the low-bidder was the one who got the job,'" laughs Jim Baxter of TRW. "Today, low-bidders do not always get the job."

In many ways, the consideration of other things aside from price has been good for companies. For too many years, American firms were haunted by a poor quality image. Most have made sincere attempts to remedy workmanship, and they expect more from both within—and outside—their company.

Baxter's company has adopted an approach where "suppliers are certified." In other words, a supplier or subcontractor on a proposal is expected to prove himself. How? In one case, suppliers are not automatically given contracts simply because of bid. If they want to do business with the defense contractor they must start with one purchase order.

When the product is delivered it must have 97 percent quality acceptability, and the supplier must have a 90 percent on-time record. Once a vendor has lived up to the purchase order and the 90–97 percent levels, he becomes a certified buyer and proposals for larger orders are accepted. Until he does, however, his proposals, regardless of price, are unacceptable. This approach is spreading across the industry, and with the increased media attention to "cost overruns" and out-of-line payments for replacement parts, it will become the norm in a short time.

Those in defense claim they have been getting a "bad rap" for the so-called high-priced wrenches and toilet seats that the media has written about. What should be understood is that prime contractors are not in the replacement or spare parts business.

"We make a point of telling that to the government or whatever agency we submit an RFP to. We are happy to give them a list of suppliers who are in the replacement business. If they used the list there would not be a high-priced replacement. Instead they call us and ask us to supply the part," says Baxter.

This is similar to a new car buyer going to the dealer and asking him for a new hood ornament. Since the dealer does not manufacture them, it would cost the consumer a small fortune to obtain an ornament from the dealer. That has happened in aerospace. The government has taken the shortcut and asked aerospace companies for spare parts instead of going to suppliers and other subcontractors—the people who are actually doing the manufacturing.

There is an exception when it comes to pricing—the RFQ. The request for quotation is exactly what it says. How much will it cost for you to supply us with 100 widgets. That same request can go to a dozen companies, thus the agency has a chance to compare apples with apples. All firms supply the same widget. In that case, pricing is everything.

The most dramatic change insofar as defense and proposals are concerned is in the area of product development. In the past, once an RFP was submitted and won by a company, the government would front or pay for the development cost of the product. That is no longer the case. Today, if a company submits an RFP for a new product and it costs (for development) $45 million, the government may ask the firm to come up with $20 million of the $45 million.

Within the industry many believe the company's required contribution for development is unfair. They point out that although a company such as General Motors pays for all its research and development, it recoups the monies through its present product line.

"That is not the case in aerospace," says Gary Minor. "Our profits are restricted and fixed. We cannot tack on development costs to an existing product line."

As a result, defense companies have taken a new approach with proposals. They are teaming with competitors and sharing the development cost. For example, TRW may team with Lockheed to develop a product. The product is jointly developed and the first-year production is shared. After the first year, each company competes against each other for the contract. The lowest bidder usually wins. Minor looks for this trend to continue, and more joint venture proposals are on the horizon.

"You have to sharpen your pencil and cut as much as possible if you are going to stay competitive in this business," says John Hamond, who has been writing proposals for nearly two decades.

"At no time have I seen the government so intense on getting a better price. Obviously, there's the deficit and pressure from Congress. I think this trend is definitely going to continue for years to come."

The impact of large budget deficits is going to be significant. Aside from causing major defense contractors to band together in partnerships, it can open the doors for smaller contractors who could not bid on an entire contract because of limited finances. Now these contractors may be able to submit answers to RFPs by splitting the obligation with other companies.

Teaming is not exclusive to the defense/aerospace industry. Universities have found valuable allies in the private sector, and will often form a partnership with a private company in order to obtain grant, foundation, or RFP monies.

A typical case may be where a university and word processing company combine efforts to hire and train employees for the word processing firm. Monies are obtained either through local agencies or foundations, and the private company has its wages subsidized by providing the training location, while the university earns money by providing the instructors.

THE COMPUTER CHANGE

Tight money is not the only thing that is causing changes in the proposal business. There is a product that has had enormous impact: the computer. The proposal that is not a letter quality document is at a disadvantage. The computer has also enabled the small firm to compete with the giant, thanks to desktop publishing and its superb graphic capabilities.

No longer does the small (or large) firm need to spend monies on an outside graphics house for proposals. Desktop publishing has perfected in-house capabilities for graphics, which are extremely important in any proposal.

Television has made everyone (even those who read the submissions for complex RFPs) more visually oriented. Graphics make it easy for those reading proposals to see complex products or services clearly. The technical product can be made less technical. Even the trained engineer or technical expert can be helped (and influenced) by well-placed graphics. Although they may say graphics do not matter, the proposal becomes easier to read and comprehend for anyone, regardless of their background, if graphics are used effectively.

In the private sector, Joe Izzo says, "When you write a proposal for a client they always expect charts and graphs. There are few prospective clients who have the patience to read pages of verbiage without visual help. In the future, we are going to see more software that will dramatically enhance even today's sophisticated proposals."

Boilerplating, the process of lifting entire sections of a proposal, saving them, and using them again in other proposals, is another capability that computers have given to proposal writers.

For smaller companies such as Bob Ritchie's communications firm, boilerplating is important. With a limited staff, he has been able to customize proposals and compete with companies that are much larger.

"The computer makes it possible. Don't ever discard or file a proposal away once it has been presented and a decision has been made. There is usually something in it that can easily be used again."

Boilerplating can have its pitfalls, however. There is a tendency to boilerplate too much. When this happens original proposals no longer appear original to the client, and there is danger of losing the prospect. The key to effective boilerplating is to lift whatever is needed, but always review and update the boilerplated section each time it is used.

Carol Geisbauer always re-reads and re-writes. "There is nothing wrong with boilerplating as long as you review the material. I find there is always a paragraph or two that can be improved."

COMMUNICATION IN PRIVATE SECTOR PROPOSALS

Computers have certainly helped proposal writers, but the one ingredient that machines have not been able to enhance is communication, the ability to talk to someone as "one person to another in the proposal," says Don Kracke.

What he means is to avoid stilted language and phrases. The proposal should be written just as if "you were talking to the person across the desk." There is a tendency with proposals to become too formal, almost pompous. RFPs are more formalized than the private sector proposals, but they do not need stilted verbiage either. Everyone appreciates straightforward writing and talk.

Bill Johnson points out that although the days of doing business with a handshake are gone, "Success in any business relationship depends upon your rapport with a client." Rapport is lost when a pre-proposal discussion is conducted in language that everyone understands, but the proposal comes out too formal and stiff.

Keep it simple, says Kracke. "Do you understand the company, what it is going through, and the help it needs. Do you understand the problems." If the proposer does, he or she should say so (in writing) and do it so everyone can comprehend what is written. In order to sell a proposal, the proposer must communicate.

"That's one element that hasn't changed since proposal writing began," says Kracke.

TEN KEYS TO WRITING SUCCESSFUL PROPOSALS

Whether the proposal is for the private or public sector, one thing has not changed—the keys to writing successful proposals.

There are ten distinct steps (each is detailed in later chapters) that must be followed if a proposal is going to win.

1. *Research.* Not a word can be written until the problem and/or company is researched. In some cases, this may involve interviewing key executives as well as employees. In others, it may require research in the library or talking to agencies or those with influence in the government. Research is required because the need that management says exists may not be the only problem a consultant has to solve. All needs cannot be determined without sufficient research.

2. *Objective Writing.* Adjectives and flamboyant language and promises do not belong in proposals. Factual writing is the language of the winning proposal.

3. *Creative Ideas.* The consultant who leaves out new and creative ideas for fear they will be stolen seldom has a chance to win. Management (and others) seeking proposals are looking for new ways and ideas to solve problems. There are ways to present ideas and protect them at the same time.

4. *USP—Address It.* To win, proposals must have a USP (Unique Selling Proposition) that sets the proposal writing firm apart from its competition. That USP can be anything from previous experience to proprietary technology.

5. *Language.* Stay away from technical jargon or acronyms that are known only to the proposal writing firm or a select few. Winning proposals are written so that anyone can understand them. There is, of course, one exception—the technical portion of a proposal which is usually written in technical terms, especially if it is earmarked only for those with a technical background.

6. *Handling Competition.* Your competitors should never be "put down." If your firm can do something that other firms

cannot do, play up your company's ability in the area. Leave it up to the prospect to detect the weakness of the competitor by comparing it with your strengths.

7. *Management Summary.* The key selling points must be reiterated in a management or executive summary that usually is placed at the beginning of the proposal. The summary contains all pertinent information so that the prospect's top managers do not have to take time to read through the entire proposal. The fee for the job is not automatically included in the summary.

8. *Strategizing.* The proposal writing firm has to determine a strategy—that is, how will the project and prospect be approached? Who are the influencers? Who has the ultimate say? What should be stressed? How should it be outlined? Whom should we be talking to? Who will our competitors be?

9. *Proper Organization.* Proposals should not ramble. They should begin with a summary. The remainder of the proposal should be carefully organized, ending with the qualifications of the firm that is going after the business. In between should be evidence that the proposal writing company fully understands the problem and has a solution.

10. *Determining Budget/Costs.* Is there a budget or does the prospect want the consulting firm to come up with a figure? Is it a budget- or task-oriented amount of money the prospect is offering? How much and for what? These are questions the proposal writer must determine in advance because they are questions the prospect will be examining when he or she sees the proposal.

INTERNAL PROPOSAL CHANGES

While external proposals have been changed by a variety of influences, internal proposals have been changed by two prime factors: time and economics.

Typically, internal proposals fall into the following categories:

1. Engineering changes
2. Ideas
3. Research and development
4. New products
5. Departmental reorganization
6. New machinery and plants

With the corporate emphasis on profits, cost cutting, and return on investment, the internal proposal is being scrutinized more carefully than ever. Management views internal proposals that concentrate on points 1–4 more favorably than 5 and 6.

The first four ultimately lead to more sales and profits. The last two do not necessarily bring any more monies into the company.

"Products that give your company a technical advantage are certainly viewed more favorably than an investment in a new plant or equipment," says Karl Brennan, "and it stands to reason."

The technologically advanced product can be sold to customers somewhere down the line. Building a new plant comes out of the company's treasury, and its return is not as obvious as the product. Each takes a different sales approach.

Brennan says that when you try to convince management to set aside funds for a new product, service, or additional research, you must answer such questions as "What are we going to do? What are we going to get? What kind of technical advantage will be ours, and possibly what kind of sales can we expect?"

There are other questions involved when it comes to selling management on spending money for a new plant or piece of equipment. Management wants to know:

1. Will it reduce costs? When?
2. How much will we save?
3. Why do we need to replace the current equipment?
4. How much life is left in the current piece?
5. What is its book value?
6. How long is the payback period?

The bottom line is: What is the return on our investment? That is what management is going to ask anyone who proposes they buy a new piece of machinery or develop another widget for internal use. It's always return on investment.

Management is going to scrutinize proposals for internal investment more closely than those for development of new products. There is a reluctance to spend money on something that does not show profit the traditional way—through sales. Board of directors and shareholders may not have the same vision as the engineering or manufacturing staff.

Most can see the value of developing a new product and selling it to others in industry. That is not the case with internal expenditures for a new plant and equipment. It is a factor that must be considered carefully by those making proposals, and the presentation must ultimately show how the new equipment will translate into a money-saving operation.

This information must be crammed into as short a time span as possible when making an internal proposal. Whereas management previously set aside long periods of time for research and development and idea sessions, that is no longer the case. Everyone has a time crunch.

Generally, management seldom has more than 30 minutes set aside to hear a proposal. The internal proposal that goes longer stands an excellent chance of losing regardless of its merit. We live in a fast-paced society, and managers, as well as others, have little patience, "so keep it short," advises Gary Minor.

THE INTERNAL "VERBAL"

The internal proposal has evolved into a well-rehearsed verbal presentation aided by a viewgraph, which is a projector that enables the presenter to write on a transparent graph that is projected on a screen.

If there is a handout, it is usually only a brief outline with copies of the viewgraph slides given to those attending after the meeting. The burden of the presentation is on the presenter and his oral communication abilities. John Hamond puts it this way, "You need personality." Years ago, it may have only been necessary to present the facts and let management make the decision. Today, it is equally as important to be "dynamic." Do not bore the boss.

The days of matchbook presentations that ramble on are gone. The boss is accustomed to seeing and hearing high-powered sales-people and presentations. Before he goes for something, he needs to be moved, and you can help your case by putting emotion, feeling, and variety in your voice. Avoid speaking in a monotone.

And, adds Karl Brennan, "Be brief. If you can do it in less than 30 minutes, do it. Say it and get off. You will be amazed at the results."

CHAPTER 2

Finding the Inside Track

For years, Don Kracke had been in one of the most competitive businesses imaginable—he would take a new idea that made sense and market it to a major company such as a Sears or Proctor and Gamble.

Although Kracke had done well, it was a tough road. He had to spend countless hours researching the marketability of the product, testing it, and finally preparing a presentation.

Along the way he marketed items such as an "executive garbage can," a colorful garbage can that had its exterior decorated with pictures of items such as the *Wall Street Journal* and Dom Perignon champagne. One of his prize ideas was a "silly pencil," a flexible, funny-looking pencil that was approximately three-feet long. All together he successfully sold nearly 200 ideas. Obviously not every one of them was a roaring success. Still, as Kracke said, it enabled him to "make a living."

Seven years ago, everything changed. Kracke hit upon an idea. Instead of selling new products to companies, why not sell them designs that could be placed on dishes, towels, and other housewares. His thought was to create coordinates for mass merchandisers. When a customer came into a department store to buy a towel, he could purchase a bath towel with a particular design and might also buy a matching dish towel. If he could not afford to buy both, he could come back to buy the dish towel at another time.

Kracke tested his theory. Customers did, indeed, prefer coordinates. And the mass merchandisers preferred them as well. It enabled stores to add on to a customer's purchase, and they could charge a slightly higher price for the coordinates as well.

Kracke's company, Design Concepts, collects fees in the form of royalties from companies that utilize his coordinates. To date, there are 30 firms that have bought Kracke's proposal and are paying Design Concepts fees for the coordinates they are utilizing on their products.

For Kracke, it has been a rewarding experience. Instead of continuing to bang his head against the wall and market new products to reluctant companies, he writes proposals to major firms and sells them on his coordinates concept. He not only has carved his own niche, but he pioneered a new industry.

He also found the inside track. For those who look closely, there are inside tracks and marketing opportunities for proposal writers in most industries.

In aerospace, the government has implemented far-reaching new policies that include competitors "sharing" plans and blueprints for proprietary products. A decade ago, the mere suggestion of making available internally created new products to others would have caused a revolution. Today, many in the defense industry are resigned to the fact that this could be the wave of the future.

PROPOSAL TEAMING OPPORTUNITIES

With the government also backing away from footing the entire bill for development costs, doors have been opened for smaller companies with less capital to team with larger ones in making proposals. Thus the two can share the cost—and the technology.

Although these developments are not welcomed by most of the large defense contractors, they may be a boon to the medium and small-sized contractor. They are also evidence of a new budget consciousness on the part of the government. Unquestionably, these constraints will have impact on RFPs in the future.

In nongovernmental sectors there has been a loosening of the rules as well that has led to opportunities. Many companies within the private sector, which once relied on "client referrals" as a source of new business, now find that their competitors are advertising, using direct mail and other forms of marketing to open a prospect's door for proposals.

Certainly referrals remain a prime source of business for many, but intense competition has become a way of doing business. Because of that competition, the written proposal has become more important than ever. It can make the difference. A company that has less resources than a competitor can suddenly find itself on the inside track thanks to a well-written proposal.

The key, however, before any prospective client is approached and a proposal written, is for a company or consultant to find the right niche if it is to successfully compete for business.

That does not mean starting a new venture as Don Kracke did. It does, however, indicate that companies should not be wasting time writing proposals just for the sake of writing. Answering RFPs that only remotely relate to a company's expertise is a waste of time.

Applying for grants without sounding out the foundation as to its attitude about the recipient's programs is another waste. Pursuing a client in the private sector without knowing everything about the prospect is another effort in futility.

KEY TO WINNING PROPOSALS

Winning proposals are written by companies that know the prospect's business and problem intimately. They also have a USP (Unique Selling Proposition) that their firm can offer. A USP simply sets one firm apart from another. It is the "hook" or "angle" by which most firms sell their products and companies. Every firm has a USP. In the automobile field, it may be a car's mileage potential, price, or luxurious interior. It may be a particular service or way of doing business. It may even be one of the principles who is noted for his or her expertise. Whatever the USP, it is a crucial part of any proposal. When Kracke entered the licensing field, his was the only company that specialized in coordinates for the housewares field. Mercedes may sell status and luxury, but Hyundai sells low price. They are all USPs.

USPs are specialized services and/or products that only one firm offers. In many cases, the USP may be present in products that two competitors have, however, the first company may bring it out and use it as a selling point while the second firm bypasses it.

USPs IN PRIVATE SECTOR PROPOSALS

Finding a special niche and USP has become of prime importance
in the private sector. Take, for instance, the accounting profession.
With the continuous flow of new tax laws, it would appear that
there is no end of business for the accountant. For some CPA firms
that is true, but for others there is a frantic scrambling underway.

There will always be tax work for the corner accountant, the
generalist, but for those desirous of landing the big accounts, audits
are out and specialization is in. You are more likely to find a CPA
firm making a proposal to design a new computer system than
to audit a firm's books. There is more money in the system and a
plethora of potential clients.

That is exactly what most Big 8 accounting firms are doing today.
They are presenting proposals to companies to design computer
systems and provide management consulting. They have found a
special niche, a unique selling proposition. Competition has forced
the majors to look for other, related sources of revenue and they
have.

The drive to specialize is topped only by the cutthroat techniques that have been adopted by many firms. "What's happened,"
says Bill Johnson with a note of sadness, "is that ethics have been
replaced by advertising and client raiding."

Johnson points out that many CPA firms will do auditing work
at cost (or even a loss) simply to "get their foot in the door. Most
large CPA firms are problem-oriented, not audit-oriented. Today,
the CPA firms want to get involved in hardware and software installation, and other areas where there is significant income."

Johnson has studied the industry closely and selected his niche
carefully. "We don't sell audit services, although we certainly
perform them. Our proposals are geared to sell our ability in
management."

Johnson's proposals revolve around troubleshooting. He will go
into a firm, define its weaknesses, needs, and strengths, plan and
implement a solution, and communicate the entire process to management with an initial proposal and follow-up reports.

In less than two years, his dollar volume has soared into seven
figures and he can hardly keep pace with the growing number of
clients. He does not advertise, nor does he make cold calls as many

other firms do. He has kept out of the rat race by finding a specialized service within the accounting field.

PROBLEM-SOLVING PROPOSALS

"We found a niche, a specialty. Anytime you are in a competitive field you must find a unique service or you are not going to grow."

Johnson's ability at management problem solving is such that he is often referred to clients by other CPA firms. It also illustrates the demand for services from firms that can solve a company's internal problems.

Johnson's proposals are of particular interest because they not only cover the cause of the problem, but they detail the problem and the solution. He finds out everything about the firm before anything is ever put on paper. Initially, he has a talk with the owner to see if "the chemistry is there. Can we work together?"

Regardless of how well-researched and accurate a proposal happens to be, it is useless if the principles cannot work with the outside firm. The account may be tempting, but if the two elements do not get along, the relationship will never work out.

During Johnson's initial meetings, the prospect "makes a commitment to us as to the availability of information, records, and people. We give him feedback as to exactly what we are going to do. We want to be sure he understands how we are going to proceed. If we pass the 'smell' test, we go ahead."

Johnson's procedure illustrates how business is changing. It is no longer just a matter of writing a proposal to see if you can sign a client. Astute firms realize that unless there is chemistry between the client and the consultant, there will be no future business, nor will there be any referrals.

Johnson understands that any long-term relationship is going to require the cooperation of all management within a firm. Thus he urges the owners/executives or whomever brought him in to bring those in management in on the pre-proposal discussions.

"If an owner is wise, he will. Sometimes if he is not he will try and solve the problem without them. We make every effort to get the management team involved because many times they know something that the owner does not."

PROPOSAL RESEARCH

Johnson follows a technique that many do prior to writing a proposal. They research, research, research. They do as much "homework" as possible. In the case where an owner or top executive brings in an outside firm, questioning the employees is an accepted part of the pre-proposal stage.

"It is difficult," he says, "to find out everything that is wrong without the cooperation of employees. You have to reassure them and let them know you are not there to take their place."

Johnson, as well as others in the proposal-writing business, have found that the major problem companies encounter is a lack of communication within the firm. People do not share knowledge, and they all go in different directions. That makes it difficult for any private firm to come in and dig out the truth that is needed in order to write a thorough proposal. If employees do not share information among themselves, will they share it with outsiders?

Johnson recognizes this difficulty. He will spend time with the owner and/or executive in charge and listen to his version of the problem and a statement of what his goals are. Then he will spend time within the company and talk to personnel. Those in the private sector have found that taking the CEO's or top management's word as to what the cause of the problem may be often does not work. When researching, those who write winning proposals spend time with those below the top management level.

PROPOSAL DIALOGUE

Johnson may spend anywhere from a few hours to a few days researching. Once he has preliminary information, he goes back to the owner/CEO and tells him what they have found. He asks if the owner has any thoughts. "Usually that starts a dialogue. Other problems and concerns are voiced. From that meeting, plus the background we have gathered, we write our proposal."

Unlike most firms that go after business, Johnson charges for the proposal and the research time. This is unique to the profession and certainly not every company can do the same.

"When someone calls us in they have already engaged us. They understand that we will do a complete study. Our proposal will carefully define the problem and will detail the solution. That is one of the differences in the way we operate. We not only offer an analysis of the problem and solution, but we outline and detail the steps to that solution."

Research and writing fees are presented to management by Johnson before the proposal is written. Management agrees and usually signs a letter in which the fees are outlined.

PROTECTING IDEAS

Because management pays for Johnson's ideas, he has no problem in detailing them. Other firms, however, are reticent about presenting ideas for fear they will be stolen. One way to prevent theft is to present the idea but not detail the steps to the solution. The firm's creativity is evident through the idea, but the process is left out of the proposal.

Management can take Johnson's proposal and run with it, because they own it. They bought it. Or they can buy part of it and have Johnson's firm conduct the program. Or they could pass on the entire proposal and call in another firm. Johnson makes sure everyone understands the rules before anything is done.

While Johnson has carved his niche in a small region of the country, Coopers & Lybrand is an accounting firm that operates nationally and is presenting proposals in numerous areas of the country at the same time.

ENTREPRENEURIAL OPPORTUNITIES

Since the advent of advertising, Coopers has become one of the most aggressive firms in the industry, and operating on a national basis it has to be. Coopers, too, has found a niche. Although a large part of its new business is composed of established businesses, one of its fastest growing areas is "emerging business services."

Entrepreneurship remains at an all-time high in the United States, and more new companies are started every year than ever before. The new companies require services as well. They may be small to begin, but they have tremendous growth potential. At the same time, most cannot afford major accounting or management service fees. Eventually they will need them—and they will be able to pay.

Coopers recognizes this potential and to accommodate the entrepreneurial firms, it provides services to them in graduated steps.

"One day," says Ms. Arrington, the firm's marketing director, "those little start-up companies will grow into large corporations. If we are with them at the beginning and follow them through as they grow, we will be doing their work when they become a large corporation."

Coopers has also targeted companies within specific industries. This is a technique that many others seeking business can utilize. Coopers may, for instance, target banking. If so, it will take a partner who has extensive experience (and clientele) in the banking field and use him to make contact. Being in the field, the partner can talk the prospect's language. Targeting is an excellent technique for opening a prospect's door for a proposal.

Knowledge of the industry becomes an important selling point when a proposal is written. (An exception would be the advertising business. For example, if an agency represented Ford, they would not be too welcome at Chrysler since both are competitors and many of their plans are proprietary.) In accounting, however, if a firm represented Ford and did a remarkable job at saving money, taxes, and so on, you can be sure Chrysler would be interested.

THE NETWORK ROLE

Like many seeking business, Coopers utilizes networking. That is, it may have a banker on its board who knows a small (or big) company that is having accounting problems. Many firms fill a number of seats on their board with "networking specialists," such as bankers, insurance people, and others who know who's who in the community . . . and which companies might be having trouble.

Networking is a scouting technique utilized extensively in the private sector. Obviously, the larger the proposal firm the more potential contacts and networking. That is one reason why firm members join community groups such as Rotary, Kiwanis, and so on. It affords them the opportunity to meet more prospects.

Coopers has also considered advertising in trade magazines, however, there has been some reticence. Many consulting firms scouting for new business have drawn back from advertising because it is relatively expensive and unless there is a firm measuring device, it is impossible to tell if the ad drew. When Chrysler buys a 30-second spot on national television, and its dealers buy ads in the local newspaper, it is difficult to tell what brought the customer in unless they are surveyed.

ROLE OF DIRECT MAIL

Direct mail is a measurable tool that is rapidly spreading across all industries. The technique is not to just send out a fancy brochure and hope for a call. What most firms are doing to open the doors is to use direct mail as a lead generator. The mailing piece is followed by a telephone call by someone who tries to set an appointment with a partner or principal who will start the proposal-writing procedure in process.

Most partners, however, are unwilling to make cold calls. They do not want to prospect. So they leave the follow-up to a secretary or assistant. That approach can work to open the doors, but it will never be as effective as having the executive or partner make the call themselves.

Another approach is to utilize a mailing piece with a postage-paid return card. Or it may have a telephone number at the end of the letter or brochure with the name of a particular person to call. This approach is not as strong as the personalized direct mail letter that closes with a line that says something like "I will give you a call to see if I can be of service." Companies seeking business find it more productive to initiate the calls and not rely on the prospect to pick up the telephone.

COLD CALLING

While some would call this "cold calling," it can be effective. Ask Jay Abraham. Abraham is an unorthodox marketing consultant who puts together unique cold calls as well as "proposal letters." His goal is to get the decision-maker on the telephone and conduct an interview with him. On the basis of what comes out of the interview, Abraham will begin to throw ideas out—at no cost—to the executive.

Obviously, it is not easy for an unknown to get a decision-maker on the telephone—ask any insurance salesman. Abraham will often precede the call with a letter in which he analyzes a small portion of the company's marketing strategy that he has seen. He will improve on it, and give the letter recipient—once again at no cost—a way to improve sales and response. Abraham may go through this process a half-dozen times before he actually gets the decision-maker on the telephone. He does not let that deter him. "If I see a company that I know I can do something for I do not give up. I keep pounding away, writing letters and making calls."

Some would call Abraham's tenacity "positive thinking." Abraham shakes his head. "In the service field you'd better stick to it if you hope to open doors. Hearing an abundance of 'no thank yous' among a few scattered 'yes or maybes' is what consultants must adapt to."

Persistence has enabled Abraham to get the decision-maker on the telephone in a majority of instances. He says there is no secret behind his technique. He is glib, light-hearted, and charming—three attributes that enable him to get beyond the secretary.

GIVING AWAY SECRETS?

Once the decision-maker is on the line his approach is straightforward. "I do what most cold callers and proposal/letter writers fail to do . . . I am specific. I do not make vague promises, nor do I write superficially. My conversation on the telephone is the same as it is in the letter. It resembles day-to-day talk. I give the prospect all the information he can use. I do not hide anything."

Some consultants may shy from that approach, fearing that once you have given away the secrets there is nothing left to sell in a proposal. Abraham does not agree with the statement. "I always come up with something new for the proposal."

Cold calls present problems other than reaching the decision-maker. Suppose the prospect is already doing business with a particular firm. How does the private firm know whether the client is unhappy with his present marketing, accounting, or other services and/or products?

They do not. That's one reason why referrals are preferred far and above the cold call. Although the prospect may have someone doing the work, the fact they have agreed to see a new firm is evidence they may be unhappy.

However, no one who is referred should make the assumption that the prospect they are seeing is unhappy with their present situation. Often they agree to talk to a new firm because of the relationship they have with the person seeking to put the prospect and new firm together. A company that has significant monies owed to a bank would certainly be "open" to talking to an accounting firm the bank's loan officer had recommended. They would not want to insult the officer by saying no.

Regardless of how the door is opened for the proposer, it is important to be careful and not say anything derogatory about the firm presently doing the work for the prospect. Putting down the opposition does little good, and often can cost a firm business before a proposal is ever written. There are ways for companies to upgrade their appearance through a proposal without ever putting down the opposition.

THE DECISION-MAKER AND THE PROPOSAL

It is important to get the proposal into the hands of the decision-maker. This is not always easy. Someone down the ladder may be screening proposals, and he or she may have been designated by top management. It is difficult to get by the person without creating an enemy. Wise proposers never bypass the go-between—they go through him. They may determine who else "may" be involved by asking questions. If another name is mentioned, the proposal company has its opportunity to suggest sending a copy to the person, or stressing the need to have him involved in the information-gathering sessions. The decision-maker may not be involved in the screening, but he or she should certainly be part of the information-gathering process before the proposal is written.

Joe Izzo seldom will meet with a firm unless there is a decision-maker present. The odds of getting the business drop about "40 percent if you cannot get the decision-maker involved."

Izzo's firm is one that has managed to carve a niche in a highly competitive field. He has become known as a data-processing troubleshooter, and his expertise is such that a company will even turn its entire data-processing department over to him in order to have it run properly.

His performance in this industry has helped him develop a practice in which more than 50 percent of his leads come from referrals. A prolific writer, Izzo also generates business from firms that have read one of his numerous articles or books on data-processing problems. He reprints articles and sends them out to prospects as well as to his present clients. As a result, he has a firm with a rapidly growing clientele.

The ability to write feature stories is markedly different from writing a proposal. There are not many writers of proposals who can do both. Those that are able to have another method for generating business.

Izzo personally gets involved in the research for every proposal that is written. Regardless of where the lead comes from, he will travel to the targeted company and spend as much time as possible gathering information.

If going out of town, Izzo says, "I demand at least eight hours in which I can meet with all the people involved. Everyone from top management and the owners down to the data-processing department. I let them talk about their problems. I might suggest a few things and ask if they have tried this or that. I try to get a dialogue going."

HOW CLIENTS PERCEIVE PROBLEMS

Izzo has found that what the client initially perceives as the problem really isn't. Many times they do not know what they want. They only know there is a problem, and he has to solve it and present it via a proposal.

Some managers feel they have a grasp on the problem, but in most cases those writing proposals find that the managers are missing key points. That only comes out when the proposal firm does its research. If it took the manager's word for everything, the proposal—and the job—would never be complete. It is essential that research be conducted among other members of the firm before the writing begins.

Izzo never begins to write until he has carefully researched and made sure he knows everything first. "If you try to shortcut and present a proposal before you know all the facts, there is a good chance you will blow it. Do your homework. There is nothing more impressive to a client than showing him you understand the problem, and his company."

Izzo has also determined when he may be competing with another firm for the job, and when he has it to himself. In the latter case, he may get a telephone call from the prospect. They say they need help, and they do not mention a competitor. Usually they ask how much it will cost and when he can get started. Their anxiety is evident.

"That's a sure giveaway that there is no competition. If there were, they would be more cautious," says Izzo.

HANDLING COMPETITION

Competition has never been a concern to Don Kracke. When he opened his Design Center a decade ago, he had none. His design creations have swept the nation. One year Sears may come out with a dish towel that has a Kracke-created elephant design. The elephant is also on bath towels and other similar items. The next year it could be a duck.

This year, about 30 major companies will utilize Kracke's coordinated designs on their products. His leads will come from housewares and other similar shows. Buyers and purchasing agents pass by booths that are utilizing Kracke's designs on their wares. The more booths they pass with the designs, the more sold they become on the validity of coordinates.

Despite the notoriety, and the growing acceptance, Kracke, who has been writing proposals for more than 30 years, has not changed his approach or thoughts on the subject.

"Regardless of the type of proposal you write, the bottom line is always money. Someone has to put it up. You have to convince someone to open their wallet. Anytime anyone contemplates spending money, they want back-up and plenty of it. That's the thought I always keep in mind when writing one . . . how will I convince this person to give me their money?

"To me the proposal is part of the selling process. It is not the end result of a series of client/agency meetings. It leads to the accomplishment of getting the order. It is designed to reinforce the reasons you give to someone to part with their funds. We are considered an expense, and many managers question whether we are really worth it. That's why our proposals have to be damn convincing."

Never forget, he cautions, that in many cases a company can get along without the proposal writer's company. They can survive and grow without your product and/or service—or they can give the job to someone else. Prospective clients are always going to ask, "Do we really need it?"

"In our case, coordinates increase business but in the eyes of many retailers they are still an 'unnecessary expense.' After all, they can still sell dish towels or plates without designs. I can't deny that. So why do they need us? Is this expense really necessary? We have to justify the expenditure in their minds."

To meet those objections, Kracke is dogmatic about the necessity to gather information. "It may be dull and boring, but if you do not do your homework, you will never put together a saleable proposal. You will never get rid of all those objections."

Kracke's homework consists of everything from gathering information on the industry (call trade papers, competitors) to investigating the company. He will call people at the firm and ask for an annual report, the most recent catalogs, brochures, and anything else that will help in learning about the prospect. He also calls people in allied industries.

After thorough research is completed there is one more step before the proposal is written. "Sit down and evaluate all the stuff you have put together. Look at the company objectively. Whether you like it or not, not everyone needs your services. Not everyone needs ours. I have learned that through the years and when I finish my research if I find we are not needed, I tell the prospect."

Turning down business is difficult, but it is done by those who feel they do not fit the prospect's plans. "Why beat something that will never work out. If you cannot offer someone solid benefits, forget it. Save yourself the time and grief," he says. Bob Ritchie knows the importance of convincing the client that his proposal is worth the expense. Unlike many who have found a corner relatively free from competition, Ritchie has always been in a highly competitive industry—communications equipment. Many of his leads come from direct mail and telephone inquiries.

As is the case with many who buy products in the private sector, the prospects are usually only interested in the price and service. They want to avoid meeting Ritchie face-to-face, and would rather give him a complete rundown on the telephone.

To overcome the telephone and to make a face-to-face presentation—which is the best way to sell someone with a proposal—Ritchie has devised several ploys that have made his company extremely successful. He will say to the prospect that he would like him "to have a better idea of what the equipment is like," and will bring equipment that the prospect can use and "play with" for a week or so.

SATISFYING PROSPECTS

Paul Hackett also deals in a competitive field. Networking got his business off the ground and supported him for the first year. He reminds others that networking does not do much good if you do not satisfy the referred prospect. "If he goes away unhappy, forget it. If he goes away smiling, it will open the doors for all the business you can handle."

For the most part, when a consultant sees a prospect through a referral the prospect has made up his mind to do some business. Whether he does it with the proposer's firm or not is anyone's guess. Even when the doors are opened by an influential referral, the proposal and business can be blown through a lack of rapport, poor research, or an inadequate proposal.

Blowing a proposal is not exclusive to the private sector. Many of those in the public sector have found that a well thought-out proposal in an area where they have expertise does not always fly.

"GRANTSMANSHIP"

Dr. Schauerman, who has written, evaluated, and overseen proposal writing at the educational level for more than three decades, is one of those who has seen seemingly well-written grants go by the wayside. He maintains that many of those lost grants went out the window because educators who were responsible for having the proposals put together were unaware of the changes going on in funding. Aside from the obvious increased competition for dollars, there are a number of subtle differences that have entered the proposal writing field.

Professional grant/proposal writers are becoming the norm. These writers, who are usually full-time educators that take on the grant writing task for their institutions, are making proposal writing a science. They study foundations and government agencies closely. They make contacts, spend time on the telephone, and often know the ins and outs of an RFP before it is even written.

That's one reason why the competition for the dollars has intensified. The people doing the writing are more sophisticated, as are the readers. That does not mean that every educational or nonprofit group has to hire a professional. There are special grant/proposal writing courses being given, and there are other sources that are willing to provide insight and training for educational institutions.

For example, in the past few years there have been numerous programs designed to get welfare recipients back into the work force and off the welfare rolls. One technique was to use educational institutions to train them in new work skills. Local governmental agencies were given federal money (through the state and federal government) and were funding educational facilities to train people in the program.

Many of these agencies held bidding sessions for the universities and colleges interested in submitted proposals. Bidding meetings are part of the RFP, RFQ procedure. When the RFPs and so on are issued, the agency that puts them out holds a "bidder's conference." At these conferences, those intending to submit a proposal for the contract can not only ask many questions, but they also have the opportunity to meet those who will be judging the proposals.

It is during these bidding sessions that the nonprofessional proposal/grant writer can learn what ingredients are needed for a winning proposal.

Still, Dr. Schauerman believes the future for those looking for grants may be in hiring the pro grant writer. "Getting dollars is becoming more competitive with each passing year. We decided that the best approach would be to hire a pro grant writer."

What makes a pro grant writer different from a grant writer? He or she has a special kind of "know how"—he or she knows how to pick up the telephone and cull information from foundations and others who are asking for proposals. He can find out the required information with one call, and his chances of getting the grant are about "15 times greater than a nongrant professional," says Dr. Schauerman. Those increased odds are not because the professional is a better writer. Most of the time he is a better researcher. He or she may also be familiar with the decision-makers at the foundation level, and those decision-makers may have a bias towards them because they have seen their proposals previously.

Professionals also keep their eyes open and their ears to the ground. Foundations that give funds do not always make elaborate announcements. Usually it is up to the institution going after the monies to find out if they are available. Some publish a book each year that gives information on the type of proposals they are interested in funding.

GATHERING INFORMATION

Carol Geisbauer does not consider herself a professional grant writer, but she has studied foundations and proposals carefully. As a result, she has had a phenomenal success ratio—more than 80 percent of the proposals she has submitted have been funded.

Geisbauer does take grant/proposal writing seriously. "It is not something you can do in your spare time. You need to know what you are after and who is giving it."

To keep abreast of what is happening, she subscribes to a statewide publication (*Guide to California Foundations*) which outlines all the foundations doing business in her state, and also tells what kind of grants they have given in the past, and what type of proposals they prefer to fund. Most states have similar publications, and there is a national book as well.

Carol Geisbauer also subscribes to several newsletters pertaining to her field. She calls local and state agencies and asks to be put on their mailing lists so she will receive RFPs. She also scours newspapers to see what bills are being funded. "That's important," she says. "When you see a bill pass that is designated for, let's say, alcohol and drug abuse, you can surmise that ultimately it will make its way down to the local level."

To make sure she knows when the funding arrives, she will call the local alcohol and drug agency of the government. She will explain to them about the funding she heard was coming, and ask if they have any idea when it will be available. If they do not know, she will call back in a few weeks. She keeps calling until she hears an RFP has been written. Then she answers it.

Geisbauer does not waste time on every bill. She mathematically determines how much money will be coming into her area. For example, if the federal government passes a drug bill, and it means $1 million will come into her state, she calculates how much of the $1 million will come to her level.

"It is not difficult. Almost always it is determined on population. My organization is in a county with seven million people. If the county represented one third of the population of the state, that means we would receive about $333,000 from the $1 million. I would then ascertain how much of the $333,000 would come to my district. If, for example, we had two million people in the district, that would mean about 2/7s of the funds, or about $100,000 would be available. With my budget ($500,000 a year) that $100,000 is significant and certainly worth pursuing. At the same time, if the total funds coming in were $5,000 I would not go for it. In the public sector, there is too much paperwork and time involved for us to get involved with a $5,000 grant. Besides you put in just as much work for the $5,000 as you would for the $100,000."

Geisbauer also determines if the monies are earmarked for programs of her type. "It is ridiculous going after money just because it is there. You must make sure the funds are designed for your program. I do the same with foundations. Before I expend the energy on a proposal, I call. I tell them I administer a center for drug rehabilitation of teenagers. I explain who I am and what we do. I ask if the type of service we provide falls within their interest area.

"If they say yes, I pursue it further. I ask if they are interested in funding anything in my area, and I explain where I am geographically. If yes, then I go further. I tell them what I want to do. If it is of interest, I do not have the funds but I know there is interest."

Carol Geisbauer emphasizes that most foundations do not put out RFPs. They wait for organizations to approach them. Foundation money, she says, is often not worth the expenditure of time and effort, "unless you are national and are after one of the big foundations. Most of the small ones, or those that fund a local organization, will only fund a few thousand dollars. Maybe even $10,000. The problem is that by the time you finish the reporting and auditing requirements, there is not enough of the funds to be utilized effectively."

Geisbauer, however, is not choosy about funding. She scours her area and knows where every possible dollar can come from. She constantly calls the offices of politicians to find out if there is any new funding coming down.

Her board of directors consists of the "movers and shakers" in the community. She has city councilpeople as well as corporate executives on board. She is known as a professional grant writer, "one of the best I have ever seen," says an educator at a local university.

Others agree with Geisbauer's theory on grant/proposal writing being a two-way street. Aside from foundations, there are many private agencies and governmental bureaus that will accept proposals although they do not have an RFP written for it.

In numerous instances, funding may be made available through legislation but the RFP is months away from being mailed to vendors. Astute companies are aware of the coming funding and they hit agencies before the RFP is published.

OFFENSIVE SELLING POSITION

Jim Baxter at TRW describes it as an "offensive selling position. We know about the appropriation bills that have passed through Congress, as do other vendors who read the newspaper and keep track of Congressional bills.

"Once the bill is through, we know the type of program and equipment that will be funded. Based upon the funding and what it is for, we know the general needs. We also know the type of technology they may be looking for and whether we have it. If we do, there is no hesitation. We approach them. That's an 'offensive' selling position."

Baxter says vendors must be able to analyze funding bills and which RFPs will emerge from it. "You cannot sit around and wait for the RFP to be produced. Successful vendors anticipate. They know what programs are 'on the street.' That is, they know which programs are being bid on and the materials that will be needed once those bids are decided."

Once they know the programs, the vendors take it one step farther. "We ask ourselves what technology and/or parts will be subcontracted out. Can we supply any of them?"

When satellites are funded, for instance, there are components ranging from oxygen systems to refrigeration. The prime contractor may not supply all the parts and/or technology required. They may subcontract, or buy from outside vendors. "There is usually," explains Baxter, "a detailed description of what material will go into the satellite and the cost. It is called a Bill of Material, and it is made public when the RFP is put out. It becomes part of the proposal. A subcontractor only needs to examine the Bill to determine what his company can supply. And he can supply it regardless of which prime contractor wins the bid."

If they can, Baxter recommends immediately calling the purchasing or buying departments of both companies that are answering the RFP. "Ask the buyer/purchasing department to include your company in the 'request for quote'."

An RFQ (Request for Quotation) is a document that the prime supplier will put out when they are awarded the contract. In it are the components that must be produced by subcontractors, and the RFQ asks the proposed subcontractors for quotes on the materials. In many cases, the RFQ contains information identical to the RFP.

"The key," explains Baxter, "is to contact the purchasing and/or buying department of the prime contractor early—before the RFP is even awarded. That means if there are two firms competing, contact both. The mistake most subcontractors make is they wait for the RFP to be decided and the contractor to be awarded the bid. That's often too late. Get your request for an RFQ in early. Tell them you want your product considered. Never wait for the RFQ or RFP to be issued before you make the call."

THE ROLE OF NEEDS

"All RFPs are the result of some need," says Pat Unangst, who administers funding for a large agency. "If you keep track of agencies, you will find many times they have the need but just have not had time to write the RFP. In that case, a query from a vendor can lead to a contract."

Although it is not common, there are cases in which some agencies will "test out" a service or program with a limited contract. If, for example, it is a job-training proposal, the agency may fund it for one trainee. If it works, the vendor may then obtain funding for a dozen or more. The point is to ask. Question the agencies, both governmental and private. Most of the time the test is more readily acceptable for a local or regional project, rather than a national one. The point is that funds are available— and waiting for proposals.

Vendors, says Unangst, also miss out by not asking to be put on the bidder's list. "You do not have to have a specific RFP in mind. Get on the list. Initially, the reason is to see what is being funded and who is getting the money. You would be amazed at the number of companies that take part in the bidding that may be in your industry."

About two-thirds of the vendors on Unangst's list are out of state. Although most never intend to answer the RFPs, they are on the list to acquire information. Any vendor can do the same with an organization.

Pat Unangst, and others in similar positions, do not object to the lengthy lists and the numbers of RFPs they have to send across the country. Public and governmental agencies are constantly searching for new bidders. Calling and asking to be placed on a list is only one way companies stay abreast of new RFPs.

In the aerospace field, most companies have a marketing department whose sole job is to be aware of what is happening in their industry and to track all RFPs and RFQs. They scour newspapers for items on appropriations, and have contacts in the defense as well as departments of the military. They also ask to be put on RFP distribution lists.

They also make it a practice to examine the *Commerce Business*

Daily, which publishes lists of proposal requests that have been published.

"We are seldom surprised at what we find," says Harold Brownell of Boeing. "We usually know about it beforehand through the activities of our marketing department. But every once in a while, one will slip through. It's well worth the time to check the *Commerce Business Daily* if you are dealing with government contracts."

Karl Brennan has seldom missed an RFP. His firm, and several of his competitors, have a unique relationship with prime contractors in aerospace. It is a relationship that others in industry are examining closely because of its effectiveness.

Brennan's firm specializes in developing proprietary products for aerospace. Thus if he supplies a certain piece of technology for one airplane, and the prime contractor wants it in a new proposed model, the prime has to return to Brennan's firm and make him aware they are working on another project, one that will ultimately result in an RFP.

"We may spend two years helping the contractor develop a piece of equipment for an airplane. The airplane may not even be scheduled for production for three years, but we are helping to develop a portion of its system. If you help develop some of those systems, you know what is going on. By the time the RFP does come out, we know everything about it. In fact, we have usually influenced it."

What Brennan means by *influencing* is that if he is successful, the RFP will specifically ask for technology that has been developed by Brennan's company. Obviously, that means Brennan's company is going to get the contract.

At the same time, other companies may be helping the prime contractor in development and they, too, will be trying to influence the RFP.

INSIDE INFLUENCE

"If you cannot influence the RFP towards your technology, then you are not going to be in a good position to answer that RFP. Our goal, and the goal of any other company that helps a contractor develop a new aircraft, is to not only develop and customize the technology that is going to be used, but have it spelled out in the RFP."

How does the influencing come about? Typically, the prime contractor will announce that they are going to work on the development of a 200- or 300-passenger aircraft. Brennan's company may be approached to develop part of the aircraft's system. As a result, his engineering staff begins a dialogue with the engineers who work with the prime contractor.

After months of talking and working together, the engineers not only know what each is planning, but one may be influenced by the technology that is offered by the other. If that happens, the RFP will reflect that influence and Brennan's company has the contract locked up before they answer a word of the RFP. In effect, the RFP has become a "closed" issue.

"In this business most of the work is done ahead of time, long before the RFP is written. If you wait for the written request, you will probably lose out. In fact, most of the time if I see an RFP that is not familiar, I will pass."

Whether it is for the private or public sector, nearly all of those writing proposals today agree it has become a sophisticated business loaded with politics and pitfalls.

Years ago, it may have been the lowest bid that won, but today there are more elements than price involved. In the next chapter, we will examine some of them.

CHAPTER 3

Politics, Grants, and RFPs

It is a classic horror story and illustration of the pitfalls companies sometimes encounter when dealing with the government and its layers of rules and regulations.

It started more than five years ago when an aerospace contractor, who had worked long and diligently on a proposal, found his document had secured a contract for his company. The contract called for his firm to manufacture an electronics part that was destined for use in a radar system.

As is the case with many who win government contracts, the aerospace contractor had the edge because his firm not only had the technology, but it knew when the RFP (Request for Proposal) was going to be issued and what it required.

There is nothing illegal about the upfront knowledge. Astute companies have marketing teams that are in constant contact with procurement offices in Washington, D.C., and at the command offices outside Washington that house the Army, Navy, Air Force, and Marines.

These marketing teams, which are more technologically oriented than sales-oriented, keep their ears to the ground, read the newspapers in search of new projects that may be considered by Congress, and talk constantly to those within the armed services to find out what future needs will arise.

When the Strategic Defense Initiative (Star Wars) first became a topic of conversation, contractors throughout the United States began visiting defense department offices to find out what technology and systems might be required. As a result, some firms were prepared to compete for multimillion-dollar contracts months before the RFPs were ever issued.

Although the electronics contract had nothing to do with Star Wars, it was a multimillion-dollar piece of business. The firm began manufacturing the component in one of its Southwest U.S. plants. Things went smoothly for more than a year. That is, the parts were going out the door and being delivered in record time and without any problems.

Then it happened. A federal government auditor visited the plant. On the exact day he dropped in, a problem developed in the manufacturing system. Part of the wiring in the system was flawed. The contractor immediately stopped manufacturing and halted all shipments until the problem could be solved.

The auditor was not satisfied. He called his superiors at one of the armed forces command posts and complained. Within hours, the general in charge of the post heard about it and called his counterparts at the other armed forces bases. Within a few hours after that, some members of Congress were informed—and the problem was no longer one of manufacturing but of politics.

Ultimately, the auditors shut down the entire plant and prevented the contractor from not only manufacturing the electronic component but all the other parts that were being produced for other customers. Although it only took three days to solve the wiring defect, it took six months before the issue was resolved and the contractor was able to resume production.

The lost dollars were in the millions and the case is an example of what can happen in an industry that is among the most competitive, political, and rewarding ($300 billion a year) for proposal writers.

OBJECTIVITY AND RFPs

Outwardly, a Request for Proposal seems to be the most objective method for the government and other agencies to ensure fairness among bidders. Everyone gets the same paperwork, and they respond to the same questions. All proposals, theoretically, are judged by the same criteria.

But like any written document that is neither true or false nor multiple choice, subjectivity on the grader's part slips in. And it cannot be helped. RFPs involve individuals and human nature, and there are few of us who do not have some bias. Judges in Olympic Games figure skating or gymnastics competition seldom agree on the performance of the athletes they are grading, and the same is true of those scoring RFPs.

If price were the sole determinant, and everyone was offering the exact same service or technology, those going through RFPs would have little difficulty picking a winner. But price is only one of many variables. Certainly it is an important one, but few of those responsible for selecting the best answer to an RFP will make a selection on price alone.

There are politics involved regardless of the size of the contract. A year after the disastrous electronic component case, a local agency issued an RFP for a $50,000-a-year contract for services that it required from a private agency.

As is the case with multimillion-dollar contracts, the $50,000 RFP was loaded with detailed questions and requirements. The outside vendor, who had never answered an RFP with a proposal, was lost as he read through the myriad sections and seemingly insignificant points.

In desperation, he approached someone he knew intimately who was involved with the agency, someone who knew what it would take to win. After an hour's conversation, he had enough insight to not only technically submit a perfect proposal, but he hit every question with an answer that almost ensured his firm of a perfect score.

Proposals in answers to RFPs are scored with each section given a different point value. A firm can score low on one or two sections, but if it does well in an area where there are many points allocated it can still win. It is advisable to not only pay close attention to those questions that give minor points, but to pay special attention to the major questions that account for the majority of points.

GENERAL VS. SPECIFIC GOVERNMENT PROPOSALS

As Pat Unangst points out, "The low bid does not always win. For example, as part of a proposal a vendor might be asked to supply a piece of equipment. A bidder may come in with the lowest price, but his equipment may be reconditioned. Which one will you pick?"

Did the RFP allow for reconditioned products? How specific was it? There are both general and specific RFPs. General RFPs are vague and leave room for interpretation. For example, the RFP that asked for a piece of equipment may not have specified whether it was new or reconditioned. It is a classic example of a general RFP. RFPs that do not spell things out in detail are general.

The general RFP allows for greater subjectivity in the judging process. RFP readers and decision-makers can delay being specific until they read all the proposals. On the basis of what they read, they can become more specific and lean towards one vendor or the other.

Sound unfair? Perhaps, but in many ways a general RFP has less bias than its counterpart—the specific RFP. Specific RFPs, where everything is spelled out in detail, are used frequently when an agency has a certain vendor in mind. The agency may want the vendor to win, and they know that he or she is the only company and/or person that can supply a certain service, product, or technology.

The specific RFP can be the result of an agency and vendor working together for a long period of time. A vendor may have one contract and the agency likes the work that has been done. As a result, when it is time for renewal, the agency slants the RFP so that only the vendor can supply the exact requirements.

In aerospace and defense, the specific RFP is commonplace. Karl Brennan's firm will not answer one that is not. Brennan's firm, however, has an edge. Long before the RFP is written, his company is called upon by either the government agency or other customers to help develop the technology for a product. Brennan's company may end up working two to three years with the customer before the issuance of the RFP. If his marketing people do the job, the RFP will be slanted towards his product.

That's standard practice in the industry. It is not much different from proposals in the private sector that generally go to the person "who knows someone." Politics are played in both fields. There are ways, however, for newcomers to take advantage of the process.

Usually, new firms trying to influence RFPs can do so through one of three ways:

1. Technological breakthrough
2. Breakthrough in manufacturing a product
3. Lower cost than competitors

The more likely technique to get in the door is the first way. It happens all the time. An upstart company has an idea for a product that will be the result of new technology. It approaches the agency (if we are talking about the defense industry, it usually goes through procurement offices in Washington, D.C., or command offices of the services outside the city) and begins to kick around possible utilization of the technology.

The agency may already have plans on the back burner for technology of this type. The conversation between the newcomer and the government ends in joint development and eventually an RFP that is geared specifically towards the newcomer.

A good portion of the people at the agencies are technically oriented or scientific. They can talk about engineering and technology without problem. At the same time, the representative from a company should have technical background as well.

The greater a firm's technical capability, the more chance it has to generate winning proposals. In Brennan's case, his company stresses products in which there is "proprietary technology."

An aerospace company could be working on plans for a new 250-passenger airplane. Within the aircraft certain technology is required, technology which Brennan's firm can produce. It may take several years of research and development before the technology is to a state where it can be applied to the aircraft. Once it is, the RFP is written by the customer and issued. At that point, anyone can answer it and compete with Brennan's firm.

"If we have done our job," Brennan says, "that will not happen. During the time we have worked with the agency that plans to issue the RFP, we have learned much about the project. We know what they want. We know what their engineers are planning. Our engineers spend a great deal of time with theirs and have the chance to influence the wording of the RFP. By the time the RFP is written, it is specific and geared towards our company. We're not a shoo-in, but we are close to it."

DOLLARS MAKE NO DIFFERENCE

There are political ins and outs at every level of RFP response. Brennan's firm operates at a national and international level. It submits proposals for millions of dollars. But the same type of insight is required whether the proposal is for a billion-dollar RFP or a $10,000 grant.

Take Carol Geisbauer's agency. Her proposals have gone to foundations, local drug prevention agencies, and even the state.

"Half the process is having a technically perfect proposal," she says. "You have to answer the RFP exactly as instructed. The other half is the political process. You cannot just write an answer to an RFP, submit it, and hope you will win. Politics have to be played."

The minute Geisbauer finds there is money available, and an RFP to be answered, she knows "someone will make a political decision as to who will get the funds."

Her first step is to determine where she stands politically. That is, where the money is coming from and who will have the influence.

If, for example, money is coming from the state and it will be funneled locally, she calls the supervisor's office. It is her local supervisor who will ultimately have the say as to which organization's proposal will be accepted. The supervisor's staff will read the proposal and rank it, but the final decision will be made by the supervisor.

Carol Geisbauer will call and say, "I understand there is money coming down from the state. Does anyone have a line on it?" (Although grants and RFPs may originate at the local level, the funding can come from the federal government. It goes from Washington, D.C. to the state, then filters down to the local level. The language and requirements become a combination of both "Washington-ianese" and whatever is conjured up by the state or local agency.)

Geisbauer is asking if any agency has the inside track. At times, monies are targeted for specific agencies and it does little good to submit an answer to an RFP if you are not connected to that agency. Carol Geisbauer has found that the "deputies or whom-ever I talk to will usually be straightforward. They will not lead me on if some other organization is going to get the funds."

Others who have been in the field for a while operate in a simi-lar fashion. They all call and find out what's going on first. No one wants to waste their time. By calling, Geisbauer has done some-thing else. She has made a sales call. In the political process of selecting a winning answer to an RFP, organizations that show they are interested and concerned generally get "points" or consid-eration. They may not talk directly to the decision-makers when they make the call, but they generally talk to his or her staff. And staff always has input in a decision.

There can be two agencies within the same community compet-ing for the same funds. Each may answer the RFP and wait. If one agency has taken the time to call and talk to the political decision-maker's office, they will be remembered. Staff people tend to view the call as an example of interest. If the other agency never calls, the staff may view this as indifference although that actually may not be the case.

The call is not only designed to find out if some agency has the inside track, but it may generate additional information about the RFP and what will be expected. Things may come out during the course of this conversation that will help one agency improve its proposal enough to win. It is part of the necessary research that goes into answering any RFP.

POLITICAL "INFLUENCERS"

The political process is not limited to calling. In Carol Geisbauer's case (and with others), once she finds out who will be making the decision she goes to work in another political area. "If," she ex-plains, "I find a certain politician will be making the ultimate decision, I find someone who knows him. That someone may be from my board of directors, or it could be another local politician I have come to know.

"It does little good for me to call a political decision-maker. I don't have the clout. But if I have the mayor of a city on my board or if I know the mayor, and he or she is willing to go to bat for us, I will ask them to make the call. First, however, I brief them about the RFP. Then I ask if they can help. Most of the time they can. At the least, they can talk to the other politician and mention us in a favorable light. That is not going to win or lose for us but in a tight contest it can make the difference."

Whether you are nonprofit, as is Geisbauer's agency, or profit-making, it is important to get key people within the community involved.

Once she submits her proposal, she writes letters to everyone on her board and sends them a copy of the proposal as well. She asks them to write to the decision-maker (if they know him or her) or to anyone they know who may be involved with the RFP. She follows her letter to board members with a telephone call about a week later to see if they have written the letter she requested.

"It is important to show agencies that you are someone in the community; that you are not just coming out of left field and looking for money," she says. "Most political figures have not forgotten CETA and the problems it created for elected officials. They are extremely cautious when it comes to local funding."

If she finds a board member or local politician with influence who is concerned about the RFP, she will ask them to follow their letter with a telephone call to the decision-maker's office. This can be particularly effective when going after a grant from a foundation.

"Most of the time local organizations do not have a chance to obtain significant funding from a foundation. We may get $2000 or $3000. That's hardly worth answering the RFP for because of the paperwork. Whereas with the government, local organizations may find $50,000 or $100,000 (or more) RFPs waiting to be answered."

WHAT FOUNDATIONS PREFER

Most foundations prefer to give their funds to regional or national organizations, or the groups that will give them high visibility. Foundations may be philanthropic but they are not adverse to positive publicity. They want the exposure but they know that a small local organization will not have a project broad enough to ensure them of it. Thus they save their funds for larger groups.

If Carol Geisbauer goes after a foundation RFP, she has one of her board members make a call about two weeks after the proposal is submitted. They will tell the foundation people that "I am on the board of such and such, and we just sent in a proposal. I wondered how it was going."

The answer they usually get is that the board has not met or it will not meet for another month or two. The important thing is that the board member has shown an interest and has met someone at the foundation via the telephone. That also shows Geisbauer's agency is interested. The board member calls again when he knows the foundation is to meet. The content of the conversation will be similar to the first call, only this time the board member will ask for the person he or she talked to previously. Familiarity begins to come into the decision-making process.

That means as much in the political proposal process as it does in business. The old adage, "It is who you know, not what you know" may not apply completely to proposals but Geisbauer believes it can count for up to 50 percent in the decision-making process.

That is why colleges, universities, and others are hiring professional grant/proposal writers—not because the professional writes better than anyone else. On the contrary, he or she may write no better than anyone else on staff, but what the professional has to offer is the political contact.

The professional usually knows people at the foundation. They know the decision-makers. Consequently, when they call they may obtain an insight into the RFP that others do not have. That, however, is not the only plus of the professional.

"He or she knows what the readers of the grant proposal are looking for," says Sam Schauerman, president of El Camino College. "They know how to state the case or need. They also know how to tie in the most important points."

One such important point is an *outcome statement*. When a college, university, or other agency is given a specific sum of money, the foundation wants to know the outcome, that is, how many people will be trained or where you expect to be at the end of the program. In other words, what the foundation can expect for its money.

THREE AREAS OF CONCERN

The three key areas of concern are the *statement of need*, the *strategy for meeting that need*, and a *way of evaluating the results*.

Intrinsic to these is the budget. A common mistake is for those preparing a grant or RFP to say they will do the job or project for the amount of dollars allocated. They fail to itemize it into a detailed budget, to show administrative costs, supplies, and all significant expenditures. Foundations and others frown upon high administrative costs or salaries. As much of the money as possible should be geared to the community or project.

Under normal circumstances, the foundation does not allow a university or agency to make a profit. If it costs $20 an hour for someone to administrate the program, that figure is entered in the budget. The university or agency, however, may come out with a profit because the administrator generally is handling more than one project. In other words, he may be administering two or three grants, and his efforts may be generating $60 an hour ($20 from each grant). The excess becomes profit.

Some grants enable the proposer to earmark a set percentage of the total funding for administration. Usually that percentage is above what is actually needed. The excess becomes profit.

There is profit in other areas as well. In budgeting supplies, it is difficult to be exact. Most of the time the figure is slightly inflated, thus the proposer has a chance to make additional monies.

Foundations are most concerned with "results." How many people will be taught to read? How many students will go on to college? If the results are in the proposal (naturally as projections), chances of winning rise.

The professional grant writer has contacts and can usually find what results are considered the most important. The professional also knows how to watch for the right grants, that is, those that will fit into the organization he or she is representing.

The professional, with his familiarity with various foundations, does not always have to wait for an RFP. If he or she has an idea for a project that they believe may be funded by a foundation, all they have to do is take it to the organization. They may get a feeling for its acceptance via the telephone, or they can write to the foundation and ask for the forms.

The nonprofessional can, of course, do the same thing. If they do not know anyone at the foundation, all they have to do is write to say they are interested in applying for dollars for this type of program and the foundation will send the forms and information. It is preferable, however, to talk to someone at the foundation first and find out if the project is something they will consider before wasting time with paperwork and filing.

The professional, through his or her experience, can also answer RFPs quicker. Generally, a professional can write four or five answers to an RFP in the time it takes a nonprofessional to write one.

The professional knows the people who are working at the agency or foundation. If he does not, he can pick up the telephone and ask the right questions. Obviously, that means anyone answering an RFP can do the same. The advantage the professional has is that he knows the questions to ask when he sees the RFP.

Those questions may not be as complex as some think, however. As Geisbauer says, anyone can pick up the telephone and ask questions, and anyone can answer the RFP if they follow the directions and questions closely.

"Frankly, I do not believe there is a difference between the professional grant writer and a good writer. I do not consider myself a professional. I write best about things I know about. If your heart is in what you know about, you will add the right ingredients to the proposal."

Sam Schauerman agrees that the nonprofessional can do it as well if they will take the time. "There is no problem with anyone picking up a telephone, calling, and asking questions. People at foundations and agencies are more than willing to provide whatever information they can. In some instances, you are able to write a proposal although there is no RFP issued. You can send it to the individual at the foundation that you may have met by placing a telephone call. You can ask them what they think and in many cases they may send it back with comments.

WHY SOME LOSE

Answers to RFPs that do not win may be sent back to the organization along with comments. The comments will tell the writer how the readers evaluated the proposal, what they thought was done right, and what they did not like. Such feedback provides excellent insight into writing style and content for the proposer.

Should Carol Geisbauer lose with her proposal, she calls the agency and tries to find out what her proposal lacked. No one likes to lose but they know they can learn from the loss. Brennan's firm holds a critique session, as does Brownell's. Jim Baxter's firm analyzes why they did not get the proposal as well.

Typically, a proposal loses in the technology area because the agency does not have enough confidence in the component. However, there can be other reasons. If there are two products, both equal in function, one company may get it over another because of previous history. One may be on-time with progress reports, the other habitually late. One may be neat, the other sloppy.

Another reason for the loss is that the competitor simply "outspent us," says Brownell. "If you invest $500,000 in a proposal, and someone else puts in $5 million and builds a model plus they do all kinds of other research and development, they are generally going to be ahead of you. They did an in-depth job with their homework, you did not. Common sense tells you why you lost."

Agencies have developed a deficiency system. If a company does something wrong, it earns a black mark. One of the trickiest marks to avoid is one for incorrect pricing which often comes about in an innocent way. A company may have a winning proposal, but that is only the first step. The second step is negotiating a contract with the agency. While the negotiation is underway, the agency will issue a letter authorizing the company to start procuring a portion of the materials that may be needed.

In the case of a theoretical $100 award, $60 may be spent internally by the company, and the other $40 for outside buys. The government letter says it is ok to buy $20 of the $40 worth of material. When the contract is signed, the remainder can be purchased.

The company instructs its purchasing department to make the buy. The purchasing department contracts and negotiates with other vendors. In the end, the parts may be bought for $15, $20, or even $25. If the contract has been negotiated and the purchase is for $20 or $25, there is no problem (if it is for $25 the company just loses). But if the purchase runs $15 there can be difficulties. In that case, the company is guilty of "defective pricing," and it may earn a black mark which can go against future contracts and its track record. A poor track record can destroy many proposals even if a company has a technologically superior product.

Feedback from a loss is critical. It is advisable for any agency or company to discover the reasons behind losing. Hidden within the answer is usually a hint on how to be successful the next time around. Those who make decisions about RFPs are often quite open when talking to a company that failed in its bid.

Losing usually stems from a lack of knowledge or insufficient insight into the RFP. If one particular firm has been awarded a contract for the past three or four years, before turning in a competing proposal, firms wishing to compete should do homework. Proposers should determine if the agency is satisfied with the current contractor. This is valuable intelligence and can help companies determine whether they should compete for a contract.

There are techniques for getting the information. In many cases, there are internal reports and memos that can be examined. If a firm was interested in entering a proposal and competing against a current trash collector for a city, county, or whatever contract, it should contact the appropriate city, or county committee that is in charge of trash. Ask questions. See if there are memos or reports that have been filed on the current vendor. There usually are and, in many cases, they are public record. "Virtually anyone who has had a contract with a public agency usually has been the subject of a public report," says Ms. Unangst. "If the odds are that a fine job is being done and there is not an open slot, why jump in . . . unless you can offer something no one else can."

Study the attitude of the committee. If it is dissatisfied, it may be worthwhile to submit a rival proposal. If not, a company may be wasting its time.

BIDDER'S CONFERENCE

For those who decide to jump in, the bidder's conference is a must for REPs that are local or regional in scope. Usually all the competitors are present as well as those who have the responsibility for the RFP.

Questions are answered and the RFP is clarified. The person who wrote the RFP—that is, the person from the department which perceives the need—is often at the conference to answer questions. By listening to what he or she emphasizes, the proposer gets additional insight into how the RFP should be answered.

The people at the conference may also end up monitoring the program. "I want them to see me," says Carol Geisbauer. "It helps establish a relationship. It is the little things that can make the difference."

A bidder's conference serves as more than a question-and-answer forum. Leading questions can be asked, and the answers provide the proposer with information that is not readily available. It also gives proposers something their competitors may not have if they do not attend the conference.

If competitors are in attendance, it gives other proposers a chance to hear what is bothering their competition. That, too, can make a difference.

Points are frequently made at the bidder's conference that are not found in the RFP. The bidder's conference is a source of additional coaching and seldom fails to help the proposer.

"We will not write the proposal for you," says Pat Unangst, who administrates an agency that puts out numerous RFPs, "but we will spend time answering questions. If we find someone who is not familiar with the RFP process, we will probably spend more time with them to familiarize them with the process."

RFPs are graded by a team of people It may be just a few or sometimes as many as a half dozen or more. Low and high scores are thrown out, and an average is taken. An odd number of readers are usually on the team. A portion of the readers come from the staff, some are from outside the agency, and others may be from private industry.

In the RFP, the grading process is spelled out, but the bidder's conference also gives a chance for a proposer to ask questions about the grading, and who might be doing the reading. Although the exact names of the readers may not be revealed, the proposer may get additional insight into the grading system by finding out if the graders are from, for example, private industry or the agency.

It should be noted that there are two distinct levels of RFPs. One is for goods and services at the local, regional, or state level that usually do not involve proprietary technology. With these RFPs, bidder's conferences are extremely important.

With high-technology, national (in scope) RFPs, the bidder's conference is usually a waste of time. These are cases in which the proposals are prepared long before the RFP is issued. They have been in the preparation stage for months, perhaps years. They are the RFPs that have been influenced by vendors, and normally they are contracts awarded through the procurement office in Washington, D.C. or one of the armed services command centers.

In this case by the time the RFP is issued, it is too late to answer. That is, there is not enough time to prepare a proposal. Typically, this is the domain of the defense and aerospace industry.

Gary Minor's firm is deeply involved in this segment of the industry. His proposals go to the SPO (Special Projects Office) of the armed service involved. One can compare the armed services to a large department store, where each SPO (Navy, Marines, Air Force, and so on) can be compared to a particular department (men's, women's, sports, and so on) within that store.

Minor's office makes it their business to maintain daily interaction with the SPOs. "We call them and talk to them, get to know them. We learn what sells, and what will sell to them. If we have an idea, we can approach them. Unfortunately, just about the time you get to know them, the government transfers personnel."

Minor's division will submit winning proposals for about 125 defense projects this year. He never misses a bidder's conference, although by the time the conference comes along the written proposal has been underway for some time. Most times, he says, he finds his competitors in attendance. The bidder's conference can get confusing, adds Minor, when there is an RFP for a new product line. "That's when you get about ten times the number of new people. Some are looking for new products that might fit existing business. Others might be looking to team up with another company. The bidder's conference turns out to be a prospecting venture for new vendors."

WHAT THE RFP REALLY SAID

Dan McClain, a former assistant city manager of a large metropolitan area, says that many proposers have problems because they do not listen carefully to the answers they are given at a bidder's conference nor do they understand what an RFP was really saying.

Those answering questions at a bidder's conference are critical sources of accurate information. Whether they wrote the RFP or not, they understand it and what the decision-makers within that entity really want.

McClain cites the case where a number of competitive cable television groups came together to answer his city's RFP for a cable television system. Although the proposal selection would ultimately be made by the seven city councilpeople who ran the city, there were a number of staff members who played key roles.

While most of the companies surveyed the community and what its people wanted, not many understood what the council and staff were after. This was a mistake since ultimately these people would be the decision-makers.

Some miscalculated, and in the end the company that won did so because of its ability to comprehend the staff's answers to questions at the bidder's conference. The city councilpeople relied greatly on staff and its opinions, because the staff understood what the councilpeople wanted. "That is going to vary from city to city, but anyone submitting a proposal should attend a council meeting and observe how the politicians rely on their staff. The greater the reliance, the more credence proposers should give to staff members."

In the RFP process, politicians are also influenced by their pet interests. For example, suppose a company was making a proposal for a contract for a busline within an area. There might be six or seven supervisors, aldermen, or councilpeople who would ultimately make the decision as to which firm would get the contract.

Within the decision-making group, one of those politicians may have an overriding interest in pollution, while another may be concerned with traffic congestion. The company answering an RFP with this scenario should pay special attention to both those areas, and address those questions in the RFP.

If those political interests are not well-known, proposers should research and question politicians and staff to determine if they have any special interests before an RFP is answered.

RENEWING THE CONTRACT

"If you prove yourself one year, you are in an excellent position to repeat the following year," says Carol Geisbauer. "It is like any other business proposal. If you do the job for a company, they are not going to be hesitant to renew, and your competitors are not going to be able to make headway."

Nothing, of course, in the RFP area is automatic. The higher up the government RFP ladder, the more impersonal and the greater the amount of paperwork.

Joe Izzo, JIA Management, refuses to submit RFPs because of the "immense amount of useless paper" that has to be filled out. Many in private industry agree. Quantity instead of quality is still found in agencies putting out RFPs. Instruction booklets for answering the RFP are becoming clearer as well. The days of the $600 hammer are gone because agencies are being pressured to approach the cheapest source for spare parts.

PROPOSALS AND COST CONTROLS

Now the public as well as politicians have become adamant about more reasonable costs. Cost control will be one of the major issues in government proposals of the future. Another issue is the auditor. There are no agencies growing more rapidly with investigators than the IRS and procurement departments. The procurement auditors are dubbed "auditators"—for audit investigators.

For some, the emphasis on cost control and auditing has gone beyond reason. In aerospace and defense, this is reflected in the disappearance of government funding of research and development costs. Today it is a partnership. If a company competes for a product and submits a proposal, it will find that Uncle Sam is only willing to pay half the front end. The remainder has to be put up by the proposer.

Companies evaluating RFPs must take that additional pricing factor into consideration. If the development cost is going to be $15 million, they will have to put up one-half of it themselves. Or if their proposal is the winner, they may have to split the cost and development technology with a competitor if they cannot afford to put up all the capital.

Sharing technology is a delicate issue. Companies that spend millions of dollars on research are not anxious to give proprietary plans to others.

Where companies share cost and plans, they must compete against each other to see who will supply the product as soon as development is finished. Usually, the company that is "dragging" the other along, that is, the one that had the prime contract, will wind up with the business the first year. After that, they are competitors.

Although both have the technology—because it has been shared—they do not operate the same and their costs will differ. One company may have different manufacturing techniques, methods that allow it to produce the product at a lower cost.

The government has also become sensitive about companies that win a long-term contract. In the past, firms that won 20-year contracts for 1000 missiles a year only had to supply the same 1000 missiles each year. In most cases, even if the missile became outdated, the government was stuck with it.

Today, a 20-year missile program with 1000 missiles a year may only be a one-year contract for 1000 missiles. The RFPs have stipulations within them that require rebidding each year, although the initial proposal and contract was multi-year.

Each year the company that won the 20-year missile award finds it has to negotiate for a follow-on contract. A follow-on is another RFP that says we bought 1000 missiles last year, and this year we will buy another 1000—but not necessarily from your company. It depends upon the quality, improved technology, and price.

If the original winner of the contract turns in a bid that fails to beat someone else, they will have to share their technology and take a licensing fee from the competitor who has won. Thus, the long-term contract is no longer long-term.

From the public's viewpoint, this technique is more cost efficient, and the government will get more for its dollars. From the proposer's view, it creates more paperwork, problems, and of course, competition.

Although some of the changes irk proposers in the defense industry, there are a number they view as beneficial. If the company wins an award, and it finds a way to improve the product during the course of the contract, they may recoup development costs for the new model from the government. Both the company and government come out on top.

DEVELOPMENTAL PROPOSALS

Winning has become a way of life for John Hamond's company. He specializes in developmental proposals. That is, his firm manufactures a proprietary technology that can be customized for different products depending upon the product's ultimate use.

Companies may approach him and ask if he can customize the technology for a projected product they have in mind. The product may not be produced for 10, perhaps 15 years, but planning begins early. Hamond answers the request with developmental proposals. The developmental proposal is similar to the answer for an RFP. It contains technological, management, and cost sections and details each.

There is no bidder's conference involved, and the bottom line is a product that will be a significant source of income for his company in the future. Hamond takes his technology a step farther, as do others who have proprietary products. He will approach agencies—because of the knowledge he gains from his marketing field force as to what may be coming in the future—and he will write an unsolicited three-to-five-page outline for an idea.

The idea is always slanted towards the agency and a problem it currently (or is about to) faces. If the agency is interested, they may put together a detailed RFQ or RFP that would ultimately go to open bid (that is, anyone could answer). The likelihood of anyone but Hamond's firm answering is slim, since the RFP is based upon the input from Hamond.

Hamond has a third way of selling. He brainstorms with others in his division about the potential use for their technology. They may come up with an idea (perhaps it ties into the SDI or some other future program) and approach the agency with it. An RFP could end up as the result.

"We become the stimulant for the RFP and more business," he says. "We've been doing that for years. In this era, you cannot sit back and wait for the RFPs. If you have a product, and you see someone or some agency that can use it, bring it to their attention."

Hamond's company does what Ed Velton, a consultant in the field, says many fail to do. They exchange ideas frequently with the technical people at the agencies and they always know what is going on. Hamond also avoids one of the pitfalls that many firms fall into—a late submission of a proposal—which, in the opinion of Tom Kaplin, another noted consultant, usually happens because companies "wait for the RFP and do not market their services early enough." In this $300 billion-a-year industry, marketing is everything.

And the political process is not far behind.

CHAPTER 4

Winning RFPs & Grants

For 10 years, Carol Geisbauer has been one of the most successful grant/proposal writers in the country. During this time, she has developed a comprehensive chart detailing everything from how money flows to the format of a grant.

Geisbauer's outline starts with the potential funding sources. These range from the federal government to private foundations and/or corporations.

Funding Sources

1. Federal
2. State
3. County
4. City
5. Private (foundations and/or corporations)

The state, county, and city may contract directly with a local organization such as Carol Geisbauer's. The federal government almost always works through the state and does not contract directly with local groups.

Federal $\longrightarrow$ Block grants $\longrightarrow$ State $\xrightarrow[\text{with}]{\text{contracts}}$ County $\xrightarrow[\text{with}]{\text{contracts}}$ Local organizations

The block grant refers to a "block" of money that goes to the state. The state divides the funds according to population, need, or some other well-defined parameter. Geisbauer tracks these funds carefully and maintains constant contact with local agencies to see if (and when) funding has arrived.

In what other ways does a consultant find out about the funding? There are seven common sources for the local organization; these are:

1. *Federal Register*
2. Newsletters
3. Mailing lists—county departments
4. State legislature
5. Ear to ground
6. Foundation directors
7. Roster of corporations

The *Federal Register,* available in most libraries, lists funding sources according to category. For example, housing falls under the "health and human resources" classification. Those seeking grants or RFPs relating to housing would consult the *Register* under that heading to find a list of possible grants. Anyone could go through this list and contact the appropriate agency (which is listed) for details.

Geisbauer has also developed a format for answering RFPs or submitting grant proposals to foundations. Although the exact requirements vary, successful grants usually have the following elements:

1. Program needs/analysis
2. Program goals
3. Program objectives (should be measurable)
4. Methodology—how the program will be carried out
5. Evaluation—how the program will be evaluated. How will it, for example, count the number of successes, people who go through the program, and so on?
6. Sponsoring organization capability—the organization's background, success, who runs it, what will be going on
7. Work plan including a timeline—when will everything happen?

8. Budget and budget narrative—including details showing where the money is going and to whom

9. Letters of support

10. Attachments—the foundation or organization putting out the RFP may ask for things such as copies of programs the proposer has been involved in, its affirmative action plan, insurance plans, and so on

When answering an RFP or submitting a grant, there are many requirements for the consultant or organization that is writing. A violation of any one of them can ruin the proposal. The requirements include:

1. Following the guidelines—*exactly*—*do not* go beyond the number of pages, signatures, attachments, number of copies, and so on

2. Writing clearly, concisely—edit—edit—edit

3. Writing well—do not use adjectives. Look at other proposals that have won to get an idea of what good writing looks like.

4. Having perfect spelling, punctuation, sentence structure

5. Having the correct form: follow the instructions—indent paragraphs—break up paragraphs—make it easy to read

6. Using a computer (letter quality) or good typewriter

7. Setting a target to complete the document a week before the deadline—in case something breaks down

Do not forget the political process. Call the staff of the organization if necessary, contact your local representatives, board members, and any other influential people you know.

By adhering to the rules and following the format, Carol Geisbauer's proposals usually win.

Recently the proposal in Figure 4–1 (pages 72–92) brought Geisbauer's organization nearly $150,000. The preparation and research paid off. She hit all the political bases as well as put together a technically perfect document—and that is what it takes to win in the public sector.

The funds Geisbauer competed for were earmarked for delinquency prevention programs for youths and adults in the County of
Los Angeles. The funds may have originally come from the state or
even the federal government. The origin is not stated in the RFP.
The RFP that she answered was typical of those that are available
to organizations throughout the country.

The funds are awarded on the basis of recommendations made to
the County Board of Supervisors by the "Justice System Advisory
Group." This group was appointed by the Board, and is responsible
to them. Although the group makes the recommendation, it was
up to the Board to approve it—a political decision.

Half the battle with RFP proposals is political. Who do you
know? In this case, Carol Geisbauer did not personally know supervisors, but there were members of her Board who did. When
she completed her proposal, a copy went to her Board members,
and she asked several to call the supervisor's office. A mayor and
several local elected officials did.

On page 73 appears the amount of the total funds ($1.9 million)
that are earmarked for *community-based organizations* (CBOs),
or funding category III. A pitfall in submitting proposals is that
overzealousness may lead organizations to apply to the right organization for the wrong funds.

These funds are countywide, and there are five supervisorial
districts within Los Angeles County. That means each district
is going to get approximately $400,000, or one-fifth of the $1.9
million.

On page 73, the funding is shown to be for one year; prior receipt of funds does not necessarily mean the recipient is going to
get this funding. Prior performance does, however, count when decisions are made. If an organization did well with its proposal the
first year, that fact is going to be taken into (subjective) consideration by the decision-making body.

On pages 78–79, there is a listing of "eligible target groups and
definitions." This gives consultants and local organizations a
chance to see if their group "fits" the RFP. It is senseless for an
organization to submit a proposal if it does not serve one of the
targeted groups or provide the services sought (page 75).

The timetable (page 80) is important. Note two significant
dates: On January 11, there is a bidder's conference, and the

deadline for proposals is February 8. The January 11 date presented Geisbauer with three opportunities. A chance to:

1. See who she was competing against
2. Meet the people who would be playing a part in the judging
3. Get her questions answered

The proposal format (page 80) is to be "brief and straightforward." That means no adjectives or superlatives. The next three pages describe what is expected.

The breakdown of how each section will be graded is on page 84. Methodology, or how the program will work, accounts for 30 percent of the points, the objectives 25 percent, and budget 15 percent. These three categories generate 70 percent of the points.

Objectives refer to what the organization hopes to accomplish. And the answer has to be specific.

The Appendix includes the raters' guide, as well as one of the most critical parts of the proposal—budget guidelines.

Figure 4–2 (pages 93–109) is a portion of the winning proposal Carol Geisbauer submitted. This proposal shows the technique that is utilized when filling out an RFP. There are few, if any, adjectives in the proposal, but Geisbauer uses *underlining* where she wants to make a point and uses indents and short paragraphs to make the reading easier.

Research is an important tool of any proposal, and Carol Geisbauer did her homework (page 94). The facts and figures she culled from census data, the supervisorial offices, local politicians, and other community-based groups, are all outlined—and impressive.

The funding is for prevention of juvenile delinquency, therefore, she establishes need by showing the problems the area has with juvenile crime through statistics gathered from various police organizations.

Every funding organization is sensitive to measurement, and Carol Geisbauer gives a thorough outline on page 97 as to how the success of the program can be ascertained. There are figures, not generalizations. Statements such as, "We hope to reduce juvenile delinquency dramatically through this program" never fly without backup. The backup is in the form of the exact numbers.

The nine-page budget beginning on page 101 is the model of how a grant budget should be detailed. It starts with a breakdown of the $150,000 and goes into detail.

Geisbauer says the "biggest mistake made when filling out a budget for a foundation or other grant, is that too much goes for administration and not enough goes into the program."

In Geisbauer's budget, $84,000 (not including employee benefits) will go directly to counselors who will be working with the youth, and $31,500 will be utilized for administration salaries. That means around 20 percent of the budget (plus benefits) will go to administration. Typically, that is a low administrative fee, and proposal evaluators will look favorably upon it.

THE BIDDER'S CONFERENCE

How Valuable Is the Bidder's Conference?

With major defense industry contracts, by the time the RFP is issued there are already firms that have the inside track. Thus attendance at a bidder's conference—where the expected proposal and its requirements are discussed—may be a waste of time.

That is not the case with Requests for Quotation (RFQs), the document that is issued by agencies when they want an independent contractor to give them a price for products or services. Nor is it the case with RFPs that are issued for new products or those seeking vendors for products or services at the local or regional level. In these cases, attendance at a bidder's conference can lead to valuable insights.

Figure 4–3 on page 110 is an invitation to a bidder's conference. Along with it is a detailed (Figure 4–4 on page 111) description of the four areas in which the agency will accept proposals.

The package given to those at the bidder's conference may be 30 or 40 pages long. At the conference, those in charge of the RFP go through the document to make sure everyone present understands it. The first page (Figure 4–5, page 113) outlines what is expected, the number of copies that must be submitted, and when it is due.

The last paragraph in Figure 4–5 says "two originals." Rather than two original copies, this phrase refers to two copies with *original signatures*. The rest can be copies. This instruction was clarified at the bidder's conference along with other important factors.

Personnel at the conference included the two people who would judge the value of each proposal. The consultants who attended had the opportunity to meet them.

Those in attendance were also made privy to information that was *not* in the RFP. One of the most important things they heard related to price—and profit. They were told that for each placement—the object of the RFP was for vendors to present programs in which the unemployed, disadvantaged, and disabled could be put back to work—they could budget $5,400. Financial information in the RFP was limited to the $45,000 that would be awarded (in total) to winning proposals.

Without that information, a bidder would have to guess as to how much he would allocate for each placement. One of the potential bidders in attendance was a school that trained and placed auto mechanics. The tuition ran approximately $2,500 for the six months of schooling and placement.

A $45,000 contract would require the firm to train and place 18 candidates at $2,500 each. At $5,400 per placement, the auto mechanics firm would only have to enroll, train, and place half as many participants. The advantage is obvious—the firm would make more than twice as much money for half the effort.

As mentioned before, a company that was not present at the conference would never have known about the $5,400 figure. Those contenders who had this information could go back and handle their budget with more accuracy. They would also know what kind of profit they could make.

At the conference, bidders were also told that the programs most likely to win were those that "linked the private and public sector." In other words, the grantor was anxious to develop programs with private firms who would be paid to train applicants and keep them in the private sector following their training.

Figure 4–6 on page 114 outlines the point evaluation system. The methodology is critically important, along with the organization's capability. Have they trained people before? How successfully? How many placements?

The budget consideration is not far behind. Figure 4–7 on page 116 breaks down cost by categories; administrative costs, which are always scrutinized, are detailed. The firm that has too great a percentage of administrative costs (20–25% is the norm) will suffer in the grading.

How does a company make its profit? If, for instance, a vendor submits a proposal and has 20 percent ($9,000 out of the $45,000 contract) for administration, that would appear not to cover the salaries for the executives, secretaries, and clerical workers involved. That would be true if each vendor had only one client—the vendor has other clients, however, each sharing in the total administrative costs.

The proposal format (Figure 4–8, page 117) differs slightly from the one Carol Geisbauer submitted. There is set space for a narrative which cannot be exceeded without disqualification.

The budget page has a statement at the end that may cause confusion. It says "describe matching funds to be used to expand or enhance this proposal."

Agencies have a fetish for "matching funds." What this refers to is the dollars that the contractor is willing to contribute to the contract. The dollars are not "hard" or actual dollar expenditures. For example, according to this RFP, the school or training facility that wins the contract has to spend money recruiting applicants. It can earmark part of the contract for advertising, but it may also put in $5,000 of its own funds as "matching."

The company may plan to advertise for students whether it wins the contract or not. It has a budget of $5,000 for ads, and it will spend the money regardless of the contract outcome. It can enter the $5,000 as "matching," that is, funds that will be spent in addition to the $45,000 grant.

Some firms demonstrate matching with secretarial services, telephone calls, or other types of administration. The important thing to remember is that matching counts—winning proposals always have them included.

COUNTY JUSTICE SYSTEM SUBVENTION PROGRAM

COMMUNITY-BASED ORGANIZATION
REQUEST FOR PROPOSALS

FISCAL YEAR 1988-1989

COUNTY OF LOS ANGELES

JUSTICE SYSTEM ADVISORY GROUP

CURT LIVESAY
CHAIRMAN

Staffed by the Department
of Community and Senior
Citizens Services

BARRY NIDORF
VICE-CHAIRMAN

Robert G. Medina
Director

FIGURE 4-1. Sample community-based RFP.

COUNTY OF LOS ANGELES
COMMUNITY AND SENIOR CITIZENS SERVICES

3175 West Sixth Street Los Angeles, California 90020-1798
(213) 738-2600

ROBERT G. MEDINA
Director

STEPHANIE KLOPFLEISCH
Chief Deputy Director

LARRY L. JOHNSON, ASSISTANT DIRECTOR
VINCENT G. TERRY, ASSISTANT DIRECTOR
LYNN W. BAYER, ASSISTANT DIRECTOR

December 21, 1987

To: Interested Community-Based Organizations

From: Henry Knawls, Chief
            Community Services Division

Subject: REQUEST FOR PROPOSALS

The County of Los Angeles Justice System Advisory Group (JSAG) is requesting proposals from public and private nonprofit, community-based organizations to operate crime and delinquency prevention programs for youths and adults in the County of Los Angeles.

The JSAG anticipates that approximately $1.9 million in Justice System Subvention Program funds will be made available to community-based organizations for the period July 1, 1988, through June 30, 1989. The final funding amount will be determined prior to July 1, 1988. All funds will be provided through the State of California, Department of Youth Authority.

Information relative to applying for funding is contained in the attached 1988-89 Community-Based Organizations Request For Proposals.

This invitation is extended to any public or private not-for-profit community-based agency which currently, and for at least two years, provides justice system programming within the County of Los Angeles.

PROPOSAL AVAILABILITY

Request for Proposal (RFP) copies may be obtained beginning January 4, 1988, between the hours of 8:00 A.M. and 5:00 P.M. at the Department of Community and Senior Citizens Services, 3175 West Sixth Street, Room 200, Los Angeles, California.

FIGURE 4-1. (*continued*)

TABLE OF CONTENTS

FIGURE 4–1.   (*continued*)

COUNTY JUSTICE SYSTEM SUBVENTION PROGRAM
FISCAL YEAR 1988–89 REQUEST FOR PROPOSALS
COMMUNITY-BASED ORGANIZATIONS

I. **INTRODUCTION**

The County Justice System Subvention Program (CJSSP) is established under Article 7, Chapter 1, Division 2.5 of the Welfare and Institutions Code (WIC), as amended by SB 789 in 1983. Under this legislation, funds are allocated annually by the State to counties to subvene the cost of selected private and public programming in support of the justice system.

The 1987–88 CJSSP allocation was $19.9 million. The 1988–89 allocation has not yet been determined, but is anticipated to be comparable.

A. The law specified that CJSSP funds be used to assist counties in protecting society from crime and delinquency by:

1. Maintaining and improving local justice systems.

2. Encouraging greater selectivity in the kinds of juvenile and adult offenders retained in the community.

3. Assisting the counties in reducing the number of offenders re-entering the local criminal justice system.

4. Assisting counties in their efforts to protect and care for children and youths who are in need of services as a result of truancy, running away, and being beyond the control of parents.

B. In order to receive funds, a county must:

1. *Establish a Justice System Advisory Group* (JSAG) to assess justice system needs, evaluate alternative programs and make written recommendations to the Board of Supervisors.

2. *Prepare an Appropriate Application*

3. *Conduct Public Hearings* to assist the Advisory Group and Board of Supervisors in its funding decisions. The JSAG held its public hearing on November 19, 1987, to invite comments on funding priorities. The Board of Supervisors will hold a hearing in the Spring to review the Advisory Group's funding recommendations.

C. *Funding Categories*

For the 1988-89 funding year, the Advisory Group has allocated funds into *three funding categories.*

FIGURE 4-1. (*continued*)

75

1. *Funding Category I*—Programs providing services which were mandated in 1976 under AB 3121 (Chapter 1071, Statutes of 1976) must be funded through the subvention program.

2. *Funding Category II*—Programs operated by County Departments.

3. *Funding Category III*—Community-based agency component. It is anticipated that approximately $1.9 million will be allocated to community-based organizations.

This Request invites Proposals under Category III as spelled out below.

II. REQUEST FOR PROPOSALS

A. *Purpose*

The purpose of this Request for Proposals (RFP) is to invite project proposals impacting crime and delinquency as specified below from community-based organizations for the tenth fiscal year (1988–89) funding.

This invitation is extended to any public or private not-for-profit community-based agency who currently, and for at least two years, provides justice system programming in the County of Los Angeles.

Applicants must meet the following conditions:

1. They should have operated effective justice related projects for at least two years.

2. They must demonstrate the capability for prompt implementation of the project submitted for funding.

3. They must provide evidence that schools and local public criminal justice agencies will participate or are willing to participate with the proposed project. Such local agencies include schools, local law enforcement, Probation Department, and the Juvenile Court. Participation includes but is not limited to:

    a. Willingness to refer designated target client population.

    b. Willingness to provide data on participating client population relating to prior arrests, re-arrests, filings of subsequent petitions, and/or court action on youths for whom appropriate release of information forms have been obtained.

FIGURE 4-1. (*continued*)

4. They must be responsive to the needs of the particular geographic area(s) of the County served.

B. *Funding Allocation Process*

This RFP solicits complete proposals. Conciseness is stressed. Proposals will be reviewed, evaluated and ranked according to the attached rating guidelines (Appendix C). A final list of funding recommendations will be presented to the Board of Supervisors by the JSAG. A tentative timetable of these events is enclosed.

C. *Duration of Funding Period*

The funding for community-based organizations' projects will be for a one-year period only. Previous or current receipt of subvention funds does not necessarily mean an agency will receive funding for 1988–89, nor will 1988–89 funding automatically qualify an agency for any future funding that may be available under this component of the Justice System Subvention Program.

D. *Overall Program Objectives of the CJSSP as Established by JSAG are:*

1. To reduce the level of serious felony behavior by juveniles and adults.
2. To increase the utilization of public and private not-for-profit youth-serving agencies by targeted youth and adults.
3. To increase the effectiveness and capacity of services available to youth and adults through coordinative efforts among both private and public service providers.

E. *Project Strategies*

The JSAG has conducted a comprehensive needs assessment to determine the most critical justice system needs. Projects focusing on one or more priority target groups and providing one or more priority services will be considered more deserving of funding.

1988–89 Priority Target Groups:

—Pre-Delinquent/At-Risk Juveniles
—Juvenile Delinquents
—Gang Members

1988–89 Priority Service Areas:

—Family Counseling
—Anti-Truancy Programs
—Substance Abuse Counseling
—Psychological Counseling

FIGURE 4-1. *(continued)*

77

Eligible Target Groups and Definitions

Target Groups	Definitions
*Pre-Delinquent/At-Risk Juveniles	Problem-prone youths referred by schools, parents and human services agencies for delinquency prevention and/or diversion services and youths referred by law enforcement to a diversion program, or informal probation supervision. This category also includes youths not receiving adequate parenting who represent a clear risk of becoming delinquent. This category includes runaways, truants, other school nonattenders, throwaways (rejected by parents), and children of incarcerated inmates.
*Juvenile Delinquents	Juveniles adjudicated under Section 602 of the WIC, for what would be, if an adult, the commission of a criminal offense and may be granted probation.
*Gang Members	Youths, including young adults, who band together with other youths in groups tending toward antisocial activities.
Juvenile Camp Releasees	Minors graduated from County residential treatment programs.
Adult Offenders	Offenders convicted and sentenced by a Criminal Court and may be granted probation.
County Jail Inmates and Releasees	Adult offenders incarcerated in County Jail facilities and released from County Jail following completion of a jail sentence.

*Priority Target Groups

FIGURE 4–1. (continued)

Eligible Services and Definitions

Services	Definition
*Family Counseling	Parenting education and services to disturbed families.
*Anti-Truancy Programs	Counseling and school reinforcement services for truants, and habitual truants and their families.
*Substance Abuse Counseling	Counseling or other medical treatment and education for drug/alcohol abuse.
*Psychological Counseling	Mental health programs involving certificated practitioners.
Child Abuse (Physical, Emotional and Sexual) Programs	Prevention, crisis intervention, protective custody and counseling.
Remedial Education	Instruction aimed at correcting educational deficiencies.
Employment Counseling, Job Training, Placement	Employment preparation, development and placement services.
Laws Governing Youths	Materials and programs designed to publicize laws governing youths.
Recreation Programs	Organized group activities designed to promote positive behavior.
Shelter Services	Protective services which include shelter, medical and counseling services.
Community Service/ Restitution	Facilitating fulfillment of community service and restitution orders of court.

*Priority Service Areas

FIGURE 4–1. (continued)

F. *Timetable* (tentative)

January 4, 1988	Request for Proposals distributed
January 11, 1988	Bidders Conference
February 8, 1988	Deadline for submission of proposals
March 17, 1988	Advisory Group meets and determines agencies to be recommended for funding to the Board of Supervisors.

G. *Funds Available*

Based upon 1987–88 funding, it is estimated that $1.9 million will be available in 1988–89 for community-based organizations.

III. PROPOSAL FORMAT

The Proposal is to be brief and straightforward. An assembled set is shown in III-H. No additional sections or pages will be considered. The Face Sheet should be the first page of a stapled set. Please submit *eight (8) copies* of the proposal, one (1) of which must be an original signed copy.

A. *Face Sheet*

Please detach and fill out Appendix A, Face Sheet. All sections must be completed and signed on page two.

B. *Organization Qualification*

Provide a brief organizational history and description of Supervisorial Districts and agencies to be served.

C. *Problem(s) Statement*

Describe the particular problem(s) addressed by your program as it relates to the overall program objectives listed in II-D and, if applicable, the priority areas listed in II-E. You should also include specific data documenting the nature and extent of the problem(s).

D. *Project Objectives*

List specific outcomes you would want to see which address the problem, i.e., what you expect your project would accomplish in lessening the problem. For each problem listed, there should be a specific objective with a *measurable* level of accomplishment within a specified time period.

FIGURE 4–1. (*continued*)

E. *Methodology*

Describe how your project would operate to achieve the desired outcomes. Be very specific about each particular component of your project. Each objective should be specifically addressed in this section. Include the approximate number of hours of service (by type) to be provided each client, the anticipated length of client participation in the program, and the expected outcome to the client, following completion of the services rendered. In addition, include information on:

1. Target Population

    Identify the population to be served. (Refer to eligible, priority client groups and definitions on page 4.) Describe how your proposed project relates to the needs of the particular clientele to be served.

2. Target Geographic Area

    Identify the geographic area to be served and the percentage of service to be allocated to each Supervisorial District. Describe how your proposed project relates to the needs of the particular area to be served.

3. Referrals Sources

    Indicate source of referrals, how referral source was developed and the approximately number of referrals to be received from each referring agency.

4. Supervisorial District Maps (Appendix D)

    Identify on the Supervisorial District Map(s), in colored pencil or ink, those areas your agency is proposing to serve. (Behind each map is a listing of cities and unincorporated areas by Supervisorial District.)

Finally, indicate here whether other funding currently allocated to your agency or which your agency intends to apply for, will be used to enhance this project. And if so, in what manner.

F. *Internal Assessment*

Describe the measurement tools you would incorporate into this project so that results can be evaluated both by your Agency and by County and State program monitors. Each project objective should be treated separately.

FIGURE 4–1. (*continued*)

G. *Letters of Support*

The only letters of support which are specifically requested are those from agencies (law enforcement, schools, probation, etc.) indicating willingness to make referrals and to provide data on the delinquency/criminal problems within the target area.

H. *Proposal Submission Format*

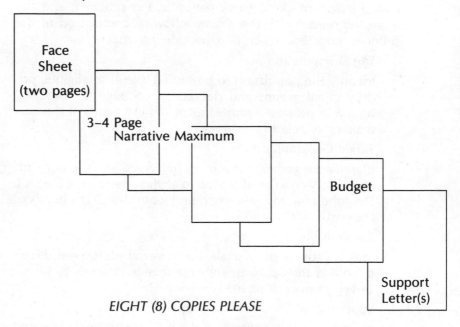

EIGHT (8) COPIES PLEASE

IV. PROPOSAL SUBMISSION REQUIREMENTS

Proposal Availability

RFP copies may be obtained beginning January 4, 1988, between the hours of 8:00 A.M. and 5:00 P.M.

Department of Community and Senior Citizens Services
County of Los Angeles
3175 West Sixth Street, Room 200
Los Angeles, California 90020

Proposals may be mailed, postage prepaid, or may be delivered in person in a sealed envelope marked "County Justice System Subvention Program Proposal—FY 1988–89."

FIGURE 4–1. (*continued*)

All proposals must be received by the Department of Community and Senior Citizens Services *no later than 5:00 P.M., Monday, February 8, 1988,* at the address listed above, to the attention of Mr. Herman Simmons.

All questions, correspondence or other matters pertaining to this RFP should be directed to Mr. Herman Simmons at the above address, or he may be reached at (213) 738-2767.

It is preferred that the narrative of the proposal be single-spaced, concise, and no more than four 8½″ × 11″ pages in length.

> Note: IT IS THE SOLE RESPONSIBILITY OF THE SUBMITTING AGENCY TO SEE THAT ITS PROPOSAL IS SUBMITTED IN PROPER TIME. SUBMITTING AGENCIES SHALL BEAR ALL RISKS ASSOCIATED WITH DELAYS IN THE U.S. MAIL. ANY PROPOSAL RECEIVED AFTER THE SCHEDULED CLOSING TIME FOR RECEIPT OF PROPOSALS WILL BE JUDGED LATE AND RECEIVE A PENALTY OF TEN (10) POINTS PER DAY. THE ADVISORY GROUP STRONGLY SUGGESTS THAT PROPOSALS BE HAND DELIVERED IF YOU ARE CONCERNED WITH POSSIBLE POSTAL DELAYS.

A. Only signed, written proposals specifically accepting responsibility for meeting the objectives and requirements specified in this RFP will be considered.

B. All costs of proposal preparation shall be borne by the applicant agency.

C. Los Angeles County reserves the right to reject any or all proposals, or any part thereof, received by reason of this request. In any event, no contract is implied merely by the submission of the proposal.

D. Los Angeles County reserves the right to retain all proposals submitted. The selection or rejection of a proposal does not affect this right.

E. Los Angeles County may terminate contracts at any time upon providing the agency with thirty (30) days' written notice.

F. Any department or agency of the County of Los Angeles has the right to use any or all ideas presented in any proposal

FIGURE 4-1. *(continued)*

submitted in response to a request without any charge or limitation. Selection or rejection of a proposal does not affect this right.

G. The face sheet must be signed in the name of the submitting agency and must bear the signature of a person duly authorized to legally commit the agency.

H. Proposals may be withdrawn either personally, by written request, or by telegraph request prior to the scheduled closing time for receipt of proposals. Thereafter, all proposals shall remain open and valid for a period of sixty (60) days.

1. The awarding of any contracts as a result of this RFP is contingent upon the receipt of sufficient funding by Los Angeles County through the CJSSP.

I. Applicants not currently funded should expect a site visit by DCSCS staff prior to any recommendation for their funding being forwarded to the Board of Supervisors.

V. SELECTION CRITERIA

The JSAG will make funding recommendations to the County Board of Supervisors who have final authority over the selection of projects and allocations of funds to be awarded through this RFP. Each proposal will be evaluated on its own merits. Previous receipt of JSAG funds does not mean automatic funding for contracts under this RFP.

The rating instrument will consist of six (6) areas of evaluation, weighted as follows:

—Problem Statement	15 points
—Organization Qualification	5 "
—Project Objectives	25 "
—Methodology	30 "
—Internal Assessment	10 "
—Budget Summary	15 "
Maximum Possible Score	100 points

The rating and selection factors include all of the following criteria:

A. The extent to which the applicant meets all agency requirements specified in the request.

FIGURE 4-1. (*continued*)

B. The extent to which project objectives, approach, and projected benefits meet criteria specified under project strategy in
this request.

C. The extent to which the project design will impact on crime
reduction and/or institutionalization.

D. The extent to which law enforcement, schools, probation, and/
or the courts have agreed to participate in the program.

E. The extent to which services are focused to enhance or aug-
ment existing services.

F. The extent to which services address the needs of the geographic area and the Supervisorial District(s) which the program covers.

G. The extent to which identified needs address a significant community and justice system concern.

H. The extent to which provision of directed services related to
priority need areas is enhanced or complemented by other
funding sources.

FIGURE 4-1. (*continued*)

APPENDIX

A. Face Sheet

B. Budget Detail Guidelines

C. Raters' Guidelines

D. County of Los Angeles

Supervisorial District Maps
Districts I, II, III, IV and V

E. General Conditions

F. Contract Responsibilities for Successful Bidders

FIGURE 4–1. *(continued)*

APPENDIX A
APPLICATION FOR FUNDING
COUNTY JUSTICE SYSTEM SUBVENTION PROGRAM
JULY 1, 1988–JUNE 30, 1989

COMMUNITY-BASED ORGANIZATION PROPOSAL

FACE SHEET

Agency Name: ___Helpline Youth Counseling, Inc.___

Agency Address: ___9820 Belmont St., Bellflower, CA 90706___

Project Name: ___Helpline Intervention Team___

Contact Person: ___Carol Geisbauer___ Telephone No.: ___(213) 920-1706___

Supervisorial District	Number of Clients to Be Served		Supervisorial District	Requested Funds
I.	100		I.	$35K
II.			II.	
III.			III.	
IV.	200 + 200	(6 SE + I B)*	IV.	$54K + 54K
V.			V.	
Total Clients	500		Total Funds Requested	$143,000

List the cities and unincorporated areas for each Supervisorial District your agency is proposing to serve.

La Mirada,
1st District ___—Norwalk, Whittier, Pico Rivera, Santa Fe Springs, Downey___

4th District___—Bellflower, Lakewood, Cerritos, Paramount, Artesia,___
___Hawaiian Gardens___

4th District___—LONG BEACH and Signal Hill___

If your agency is currently funded under this program, please answer the following questions:

CJSSP Funds received for FY 1987–88 ___$97,034___

Total Planned Number of *Clients* for FY 1987–88 ___400___

Average Cost Per Client FY 1987–88 ___$242___

*6 Southeast Cities + Long Beach

FIGURE 4-1. (*continued*)

Appendix A (*continued*)
APPLICATION FOR FUNDING
COUNTY JUSTICE SYSTEM SUBVENTION PROGRAM
JULY 1, 1988–JUNE 30, 1989

COMMUNITY-BASED ORGANIZATION PROPOSAL
FACE SHEET

Agency Name: ___Helpline Youth Counseling___

_ _

Brief Description of Proposed Program Project: _____

The focus of the HIT Program is to reduce recidivism by working

intensively with known juvenile delinquents and other identified

at-risk youth. A non-traditional approach is utilized which combines

camping, on-campus group counseling, rappelling and therapeutic

recreation with more traditional services—family counseling, group

and individual therapy.

Current Agency Funding (Use additional sheet if necessary):

Source	Amount	Funding Period
CA Youth Authority	$ 91,600	1987–88
OCJP-2 projects	$100,000	1987–88
United Way	$ 73,430	1987–88
8 Cities	$ 60,000	1987–88
Other	$174,970	1987–88
	$500,000	

This applicant certifies that to the best of his/her knowledge and belief, the data in this document is true and correct, and the filing of this proposal has been duly authorized by the governing body of the applicant agency.

Typed Name: ___Carol Geisbauer___ Title: ___Executive Director___

Signature: _____ Date: ___January 15, 1988___

FIGURE 4–1. (*continued*)

Appendix B
BUDGET DETAIL GUIDELINES

On a separate sheet, complete in line-item detail with each line showing the basis for computation of the cost, along with a justification and explanation of the budget items. Each item is to be broken down by administrative and direct service costs. The totals of each category are also to be included (see example, Page 3). Round amounts to the nearest dollar.

A. *Personnel Services — Salaries*

Each position filled by employees of the project must be listed as follows:

No. of Persons	Position or Title	Actual Monthly Salary	% of Time on Project	Months to be Employed	Total
_____	_____	_____	_____	_____	_____
_____	_____	_____	_____	_____	_____

B. Describe briefly the duties of each position as it relates to the project.

_____

_____

_____

— Step increases are allowed as provided for in the agency's approved personnel policies and procedure manual.

ONE COPY OF THE PERSONNEL POLICIES AND PROCEDURE MANUAL IS TO BE SUBMITTED WITH PROPOSAL.

— Cost of living increases are allowed once a year provided they are included in the approved personnel policies manual and approved by the agency's Board of Directors.

C. *EMPLOYEE BENEFITS*

Fringe benefits must be shown separately; for example:

1. FICA = gross salaries × the established rate;
   SUI-1st $7,000 × the established agency rate.

FIGURE 4-1. (*continued*)

2. All applicable fringe benefits must be shown. Workers' Compensation is mandatory for paid staff of all agencies.

3. Health insurance, life insurance and retirement are acceptable fringe benefits. However, these items must be provided for both high and low salaried employees. Compute these items for each person. Do not use lump sums.

4. Workers' Compensation is not mandatory for volunteers; however, it is desirable.

D. *CONSULTANTS AND CONTRACT SERVICES*

List each type of specific services to be rendered through purchase of service or subcontract, showing the proposed fee rate per hour and/or per client, and the number of clients to be serviced/hours of services to be provided.

E. *TRAVEL*

Itemize travel expenses of project personnel by purpose and show the basis for computation. Charges must be consistent with those normally allowed by agency's policies and practices.

No travel or any related expenses will be reimbursed for trips outside of the County.

F. *SPACE*

Determine total square feet need for the project. Multiply total square feet by monthly rate per square foot and number of months. (If successful, your agency will be required to provide a copy of the rental/lease agreement.)

G. *CONSUMABLE SUPPLIES*

Provide a description of types of supplies and approximate cost.

H. *RENTAL/LEASE OF EQUIPMENT*

List each proposed equipment rental (i.e., calculator, typewriter, copier, etc.) and monthly rate.

No equipment purchases will be allowed.

I. *OTHER COSTS*

This category includes costs not in the above categories such as:
Insurance i.e., Liability, Crime, etc.
Telephone
Utilities

FIGURE 4–1. (*continued*)

BUDGET DETAIL GUIDELINES

COST CATEGORY TOTALS

Prepare a separate budget summary for cumulative program estimates as follows:

Cost Category	Direct Service	Admin.	Total Funds Requested
Personnel—Salaries	XXXX	XXXX	XXXX
Employee Benefits	XXXX	XXXX	XXXX
Consultants & Contract Services	XXXX	XXXX	XXXX
Travel	XXXX	XXXX	XXXX
Space	XXXX	XXXX	XXXX
Consumable Supplies	XXXX	XXXX	XXXX
Rental/Lease of Equipment	XXXX	XXXX	XXXX
Other Costs	XXXX	XXXX	XXXX
TOTAL	XXXX	XXXX	XXXX

NOTE: TOTAL ADMINISTRATIVE COSTS MAY NOT EXCEED 15 PERCENT OF REQUESTED AMOUNT.

FIGURE 4-1. (*continued*)

Appendix C
RATERS' GUIDE

AGENCY NAME _____

PROJECT TITLE _____

1. Problem Statement _____ (15)

   Are the problems to be dealt with clearly spelled out and "solvable"? (0–10)

   Do the stated problems involve CJSSP priorities? (0–5)

2. Organization Qualification _____ (5)

   Is a description of the agency history (at least two years' experience), and activities in proposed Supervisorial District(s) provided? _____ (0–5)

3. Project Objectives _____ (25)

   Are the objectives truly measurable and do they relate to the provision of specific services to accomplish them? (0–25)

4. Methodology _____ (30)

   Is it clear how the agency will operate the program to achieve its stated objectives? (0–5)

   Does the methodology address the stated problems? (0–10)

   Is it clear how the proposed project will actually have an impact on the CJSSP priorities? (0–5)

   Do other existing or proposed funding sources assist the project and enhance services? (0–5)

   Is it clear (through narrative *and* support letters) that the agency will receive an appropriate number of qualified referrals? (0–5)

5. Internal Assessment _____ (10)

   Is it clear how the agency will monitor and track progress toward the achievement of each objective? (0–10)

6. Budget Summary _____ (15)

   Do overall budget categories appear to match proposed agency activities? (0–10)

   Is the direct/administrative breakdown acceptable? (0–5)

TOTAL POINTS _____ (maximum possible = 100)

FIGURE 4–1. (*continued*)

B. ORGANIZATION QUALIFICATIONS

Organizational History—Helpline Youth Counseling was created in 1967 as part of a plan of action formulated at a public meeting at Cerritos College, attended by 3,100 concerned residents of Southeast Los Angeles County, to provide crisis counseling to youth abusing drugs. Helpline was incorporated on August 10, 1971, for the purpose of providing psychological counseling and therapy to troubled youth and their families, and has been in continuous service for 17 years.

The major *focus of the agency is on the prevention and treatment of juvenile delinquency,* to reduce recidivism by working intensively with known juvenile delinquents and other identified pre-delinquent and high-risk juveniles.

Service Area—Helpline services the 1st and 4th Supervisorial Districts including all cities in the geographic area called Southeast Los Angeles County.

Treatment Model—Helpline Youth Counseling is a community based organization and community supported since its inception. Our model of intervention with youth is unique in that individual and family counseling in a clinical setting is supplemented by non-traditional methods (on-campus group counseling, therapeutic recreation, socialization activities, developmental field trips, managed risk wilderness programs). A *non-traditional approach* is needed to address the issues of resistance among at-risk youth and juvenile offenders to combat drug and alcohol abuse among teens, to intervene with runaways and homeless youth, to enhance school attendance among truant youth, to reach youth described as incorrigible.

Past and Current Subvention Record of Service—Helpline's Intervention Team (HIT) is the *only agency in the target region* which is specifically designed for the purpose of implementing an intensive treatment plan for pre-delinquent youth, juvenile delinquents on probation, and other at-risk youth including gang oriented youth. Helpline has successfully operated a County Subvention Program for 9 years, serving 3,600 youth.

During 1986–87 Program year, 450 youth were referred by schools, Probation Officers, Juvenile Court personnel, and deputy sheriffs. Of these 450 youth, 220 were on Probation, 180 were juvenile delinquents, and 50 were considered to be high-risk. Of these 450 youth, 415 were not arrested or re-arrested during their

FIGURE 4–2. Sample partial response to community-based RFP.

involvement in counseling at Helpline (which averages 6 months of contact), for a recidivist rate of less than 8%.

The Helpline Intervention Team targets youth residing in Southeast Los Angeles County in—

1st Supervisorial District— Norwalk, Whittier, Downey, Pico Rivera, Santa Fe Springs, La Mirada

4th Supervisorial District—Bellflower, Cerritos, Lakewood, Paramount, Artesia, Hawaiian Gardens

4th Supervisorial District—Long Beach, Signal Hill (NEW SERVICE AREA)

C. PROBLEM STATEMENT

The target area is characterized by a blue-collar working population, pockets of extreme poverty (in Norwalk, Paramount, and Hawaiian Gardens) contrasted with areas within cities which have middle class and upper middle class affluence.

Communities with minority concentrations in the 1970s become even more so by the 1980s, particularly in low-income areas. Several cities underwent major "tipping" or transition from predominantly Anglo to predominantly minority population. Hispanics comprise 25% of the population, Blacks 6%, Asians 7%, and Anglos 61%, according to the 1980 Census.

The target area has the highest ratio of children to adults in Los Angeles County—over 30% under 18 years of age. Some areas have as high as 40% children under age 18 (Paramount 35.5%, Hawaiian Gardens 40%, Norwalk 33%, Pico Rivera 33.8%, Santa Fe Springs 33.8%).

Six targeted cities for treatment services to juvenile delinquents have a high percentage of families living in poverty:

City	Families in Poverty	% of Families in Poverty with Children
Norwalk (1st)	8.3%	80.0%
Pico Rivera (1st)	8.8%	84.3%
Santa Fe Springs (1st)	8.3%	89.8%
Paramount (4th)	16.0%	89.3%
Bellflower (4th)	8.1%	76.7%
Hawaiian Gardens (4th)	25.0%	96.0%
Long Beach	10.2%	83.6%
Signal Hill	7.6%	76.2%

FIGURE 4–2. (continued)

94

Poverty as a single factor is not a predictor of juvenile delinquency. However, poverty stricken neighborhoods have high crime rates including gang activity and violence which leads to high police visibility and many juvenile arrests. Also, youthful offenders from low income families are referred to Helpline while more affluent youthful offenders seek and receive treatment in the private sector.

The Norwalk Sheriffs Station, covering the cities of Norwalk, Pico Rivera, Santa Fe Springs and La Mirada in the 1st Supervisorial District, reports 1,482 juvenile arrests in 1985–86 and 1,208 in 1986–87.

The Downey Police Department reports 509 juvenile arrests in 1985. The Whittier Police Department reports 687 juvenile arrests in 1985, 794 in 1986, and 856 in 1987.

The Lakewood Sheriffs Station, covering the cities of Bellflower, Paramount, Lakewood, Artesia, Cerritos, and Hawaiian Gardens, in the 4th Supervisorial District, reports 2,254, in 1985, 1,920 in 1986, and 1,719 in 1987.

The Long Beach Police Department reports 4,295 arrests of juveniles in 1985–86, 3,958 in 1986–87.

In the target area of Southeast Los Angeles County, 26 youth gangs exist.

Gang involvement includes Hispanic, Black and Anglo youth. The degree of involvement by youth varies from loose affiliation to weekend activity to full participation creating a highly volatile situation characterized by raids into neighboring communities, assaults on individual gang members and their families, drive-by shootings, and destruction of property of non-involved parties.

Probation officers carry caseloads in excess of 150 cases. Rio Hondo and Long Beach Probation refer youth to Helpline for counseling and diversion, and interact with counselors to monitor and follow-up referred youth. Schools refer truant youth.

There is an obvious and overwhelming need to divert delinquent youth from further penetration of the Juvenile Justice System. Incarceration in a California Youth Authority Institution costs approximately $28,000 per year and institutions are overcrowded. Delinquent youth can be successfully rehabilitated in the community by agencies like Helpline Youth Counseling, Inc.

D. PROJECT OBJECTIVES

The purpose of the HIT Program is to substantially reduce or eliminate delinquent behavior and criminal ideation through intensive individual and group work.

FIGURE 4–2. (*continued*)

Priority Target Groups Include:
—At-Risk Youth, Pre-delinquent and Status Offenders
—Juvenile Delinquents and Juvenile Probationers
—Gang Members—Youth
—Juvenile Camp Releases

Measurable Objectives

1. To provide intervention services for 500 youth in the *1st* and *4th Supervisorial District* of SE Los Angeles County

   1st District— 100 (Norwalk, Santa Fe Springs, Pico Rivera, Downey)
   4th District—200 (Long Beach & Signal Hill)
   4th District—<u>200</u> (Bellflower, Paramount, Cerritos, Lakewood, Hawaiian Gardens, Artesia)
          500

   a. 200 youth will be at-risk, pre-delinquent youth with no prior arrests.

   b. 200 youth will either be juvenile delinquents on active probation or youth who have had a prior arrest within the last six months (not gang involved);

   c. 100 youth, gang involved, will be on active probation or have had a prior arrest within the last six months;

2. Of the 200 youth with no arrest history or gang involvement but exhibiting at-risk, pre-delinquent behavior, 80% (160) will have no formal arrest beginning one month following entry into Program.

3. Of the 200 youth with a recent arrest history or on active probation (non gang involved), 80% (160) will have no further arrest while in the Program.

4. Of the 100 youth, gang involved, 40% (40) will have no further arrests while in the Program beginning one month after entry into the Program.

5. To develop an individualized treatment plan for each youth with an average of 60 days involvement of 2 hours per week (total of 16 hours of service per client.)

Service Areas Include:
   —Family Counseling
   —Truancy Reduction Programs

FIGURE 4–2. *(continued)*

—Substance Abuse Counseling
—Psychological Counseling
—Employment Counseling, Job Training and Placement*
—Therapeutic Recreation Programs

E. METHODOLOGY

Target Population

Youth ages 9–18 who may be categorized as at-risk, pre-delinquent, juvenile delinquents, police diversions, youth on Probation, gang-involved youth. Target youth are those with a prior arrest history or youth who exhibit a predisposition toward juvenile delinquency using the following indicators: law-breaking, poor school attendance/chronic truancy, runaways or throwaways, repeated misconduct or displays of deviant behavior, substance abuse, participation in gangs, emotional maladjustment, serious family related problems including neglect and abuse.

Target Geographic Area:

1st Supervisorial District in SE Los Angeles County including Cities of Norwalk, Downey, Pico Rivera, Santa Fe Springs, Whittier, La Mirada—20%

4th Supervisorial District in SE Los Angeles County including the Cities of Artesia, Bellflower, Cerritos, Lakewood, Hawaiian Gardens, Paramount—40%

4th Supervisorial District in SE Los Angeles County including the Cities of Long Beach and Signal Hill—40%

Supervisorial District maps are attached.

Funding used to enhance the staffing of the AB90 Program is provided by the City of Long Beach $24,000 (staff), United Way $10,000 (staff), the Cities of Bellflower, Norwalk, Paramount, Cerritos, Santa Fe Springs, Lakewood—$33,000 (overhead costs).

Treatment Plan

The Treatment Plan includes a combination of the following types of services:

a. therapy—family counseling, individual psychological counseling, group counseling, crisis intervention

b. extended social system intervention—advocacy, networking and case consultation with school personnel, Probation Officers, Juvenile Court personnel, Law enforcement officers; employment counseling and placement,

---

*Service funded by another source.

FIGURE 4–2. (*continued*)

c. group socialization—on-campus group counseling on a variety of issues: school attendance, truancy, dropping out, decision-making, values clarification, achievement, substance abuse, teen sexuality and teen pregnancy; Peer Counselor Training

d. experiential growth—personal growth through camping, rappelling, trust walks, field trips, team sports and tournaments, Talent Show, recreation wilderness challenge.

F. INTERNAL ASSESSMENT

HIT staff will establish and maintain case files on all clients entering the Program, including intake, monthly summary, and termination.

HIT staff will conduct monthly recidivism checks on all active clients through contact with the Probation officers, parents, or other reliable sources. HIT staff will provide the County with a ten-month recidivism report by June 30, 1989.

As stated in Program objectives, 455 out of 500 youths served will not be rearrested following Program involvement, for a rearrest rate of 9%.

FIGURE 4-2. (*continued*)

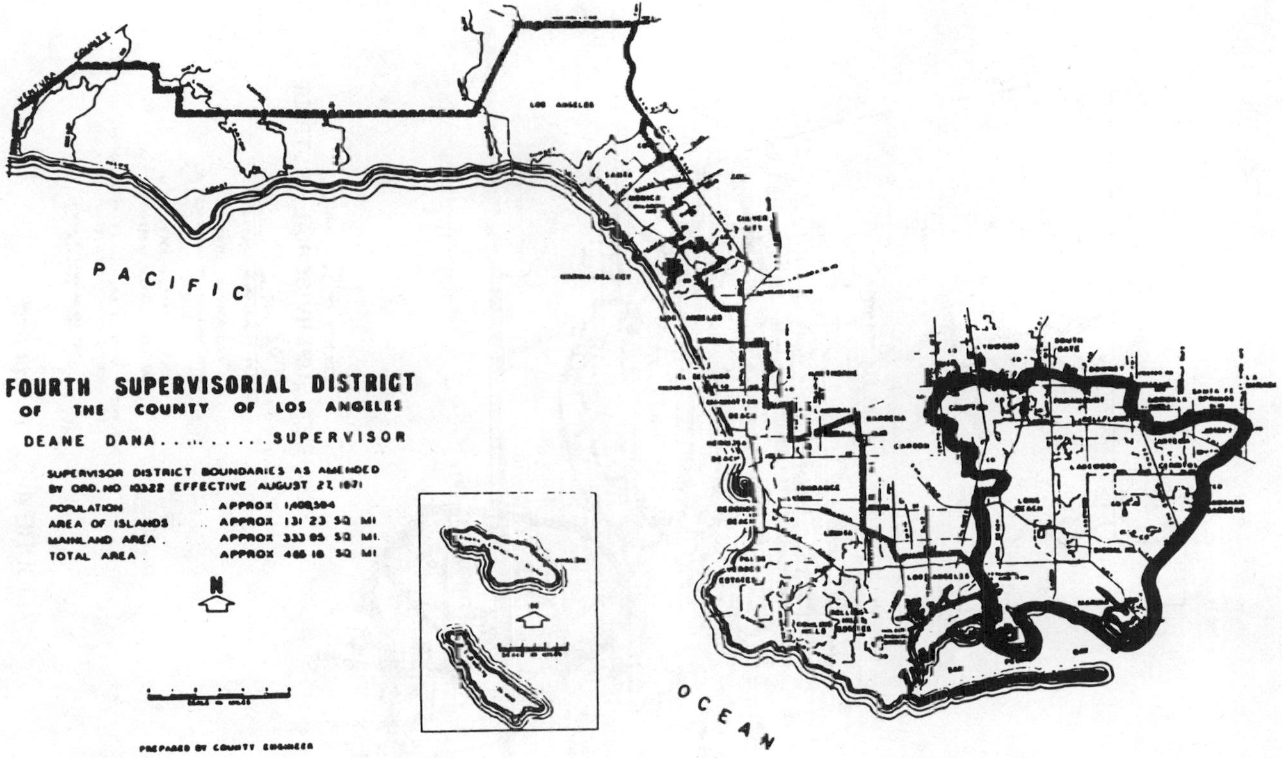

FIGURE 4-2. (continued)

99

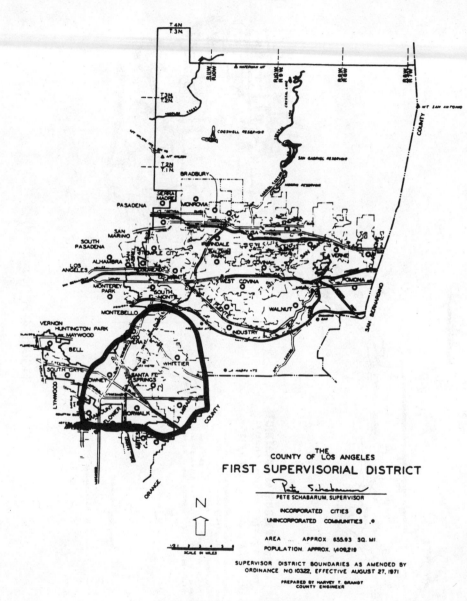

THE
COUNTY OF LOS ANGELES
FIRST SUPERVISORIAL DISTRICT

PETE SCHABARUM, SUPERVISOR

INCORPORATED CITIES ⊙
UNINCORPORATED COMMUNITIES ·⊙

AREA .... APPROX 655.93 SQ. MI
POPULATION. APPROX. 1,408,219

SUPERVISOR DISTRICT BOUNDARIES AS AMENDED BY
ORDINANCE NO. 10322, EFFECTIVE AUGUST 27, 1971

PREPARED BY HARVEY T. BRANDT
COUNTY ENGINEER

FIGURE 4–2. *(continued)*

BUDGET

A. *PERSONNEL SERVICES—SALARIES*

No. of Persons	Position or Title	Actual Monthly Salaries	% of Time on Project	Months to Be Employed	Total
1	Program Director	2,000/mo.	100%	12 mos.	$ 24,000
4	Counselors	1,750/mo.	100%	12 mos.	21,000
					21,000
					21,000
					21,000
1	Bookkeeper	1,500/mo.	25%	12 mos.	4,500
1	Secretary	1,000/mo.	25%	12 mos.	3,000
					$115,500

B. PROGRAM DIRECTOR—Provide administrative and clinical Supervision to Program staff; provide direct service to clients.

COUNSELORS—Provide direct services—family, individual and group counseling—to target youth and their families.

BOOKKEEPER—Responsible for full charge bookkeeping services for the Program which constitutes 25% of the Agency fiscal activity.
SECRETARY—Responsible for intakes, client record keeping, client charts, typing, copying; 25% of her time will be utilized by Program activity.

C. *EMPLOYEE BENEFITS*

1. F.I.C.A. = 115,500 × 7.51% = $ 8,674.00
   S.U.I. = 38,500 × 4.9%
             (7,000 + 7,000 + 7,000 + 7,000
             + 7,000 + 1,750 + 1,750) =   1,886.00

2. Workman's Compensation = 115,500 × 1.63% =   1,883.00

3. Medical & Dental Insurance $91/mo. ($1,092
   + 1,092 + 1,092 + 1,092 + 1,092 + 273 + 273) =   6,006.00
                                                             $18,449.00

D. *CONSULTANTS AND CONTRACT SERVICES*   NONE

FIGURE 4–2. (*continued*)

E. *TRAVEL*

    714mi/21¢ = $150 per person × 5   750

    714mi/21¢ = $150 gas for Van   150

F. *SPACE*

    Bellflower office—2,500 sq.ft. × 40¢/sq.ft.

                 = $1,000/mo. × 12 mos. = 12,000

                 × 25% = 3,000 – 95/mo. × 12 mos.

                 = <u>1140</u>

    Norwalk office   —3,400 sq.ft. × 50¢/sq.ft.

                 = $1,700/mo. × 12 mos. = 20,400

                 × 25% = 5,100 – $66.08/mo.

                 × 12 mos. = <u>$793</u>

G. *CONSUMABLE SUPPLIES*   749

Scotch Tape	$19/carton of 12
Copier Paper	$35/case
Manila Folders	$17/case of 25 ea.
Envelopes	$17/box of 500
Typewriter ribbon	$18/box of 6 ea.
Erase Ribbon	$19/box of 100
Pencils	$ 3/box of doz.
Pens	$ 1/box of doz.
Paper Towels	$25/case
Toilet Tissue	$25/case
Binders	$ 8/each

H. *RENTAL/LEASE OF EQUIPMENT*

    Copier $245/mo. × 12 mos. = 2,940 × 25% = 735   125

I. *OTHER COSTS*

    Liability Insurance   —15,000 × 25% = 3,750

    Automobile Insurance— 5,000 × 25% = 1,250

    Telephone   — 6,000 × 25%   104

    Postage   — 1,450 × 25%

                 = 363   240   5,344

FIGURE 4–2. *(continued)*

COST CATEGORY TOTALS

Cost Category	Direct Service	Admin.	Total Funds Requested
Personnel—Salaries	115,500		115,500
Employee Benefits	18,449		18,449
Consultant & Contract Services	0		0
Travel	900		900
Space	1,933		1,933
Consumable Supplies	749		749
Rental/Lease of Equipment	125		125
Other Costs	5,344		5,344
TOTAL	143,000		143,000

FIGURE 4–2. (continued)

BUDGET

A. *PERSONNEL SERVICES—SALARIES*

No. of Persons	Position or Title	Actual Monthly Salaries	% of Time on Project	Months to Be Employed	Total
1–100%	Program Director	2,000/mo.	24%	12 mos.	5,760
1–100%	Counselor	1,750/mo.	100%	12 mos.	21,000
1– 25%	Bookkeeper	1,500/mo.	24%	12 mos.	1,080
1– 25%	Secretary	1,000/mo.	24%	12 mos.	720
					$28,560

B. PROGRAM DIRECTOR—Provide administrative and clinical Supervision to Program staff; provide direct service to clients.

COUNSELORS—Provide direct services—family, individual and group counseling—to target youth and their families.

BOOKKEEPER—Responsible for full charge bookkeeping services for the Program which constitutes 25% of the Agency fiscal activity.

SECRETARY—Responsible for intakes, client record keeping, client charts, typing, copying; 25% of her time will be utilized by Program activity.

C. *EMPLOYEE BENEFITS*

1. F.I.C.A. = 28,560 × 7.51% =   2,144
   S.U.I. = 4.9% × 9522 = (1,680 + 7,000 + 421 + 421)   466
2. Workman's Compensation = 28,560 × 1.63%   465
3. Medical & Dental Insurance $91/mo.
   (262 + 1,092 + 66. + 66.) =   1,486

          $4,561

D. *CONSULTANTS AND CONTRACT SERVICES*   NONE

E. *TRAVEL*

714mi/21¢ = $150 per person × 1.24   186

FIGURE 4–2. *(continued)*

F. *SPACE*

Norwalk office —3,400 sq.ft. × 50¢/sq.ft.
= $1,700/mo. × 12 mos.
= 20,400 × 25%
= 5,100 ($66.08/mo. × 12 mos. = 793) 793

G. *CONSUMABLE SUPPLIES*— 0

H. *RENTAL/LEASE OF EQUIPMENT*— 0

I. *OTHER COSTS*

Liability Insurance—15,000 × 25% = 3,750 × 24% = 900
1,879

COST CATEGORY TOTALS

Cost Category	Direct Services	Admin.	Total Funds Requested
Personnel—Salaries	28,560	0	28,560
Employee Benefits	4,561	0	4,561
Consultant & Contract Services	0	0	0
Travel	186	0	186
Space	793	0	793
Consumable Supplies	0	0	0
Rental/Lease of Equipment	0	0	0
Other Costs:			
Liability Insurance	900	0	900
	35,000	0	35,000

FIGURE 4–2. (*continued*)

BUDGET

A. PERSONNEL SERVICES—SALARIES

No. of Persons	Position or Title	Actual Monthly Salaries	% of Time on Project	Months to Be Employed	Total
1	Program Director	2,000/mo.	38%	12 mos.	9,120
1	Counselor	1,750/mo.	100%	12 mos.	21,000
1	Counselor	1,750/mo.	50%	12 mos.	10,500
1 25%	Bookkeeper	1,500/mo.	38%	12 mos.	1,710
1 25%	Secretary	1,000/mo.	38%	12 mos.	1,140
					$43,470

B. PROGRAM DIRECTOR—Provide administrative and clinical Supervision to Program staff; provide direct services to clients.

COUNSELORS—Provide direct services—family, individual and group counseling—to target youth and their families.

BOOKKEEPER—Responsible for full charge bookkeeping services for the Program which constitutes 25% of the Agency fiscal activity.

SECRETARY—Responsible for intakes, client record keeping, client charts, typing, copying; 25% of her time will be utilized by Program activity.

C. EMPLOYEE BENEFITS

1. F.I.C.A. = 43,470 × 7.51% =   3,265
   S.U.I. = 14,490 × 4.9% = (2,660 + 7,000
              + 3,500 + 665 + 665)   710
2. Workman's Compensation = 43,470 × 1.63%   709
3. Medical & Dental Insurance—$91/mo.
   (415 + 1,092 + 546 + 104 + 104)   2,260
                                                               $6,944

D. CONSULTANTS AND CONTRACT SERVICES

E. TRAVEL

714mi/21¢ = $150 per person × 188%   282
              (150 + 75 + 57
                100% 50% 38%)
714mi/21¢ = $150 gas for van   75

FIGURE 4–2. (continued)

F. SPACE—

Bellflower office—2,500 sq.ft. × 40¢/sq.ft.
$$= \$1,000/mo. \times 12 \text{ mos.}$$
$$= 12,000 \times 25\% = 2,000 \times 38\% = \qquad 1,140$$

G. CONSUMABLE SUPPLIES—   560

Copier Paper	$35/case
Manila Folders	$11/case of 25 ea.
Envelopes	$17/box of 500
Typewriter ribbon	$18/box of 6 ea.
Erase Ribbon	$12/box of 100
Pencils	$ 3/box of doz.
Pens	$ 1/box of doz.
Paper Towels	$25/case
Toilet Tissue	$25/case
Binders	$ 8/each

H. RENTAL/LEASE OF EQUIPMENT—   0

Copier $245/mo. × 12 mos.   125
$$= 2,940 \times 25\% = 735$$

I. OTHER COSTS

Liability Insurance	—15,000 × 25% = 3,750/1425 2,544
Automobile Insurance	—5,000 × 25% = 1,250/775
Telephone	—6,000 × 25% = 1,500/104
Postage	—1,450 × 25% = 363/240

COST CATEGORY TOTALS

Cost Category	Direct Services	Admin.	Total Funds Requested
Personnel—Salaries	43,470	0	43,470
Employee Benefits	6,944	0	6,944
Consultant & Contract Services	0	0	0
Travel	357	0	357
Space	0	0	0
Consumable Supplies	560	0	560
Rental/Lease of Equipment	125	0	125
Other Costs	2,544	0	2,544
TOTAL	54,000	0	54,000

FIGURE 4-2. (continued)

A. *PERSONNEL SERVICES—SALARIES*

No. of Persons	Position or Title	Actual Monthly Salaries	% of Time on Project	Months to Be Employed	Total
1	Program Director	2,000/mo.	38%	12 mos.	9,120
1	Counselor	1,750/mo.	100%	12 mos.	21,000
1	Counselor	1,750/mo.	50%	12 mos.	10,500
1 25%	Bookkeeper	1,500/mo.	38%	12 mos.	1,710
1 25%	Secretary	1,000/mo.	38%	12 mos.	1,140
					$43,470

B. PROGRAM DIRECTOR—Provide administrative and clinical Supervision to Program staff; provide direct services to clients.

COUNSELORS—Provide direct services—family, individual and group counseling—to target youth and their families.

BOOKKEEPER—Responsible for full charge bookkeeping services for the Program which constitutes 25% of the Agency fiscal activity.

SECRETARY—Responsible for intakes, client record keeping, client charts, typing, copying; 25% of her time will be utilized by Program activity.

C. *EMPLOYEE BENEFITS*

1. F.I.C.A. $= 43,470 \times 7.51\% =$ 3,265
   S.U.I. $= 14,490 \times 4.9\% = (2,660 + 7,000$
   $+ 3,500 + 665 + 665)$ 710

2. Workman's Compensation $= 43,470 \times 1.63\%$ 709
3. Medical & Dental Insurance $91/mo.
   $(415 + 1,092 + 546 + 104 + 104)$ 2,260
       $6,944

D. *CONSULTANTS AND CONTRACT SERVICES*

E. *TRAVEL*

714mi/21¢ = $150 per person × 188%   282
   (150 + 75 + 57
    100% 50% 38%)
714mi/21¢ = $150 gas for van   75

FIGURE 4-2. (*continued*)

F. SPACE—

Bellflower office—2,500 sq.ft. × 40¢/sq.ft.
= $1,000/mo. × 12 mos.
= 12,000 × 25% = 2,000 × 38% =   1,140

G. CONSUMABLE SUPPLIES—   560

Copier Paper	$35/case
Manila Folders	$11/case of 25 ea.
Envelopes	$17/box of 500
Typewriter ribbon	$18/box of 6 ea.
Erase Ribbon	$12/box of 100
Manila Envelopes	$19/box of 100
Pencils	$ 3/box of doz.
Pens	$ 1/box of doz.
Paper Towels	$25/case
Toilet Tissue	$25/case
Binders	$ 8/each

H. RENTAL/LEASE OF EQUIPMENT—   0

Copier $245/mo. × 12 mos.   125
= 2,940 × 25% − 735

I. OTHER COSTS

Liability Insurance   —15,000 × 25% = 3,750/1425   2,544
Automobile Insurance—5,000 × 25% = 1,250/775
Telephone   —6,000 × 25% = 1,500/104
Postage   —1,450 × 25% = 363/240

COST CATEGORY TOTALS

Cost Category	Direct Services	Admin.	Total Funds Requested
Personnel—Salaries	43,470	0	43,470
Employee Benefits	6,944	0	6,944
Consultant & Contract Services	0	0	0
Travel	357	0	357
Space	0	0	0
Consumable Supplies	560	0	560
Rental/Lease of Equipment	125	0	125
Other Costs	2,544	0	2,544
TOTAL	54,000	0	54,000

FIGURE 4-2. (continued)

February 10

TO: **ALL PROSPECTIVE COMPETITORS**

SUBJECT: **REQUEST FOR PROPOSALS (RFPs) AND
          BIDDERS' CONFERENCE NOTICE**

The Private Industry Council (PIC) of the Carson/Lomita/Torrance Consortium is issuing a Request for Proposals (RFP) for interested organizations to provide placement-oriented training for economically disadvantaged residents of Carson, Lomita and Torrance.

It is anticipated that funding approval for each project will average at $45,000. Proposals which exhibit the most cost effective means of accomplishing the attached objectives and document private sector and community linkages will have a competitive edge.

RFP packets will be available at a Bidders' Conference on Monday, March 7, 1988 at 3:00 P.M. The Conference will be held in thew West Annex Building of the City of Torrance, 3131 Torrance Blvd., Torrance CA. After the conference, applications may be obtained by writing or phoning the Carson/Lomita/Torrance PIC, 3231 Torrance Blvd., Torrance CA 90502, (213) 618-2985.

The deadline for submitting proposals is 5:00 P.M., Friday, April 1, 1988. Proponents are urged to hand-deliver their proposals; however, if mailed, they must be postmarked by April 1, 1988.

Sincerely,

James Slayden
PIC Chair

JS:mlt

In an effort to update our RFP list, the PIC is asking that you complete the enclosed postcard, and return it to this office by March 3, 1988. Postcards not received will be an indication that your organization does not wish to be notified of future RFP notices.

FIGURE 4–3.   Sample letter invitation.

DESCRIPTION OF OBJECTIVES

To be considered for funding, all proposals must address one or more of the following objectives. These objectives are not listed in any order of priority. Services provided under these objectives are restricted to economically disadvantaged residents of Carson, Lomita and Torrance.

OBJECTIVE A—PROMOTE THE PREPARATION OF YOUTH FOR ENTRY INTO THE LABOR MARKET

- Increase youth employment in the private sector through the use of on-the-job training.
- Facilitate the transition of youth from school to work by including private employers in the design of training programs, and by combining vocational classroom training with related private sector on-the-job training.
- Provide Try-Out Employment (TOE) at private for profit worksites, which will lead to permanent, unsubsidized employment.

OBJECTIVE B— INCREASE JOB TRAINING OPPORTUNITIES FOR HARD-TO-SERVE GROUPS

- Provide placement-oriented job training programs to serve individuals who are experiencing the most severe barriers to employment. Emphasis should be on the following target groups:
  - —Youth
  - —Ex-Offender
  - —High Risk Youth
  - —Welfare Recipients
  - —Handicapped
  - —High School Drop Outs
  - —Persons of Limited English Proficiency

OBJECTIVE C—PROMOTE EMPLOYMENT AND TRAINING IN NEW TECHNOLOGIES AND GROWTH INDUSTRIES

- Training and employment in new technologies or growth industries such as aerospace, electronics, health, banking, retail, etc. Priority consideration will be given to proposals that involve employers, unions, educational agencies, and the PIC which involve these groups in designing training curricula to meet specific employer needs.

FIGURE 4–4. Description of objectives in letter invitation.

111

OBJECTIVE D—PROMOTE PARTNERSHIPS AMONG THE PRIVATE SECTOR AND PROVIDERS OF EMPLOYMENT AND TRAINING SERVICES

- Employer-specific training to meet the hiring needs of a *pre-identified* employer or employers. It can be done for a single firm or for a group of firms with *similar* training needs. In training for a group of firms, the employers may choose to form a consortium in which they design, oversee and manage the skill straining program. Employer specific training can also be done through a training contractor who will manage the training program on behalf of the participating employers.

- On-the-job training in the private sector provided to a participant who has been hired first by the employer, and which occurs while the participant is engaged in productive work which provides knowledge in skills essential to the full and adequate performance of the job.

FIGURE 4–4. (*continued*)

March 7

TO: All Prospective Competitors

SUBJECT: Request for Proposals

The Private Industry Council (PIC) of the Carson/Lomita/Torrance Consortium is accepting Proposals in response to the attached specifications for the provision of employment and training programs.

The Consortium manages a wide variety of employment and training services funded under the Job Training Partnership Act (JTPA). These services are designed to develop employment potential and to assist those who have obstacles in gaining employment.

It is anticipated that funding approval for each project will average at $45,000. Proposals which exhibit the most cost effective means of accomplishing the attached objectives and document private sector and community linkages will have a competitive edge.

Please read the instructions in the enclosed packet carefully. The competitiveness of your proposal will rely on its being carefully and correctly prepared. If you need assistance or clarification of the instructions, you may call the PIC office at (213) 618-2985.

Two (2) originals, plus six (6) copies of the completed proposal are due at the PIC office by 5:00 P.M., Friday, April 1, 1988. Proponents are urged to hand-deliver their proposals. If RFP packets are mailed, they must be *postmarked no later than April 1, 19__*. Mail or deliver to:

> Carson/Lomita/Torrance
> Private Industry Council
> 3231 Torrance Boulevard
> Torrance, CA 90503
>
> Attn: Elsie Manson, Control Clerk

FIGURE 4–5.   Sample RFP.

PROCEDURES FOR SUBMITTING PROPOSALS

1. *FORMAT*

   A. All proposals must follow the attachment format and use the attached forms.

   B. Two (2) originals and six (6) copies must be submitted. This is necessary for PIC committee review.

   C. Proposals must be complete when submitted in order to receive full review by the PIC. Completion includes all items listed under "Instructions and Proposal Review Point Values."

   D. All proposals must be signed by an authorized representative of the organization using the form provided.

2. *MAXIMUM SIZE OF PACKAGE*

   In an effort to reduce the volume of paper, proposal, narratives and attachments will be strictly limited to a total of ten (10) pages. The forms provided give specific limits by section. All pages in excess of the limit will be disregarded. The balance of the proposal will be considered as it remains.

3. *EVALUATION AND SELECTION*

   Proposals will be evaluated as follows:

   - Methodology (Point Value: 50)
   - Timelines (Point Value: 5)
   - Organizational Capability (Point Value: 25)
   - Budget (Point Value: 20)

   Bidders are advised that final selection of service providers will be recommended by the PIC to the Torrance City Council. Organizations will be notified in writing within sixty (60) days regarding final selections.

4. *PROGRAM OPERATING DATES*

   Program contract starting and termination dates will be determined during the negotiation process, however, should not exceed twelve (12) months in duration.

FIGURE 4–6. Sample point evaluation system.

5. DELIVERY OF PROPOSALS

Mail or hand deliver the proposal package to the following address, unless otherwise stated in the RFP cover letter:

Carson/Lomita/Torrance
Private Industry Council
3231 Torrance Boulevard
Torrance, CA 90503
Attn: Elsie Manson, Control Clerk

Proponents are urged to hand-deliver their proposals to the Control Clerk named above. Written receipts will be provided for all hand-delivered proposals, upon request. Such receipts will not be available for proposals delivered by regular mail.

FIGURE 4-6. (*continued*)

CLASSIFICATION OF BUDGET COSTS BY CATEGORIES

ADMINISTRATION	PARTICIPANT SUPPORT	TRAINING
• Direct and indirect costs associated with the administration of the programs • Salaries and fringe benefits of personnel engaged in: —executive —fiscal —data collection —personnel —legal —audit —procurement —communications —maintenance —similar functions • Materials, supplies, equipment, office space costs, and staff training related to administration • Salaries and fringe benefits of program administrative positions such as: —supervisors —program analysts —labor market analysts —project directors —clerical personnel	• 50 percent of work experience expenditures that meet the requirements of Section 108 (b)(3) of the Act • 100 percent of the cost of all work experience program expenditures which do not meet the requirements of Section 108 (b)(3) of the Act • Supportive services (see glossary)	• Costs associated with on-the-job training services • Employer outreach; advertising • Salaries, fringe benefits, equipment, supplies of personnel directly engaged in providing training • Books and other teaching aids • Equipment and materials used in providing training to participants • Classroom space and associated utility costs • Tuition and entrance fees • 50 percent of the costs of a "limited" work experience program as defined in Section 108 (b)(3) of the Act • Single unit charges that: —are for training; —are fixed unit price; and —are performance based requiring placement into unsubsidized employment • Construction-related costs for purchasing equipment, materials and supplies • Applicant outreach and intake; advertising

FIGURE 4-7. Sample cost breakdown.

	Proposal #
	(Office Use)

CARSON/LOMITA/TORRANCE PRIVATE INDUSTRY COUNCIL
APPLICATION FOR FUNDING CONSIDERATION

Organization Name: _____

Mailing Address: _____

Contact Person/Title: _____

Telephone: _____

Training Site Location(s): _____

Title of Proposal: _____

Training occupation(s): _____

PROPOSED ACTIVITY: TYPE OF ORGANIZATION (CHECK ONE)

_____ Classroom Training   _____ Private Business of Industry

_____ On-the-Job Trianing   _____ Private Non-Profit Organization

_____ Customized Trianing   _____ Public Agency

_____ Industry-Based Training   _____ Education Agency

_____ Summer Youth   _____ Other: _____
                                              (Specify)

_____ Exemplary Youth Program

_____ Other (Specify): _____   Special Target Group, if any: _____

_____   _____

Total Funds Requested: $_____   Number to be Served: _____

Duration of Project: From _____ to _____

I certify that this is a firm offer by the proposer to provide the services as described in this proposal and that this offer is good for a minimum period of 120 days. I further certify that this proposal has been duly authorized by the below listed organization's governing body; or, (if the proposer is a corporation) the undersigned hereby certifies and warrants that the corporation is duly incorporated and in good standing in the State of California.

Dated: _____   _____
                                              (NAME OF PROPOSING ORGANIZATION)

                 by _____
                                              (NAME)

                                   _____
                                              (TITLE)

FIGURE 4–8. Sample proposal format.

NARRATIVE

A. *Program Methodology*   (Point Value: 50)

    1. Provide a brief synopsis of your proposed program and its objectives. In addition, attach a one to two page curriculum. Include training hours for each subject.

    2. Describe the problem or condition which makes this project necessary, i.e., local labor market demand.

B. *Timelines*   (Point Value: 5)

    1. Is your program open entry/open exit, or operated on a fixed schedule? Provide your proposed schedule by completing Enrollment Schedule (E-3)

FIGURE 4–8. (*continued*)

2. Indicate completion dates for the following pre-employment activities (if approved):

   a. Pre-Enrollment Activities

Activity	Completion Date(s)
Hiring of Project Staff	_____
Recruitment of Participants	_____
Selection of Enrollees	_____
First Participant Enrollment	_____
Last Participant Enrollment	_____

   b. Classroom Activities (Educational Components Only)
   Length of Training = _____ weeks
   Number of Classes During Contract = _____

   c. On-the-Job (OJT) Activities:
   Average number of weeks of training: _____
   Planned percentage of reimbursement to the employers: _____

3. Describe the methods and/or procedures to be utilized to accomplish the following objectives:

   a. Recruitment of eligible applicants

   b. Assessment, selection and orientation of potential participants

   c. Training techniques (including books, tools, etc.)

   d. Job development, placement and retention follow-up

   e. Supportive services to participants

4. Performance Objectives

   a. Of the total participants enrolled
   _____% will be placed in unsubsidized training-related employment.

   b. Of the total participants placed
   _____% will be retained 60 days
   _____% will be retained 90 days

FIGURE 4–8. *(continued)*

ENROLLMENT SCHEDULE

Month/Year	A. Enrollments		B. Completions		C. Job Placements		D. Other Positive Terminations		E. 60 Day Job Retention		F. 90 Day Job Retention	
	This Month	Cumu- lative	This Month	Cumu- lative	This Month	Cumu- lative	This Month	Cumu- lative	This Month	Cumu- lative	This Month	Cumu- lative

Job placements must occur within ___90___ days after participant completes/exits training.

(See reverse side for Instructions)

FIGURE 4–8. (continued)

DEFINITION OF TERMS

A. ENROLLMENT— Occurs when an **eligible** individual begins his/her first training activity

B. COMPLETION— Satisfactory completion of the actual training portion of an activity **(occurs prior to 45/90 day holds, job placement, and transfers)**

C. PLACEMENT— Entered **unsubsidized** employment within 45 or 90 days after completion of training **(applicable to contract terms)**

D. OTHER POSITIVE TERMINATIONS **(YOUTH ONLY)**—Youth participant did not enter unsubsidized employment but terminated for the following reasons:

    (1) Returned to full-time school
    (2) Completed major level of education
    (3) Completed program objectives (YEET 14–15 years old)
    (4) Enrollment in Non-Title II training
    (5) Attained employment competency

E. 60-DAY RETENTION—60 days retained in unsubsidized employment

F. 90-DAY RETENTION—90 days retained in unsubsidized employment **(applicable to contract terms)**

INSTRUCTIONS

Start MONTH/YEAR column with the date program activity will begin. Show the number of participants for the month, along with cumulative totals for each section. Schedule should cover entire contract period. Enrollment column should show total number of participants by the last date to enroll.

NOTE: Enrollment column should show total number of participants by the last date to enroll.

FIGURE 4–8. *(continued)*

c. $_____ minimum starting wage at placement

d. $_____ average starting wage at placement

5. Describe the minimum qualifications (academic, occupational, physical) that an applicant must possess and demonstrate before entering your proposed program.

6. Describe skill levels, certifications, and licenses that a participant will possess upon completion of training.

7. List types of employment reasonably obtainable after completion of training. (list specific job titles)

C. *Organizational Capability* (Point Value: 25)

1. Describe other employment and training programs your organization has operated which provided services similar to those requested herein and demonstrated effectiveness in:

    • Placing individuals in jobs

    • Ensuring jobs are above minimum wage

    • Include a list of not less than TEN (10) employers with whom your organization has placed individuals in occupations specific to this program during the past year (if applicable)

If you are a *school*, attach evidence of license and/or accreditation for school and training courses.

FIGURE 4–8. *(continued)*

2. For the aforementioned programs, list previous and current funding sources.

1. _____   _____
    Name of Funding Agency   Dates of Funding

   _____   _____
    Address   Type of Program

2. _____   _____
    Name of Funding Agency   Dates of Funding

   _____   _____
    Address   Type of Program

3. _____   _____
    Name of Funding Agency   Dates of Funding

   _____   _____
    Address   Type of Program

3. Identify the headquarters, site(s) and location(s) of the project activities. Detail availability of public transportation and parking, as well as accessibility for the handicapped.

4. Identify the proposed staffing for this project, specifying the number of staff in each classification, their qualifications, and accreditations, project responsibilities, and proposed salaries.

5. Describe your accounting and programmatic reporting systems; and your organization's internal system of checks and balances; i.e., attendance, payroll, supervisory verification.

FIGURE 4–8. (continued)

Applicant
Organization _____

D. *BUDGET* (Point Value: 20)

  1. Total Funds Requested $_____

COST CATEGORY	REQUESTED	% OF TOTAL
A. Program Administration		
		%
B. Training		
		%
C. Participant Services		%
TOTAL FUNDS REQUESTED		100%

  2. Describe matching funds to be used to expand or enhance this proposal.

FIGURE 4–8. (*continued*)

CHAPTER 5

Private Industry Proposals

A decade ago, there was a $50 million-a-year company that specialized in selling collectibles. When inflation was high, the firm had little trouble selling its wares to consumers anxious to find a hedge against inflation. But when the cost of living dropped and inflation was halved, the company began to experience difficulty.

It was during one of those problem periods that marketing consultant Jay Abraham saw one of the company's ads. Within the ad, he saw the potential for a new client.

Abraham decided to launch a campaign to capture the firm's business. In his usual unorthodox approach, he picked up the telephone, called the company, and asked for the president. As you might expect, he spoke to the president's secretary, who was determined that he was not going to get through.

Abraham, however, was persuasive—and smooth. He has been cold calling for more than a decade, and the secretary was on his side within a matter of minutes. Abraham surprised the president with free advice as to how he might improve his market share. The conversation lasted 30 minutes, and before it was over, the president was impressed—but not convinced.

Abraham followed the call with a lengthy proposal/letter, outlining ideas and concepts that could be used by the firm. For three months, every other week, another proposal/letter arrived on the president's desk. Each had a fresh money-making idea in it.

By the end of the fourth month, Abraham's proposals had hit home, and the president invited him to the midwest to sign a consulting contract with his firm—a company that was destined to grow tenfold during the next five years.

Today, Jay Abraham still generates clients in the same manner. He cold calls and follows with a proposal/letter. It is a technique that few practice because of the difficulty in getting by a secretary to the CEO. Thanks in part to a glib tongue, Abraham not only gets by executives' secretaries, he does the same with nearly every other "barricade" he encounters.

Abraham's approach is an example of what proposal writing in the private sector shares with proposal writing in the public or governmental sector—the need to market services; to keep one's eyes and ears open for opportunities.

That, however, is where the similarity between the private and public sectors end. Those answering RFPs must adhere to the rules, follow the guidelines, and be technically perfect in order to win. You do not deviate from the RFP's instructions.

On the other hand, independent consultants and firms writing proposals follow no set format or guide. There are no hard and fast rules. Most of the time there is no budget to work within, either. Whereas the RFP generally has at least an upper limit cost, those seeking business from companies in the private sector usually have to guess as to the funds available.

PERSONALITY AND PSYCHOLOGY

There are other factors that weigh heavily in the private sector—personality, psychology, and politics. Usually the person who reads the proposal is the decision-maker. He or she may be the CEO or a high-ranking executive whose job it will be to work with the outside firm. If the decision-maker does not like the color of the consultant's hair, eyes, or the way he or she speaks or laughs, that means trouble—and no business.

Almost every decision-maker has an "influencer." The CEO may realize he needs a new accounting firm, but he may be influenced by the vice president of finance before making the decision. Similarly, the need for help in the data processing area may depend on the director of the data processing department, even though the decision is made by the CEO.

Top management could decide they want to bring in coordinated designs for their housewares, but they want to see what the marketing director has to say about it before making a decision.

Not every influence on the decision-maker is as obvious. The departmental supervisor who is screening presentations may—or may not—have the ear of the decision-maker. Either way, the proposer must tread lightly.

Proposers should never step on toes because decision-makers, especially CEOs, do not operate in a vacuum. They go on past experience, instinct, and what their managers will support.

WHO HAS THE INFLUENCE?

Some proposal firms deplore making a presentation to anyone other than the decision-maker, and there is validity in that objection. No one wants to waste time or effort, and no one wants to be stonewalled by a lower management employee who has little influence.

However, there is a problem: Proposers can never be sure who has influence and who does not.

Don Kracke never forgets that. "I am perfectly content to work my way up the ladder with a proposal. I am willing to take the additional time necessary to get the OK from the decision-maker. What you have to keep in mind is that even if a proposal is presented at a lower management level, the person reading it is going to have an opinion. If they like it, they will send it up the ladder with favorable comments. If they do not, they may kill it. That's why it is important to have rapport with everyone you deal with at a prospect's company, and not just the decision-maker."

Paul Hackett believes the key is finding out who the decision-maker is going to be and doing as much of your pre-proposal work with him or her as possible. If Hackett thinks he is being shuffled down the ladder simply because the company wants to get rid of him, he will bow out gracefully.

"But if I am being shifted to someone who has responsibility for sifting through proposals, I have no problem working at that level," says Hackett. "As long as you are working towards an objective, and as long as all your competitors have to go through the same process, there is no problem working downline."

There are questions that help the proposal writer determine who will make the decisions. They range from "Will there be anyone else using the system (or service)?" to "Is anyone else involved in making the decision?" All queries are designed to determine if the proposer is talking to the only decision-maker, just one of many, or perhaps to someone who will screen the proposal.

THE FIRST MEETING

Initial client meetings are critical. That is when the goals and objectives of the prospect are determined, but it is also when the prospect sizes up the outside firm and its people, and determines if they can get along. Services and products cannot be sold without rapport between the proposer and the prospect.

"Most people would rather deal with people they like, rather than those they do not know," says Don Kracke. "The proposal may be great but if they don't like you . . ."

When the decision-maker/prospective client and the proposal firm meet, there should be feelings either "towards" or "against" you. Says Joe Izzo, "They must have some emotion. They either love or hate you."

If they feel neither, there is a good chance you will not get the business. If they hate the proposer, the proposal is in trouble. Emotions surface when the proposer does his research and begins to interface with management. Is management cooperative? Do they open doors for the proposal firm? Do they put the proposal firm off? Is there suddenly a delay in the project without good reason? These are all questions whose answers may indicate how a proposal firm stands during the initial meetings.

The personality of the consultant gathering the information has an impact on the prospect, but the client's personality should be carefully defined by the proposal writer, too. The "personality of the company" serves as background for every written (or oral) presentation.

Each company has its own behavior patterns and characteristics. One might be hierarchical and have free coffee for executives, while those in the nonexecutive category may find themselves paying for each cup.

There is one well-known large corporation that not only practices the "free/pay" coffee policy, but has also found a way to differentiate employees within the two-story building it occupies. Executives—that is, all employees with the rank of department director and above—are housed on the second floor. The remainder of the staff is on the first floor, including a large data processing and an accounting department.

In this case, all decisions are made by those on the second floor. The outside firm that presents a proposal for a new or revised data processing system to managers on the first floor is wasting its time. In fact, it may even be damaging its case since there is little dialogue among employees on the first and second floors. The vice president of accounting is, of course, located on the second floor. He is the one to make the decision on any proposal.

This separation of employees is part of the company's personality. Whether it is good or bad is not the point. It is simply something prospective proposers need to know before presenting a proposal.

Information gleaned from top management may reveal only a small portion of the company's personality and problems. It may not be possible to discern the true character of a company without talking to employees at numerous levels. In the case of the "structured two-story company," with proper research the proposer would know that his or her proposal would do little good unless it is eventually read upstairs where the executives reside.

DEFINING THE PROSPECT'S PERSONALITY

Accurately determining a company's personality is one key to winning the contract. For example, Raelene Arrington's prestigious national accounting company was called in to make a proposal to a large manufacturer. While researching the needs of the corporation, Arrington's associates talked to a number of employees. What began to surface was the firm's personality—a fun-loving group with a sense of humor.

CPA firms usually do not have "fun-loving" images. They are thought of as stodgy, stiff, and conservative. Arrington's company decided that if they wanted the business they would have to make a different impression on the prospect.

One of the prospect's products was a children's trivia game. When Raelene Arrington's firm came back with its proposal, it turned the last page into an "accounting trivia game" based upon the children's game. Questions about accounting were asked and each multiple choice answer consisted of Arrington's firm as well as three of its competitors.

A hand wand was given to each reader and when the wand passed over the correct answer (which was always Coopers & Lybrand), the wand made a noise. The proposal readers thought the game clever. It also showed that Arrington's group had something in common with the prospective client—a sense of humor. It helped win the account.

Know the prospective client. Do your homework. A short time ago, one of the largest builders in California was about to embark on a $300 million housing project. He was anxious to find an advertising and promotion agency to help market the project. The fees would be substantial.

Several executives within the builder's firm thought they knew what he wanted. They invited a half-dozen ad/promotional firms to put together proposals, and they outlined the project and how *they* saw it.

While the other firms thought they had all the information they needed, one firm asked for a brief meeting with the builder himself. They got it and found that his thinking was slightly different from the executives who worked for him. He had several thoughts in mind that had not been mentioned to the other proposers.

When the firm came back with its proposals, it was radically different from its competitors. It also encompassed the one element the others had missed, the factor the builder/owner had stressed. As a result, this firm's proposal won, and the company was awarded the ad/promo contract even though it had never done anything in the building industry previously.

Research and know the client's needs. That theme is preached continuously by firms putting together proposals. While answers to some RFPs may be written by people who never meet the customer, that is not the case with proposals in the private sector.

INITIAL PROPOSAL STEP

The initial step in writing is interviewing, talking to people within the prospective client's firm. But how do you get them to talk? The key is to see the CEO or decision-maker and obtain his or her blessings and cooperation. Once that is done, it should be stressed to the CEO that it is important—before any proposal is written— that the proposal firm gets to meet and talk to key executives and employees. Most CEOs and/or decision-makers are happy to arrange the meetings. They admire the interest and the time the proposal firm is willing to put into the project.

The firm that operates with only the CEO's input is at a disadvantage. Certainly they may come back with a winning proposal, but once the project is underway they may find unexpected difficulties because they did not learn the entire story. Ultimately, an outside firm has to solve problems and this usually takes more than just interfacing with the CEO. The CEO only has his own perspective of the difficulty. Those down the line may have other, enlightening ideas as well.

Some proposal firms, however, never get the chance to meet the downline employees or the CEO. The only "meeting" they may have is on the telephone, and their interview is restricted to a long distance question-and-answer session.

Bob Ritchie encounters that situation more often than not. He markets communications equipment, a highly competitive product that is price-sensitive.

To Ritchie, selling the telephone system is not as difficult as some would imagine. The key is to plan for questions beforehand. Be ready for every telephone inquiry. Ritchie does exactly that. He finds out who will be using the equipment, how, and if they have expansion plans.

He goes beyond the firm's initial needs and probes what they may require in the future. He is even willing to sacrifice a profitable sale for one piece of equipment if he finds it will not satisfy the company's long-range needs. Ritchie's technique does not always get him in the door, but it shows the prospect he has vision and thinks about the future.

He makes it a point to deliver the proposal in person and always tries to meet with the decision-makers not only to explain the proposal, but to lend them a sample (or samples) of the equipment he has been describing. Lending a prospect a piece of expensive equipment is a smart ploy. Once it is in the prospect's hands, the proposer has the opportunity to reschedule an appointment (to pick up the equipment) at a time when the prospect has had a chance to study the proposal.

INCOMPLETE INFORMATION

At times, telephone information may be incomplete or even inaccurate. When Ritchie finds himself in a room with decision-makers and needs arise other than those he was given, he uses the change in direction to his advantage. "Well," he might say, "from what was told to me previously (on the telephone), here is what we can do. Now we can add this—and this—and this . . ."

Management will usually excuse any oversights in Ritchie's proposal because the contact was made over the telephone and he may not have been given a thorough rundown. That is not the case with the proposer who gets to meet and interview everyone within a firm he desires. If that person makes a mistake or comes to an inaccurate conclusion, they are going to lose points for their company.

To avoid misinformation, proposers always try to get to the decision-maker. But in their anxiety to get to that person, Ritchie cautions, "Never put someone from the company in a position where they appear to be less than they are. Do not put them down. If you try to bypass them and only give them cursory attention, you can create a damaging enemy. You can never tell about the influence they are going to have with the decision-maker."

Many service-oriented firms find it impossible to write a sensible proposal without meeting the prospect face-to-face, as well as talking to others within the firm. Management may be in dire straights and they may try to rush the proposal, but smart proposers avoid the temptation to get it done quickly.

Joe Izzo is one of those. He makes it a practice to never write a proposal until he has done a "thorough study" of the business and the area he was called in to examine. He may spend from a few hours to a day or more talking to the decision-maker as well as to others within the company.

"If a person calls us in and only has an hour or two, I spend the time trying to dig out the needs and any problem areas. I go back to my office and dissect the problem with my associates. At that point, we structure our strategy."

THE STRATEGY

Strategies are the outline or procedure a firm will follow before writing and submitting a proposal. The personnel of the proposal company discuss the situation and formulate a list of key questions that must be answered. These questions will supply the material for the proposal.

Questions that belong in a strategy formulating session include the following:

Who will we interview?

What type of questions and answers should be asked?

What is the personality of the company?

How deep does the problem go?

Does there seem to be differences of opinion within the firm?

Have we faced similar situations in the past?

Who are our competitors? What are their strengths?

Who will be the decision-maker(s)?

Is there a planned budget?

Will this take the time of the principals of our company, or can staff accomplish the task? Will the prospect's management be satisfied with staff? If not, how do we approach?

Izzo and whoever accompanied him to the initial meeting formulate their strategy along with staff members. They put together everything they know and call management for a second meeting.

The second session is informal, much like the initial meeting. Izzo outlines how he sees the situation. It is still early in the game, and he does not want to say something that will brand his firm as one that jumps to the wrong conclusions. He softens his initial impressions with a statement such as, "These are our thoughts and ideas, and some of the interpretations we would like to share. They are based on our initial session."

This pre-proposal meeting is meant to generate additional ideas, determine if Izzo is on the right track, and find out what turns management on (and off). It is a "feeling out" session, a low-risk approach because the proposer has not come in with definitive statements but only with "initial thoughts and ideas" that can be modified.

During this type of probing session, proposers must watch and listen to the prospect—carefully. If a prospect asks a great many questions, he may be confused. Remember, a company CEO may know everything there is to know about his firm and industry, but he may not have any knowledge of the proposer's field, hence the confusion. Even if there are not many questions, proposers should explain any concepts that may be foreign to the decision-maker. The language of the consultant's industry is not that of the prospect's. Translation in clear, understandable terms is required. Do not use acronyms or in-house terms that may be unfamiliar.

It is during this session that Izzo determines what interests a prospect. "When I hit something that really concerns them, they get excited. There's a great deal of feedback, and you must listen. These oral sessions are not meant to be one-sided lectures by our company."

Note taking, by someone from Izzo's firm, is critical. When the meeting is finished and Izzo goes back to prepare a proposal, he does not want any guesswork. Even though he has had limited research time, Izzo's proposals are on the mark—"if we have asked the right questions and listened."

Even in situations where he spends six or eight hours at the firm talking to other managers and employees, Izzo will spend more time with the decision-makers to make sure he has everyone's thoughts. "And to make sure we are on the right track. If you rush the proposal and cut down your research time, there is a good chance you are going to have a mis-statement in it. You may come to the wrong conclusion, and once you have an incorrect statement in writing and you present it to the prospect, your proposal—and you—are dead."

There are countless techniques for gathering information. Executives, decision-makers, employees—they all have input that can be valuable. One method that proposers use in situations where there may be a complex problem is called the "skunk works" approach.

The term stems from idea-generating sessions that Lockheed Aircraft used a number of years ago. The company put its brightest engineers together in one room and let them throw out as many far-out and creative thoughts as possible for one session. It was called "skunk" because no one within the company wanted to get near the engineers during these creative sessions.

Top management may see a need for outside help within a department, but the managers may not be familiar with the inner workings of that department. An analysis of the department may lend itself to the "skunk works" approach, particularly if the company supports openness among employees.

INDUSTRY RESEARCH

Don Kracke spends days, sometimes weeks, researching and doing his homework. He was called by a major soft drink company that asked if he was interested in submitting a proposal to handle its licensing. (Companies that have proprietary trademarks or products may license the use of the trademark to others. The licensees pay the soft drink company a royalty on its sales.)

The soft drink company had spent many years establishing its trademark, and it was of considerable value to licensees who could use it on t-shirts, cups, glasses, and a variety of products. Typically, Kracke licenses his own designs and does not handle licensing for others. The account, however, was substantial and it intrigued him. Kracke began to delve into the firm and its industry. He dissected trade papers, talked to executives within the soft drink company, and spent much time talking to existing licensees who already had agreements with the soft drink firm.

When the research was completed, Kracke turned in a proposal that got a response from the firm within an hour after it was read.

One line said, "What your licensees think about you is that you are not the licensor but the rippor, and the licensees the rippees."

Kracke's point was that licensees suspected that the soft drink company was doing absolutely nothing for them. Their fees went for naught. That feeling is prevalent in many franchise businesses as well. The franchisees resent paying royalties and fees from which they cannot see immediate results. The soft drink manufacturer's licensees were no different.

When the "rippor/rippee" statement was read by the decision-makers in the company, Kracke says, "I know they said 'he is right'."

That approach can be hazardous, especially if a proposer does not know the client well or if he has failed to do adequate research. "If you lay something out that you know is true, and put it in simple terms, everyone catches on," says Kracke. It is a risk, but it may set your proposal apart from the competition.

The same situation can arise when a proposal company's research indicates that the decision-maker or CEO is off-base as far as the problem is concerned. His or her opinion may differ substantially from everyone else's within the firm. What should be done?

A firm can play it safe and reiterate the CEO's concerns, and base its plan of action on them. It may get the business, but it may never solve the problem. In the end it may lose. Alternatively, it can take the Kracke approach and tell it like it is. Not all CEOs will take kindly to the "rippee/rippor" approach, but there are gentler terms and ways to proceed. Instead, it is wise to point out other things uncovered while "the proposal firm did its research" that it considered strongly when formulating its proposal.

A proposal gives "personality" to a firm, maintains Kracke. "It enables you to stand out from the crowd. There may be risks in taking that approach, but I think it is worth it."

If the proposal is dry, put a cover letter on it and strive to give the reader an idea of the proposal company's personality. "Everything we do," he continues, "is designed to help us establish a personality in the decision-maker's eyes."

In the end, proposals are merely vehicles for one person to talk to another. Too many are cut and dried and boring. The language is stilted. Prospects will never be convinced to spend money with a firm unless they are convinced the firm is human.

PROPOSAL TONE

Every proposal can read as if it were a one-on-one document if proper research is done. It can appear to be personal—and human. Personalization also means, as Kracke puts it, "an absence of the b.s. factor. I stress honesty, integrity, and clarity. Most people buy that. If they do not, you will probably be better off without the business."

Kracke says, "Too many proposals never allow the proposer to be nailed down. They have the 'trust me baby' syndrome. That's terrible. Clients are sophisticated. This is a subjective area, but always deal in specifics and facts. Our proposals are always straightforward, but not dry. The two terms need not be synonymous."

Proposals should be specific, not general; eliminate vague promises. A proposal should be articulate and have sufficient logic within it to support statements. The client should be reading and nodding his or her head in agreement at the same time.

Writing about a proposal firm's qualifications is an area that poses difficulty for most writers. They get tangled up in superlatives and adjectives. Neither is necessary. The approach should be factual and to the point. If a proposer has represented clients in the same industry, say so. If there were any special accomplishments for those clients, state them but do so without adjectives.

Tone is important. The proposal not only presents a firm's qualifications and ideas, but its tone also exhibits the confidence a proposer has. There is a big difference in "we will" and "we have" versus "we will try." Clients go for outside help because they want the expertise. They do not want someone to try, they want someone to "do." The proposer should demonstrate that in the proposal.

That does not mean bragging about abilities, but it is a "knowledge-based confidence." If a firm has done the job for others, it can do it for the prospect's company. Cite examples, mention names. One key is for the proposal company to put itself in the place of the prospective client. The writer should try and imagine that it is his company that is going to read the proposal and hire the outsider. What things would be of concern? The proposer should ask himself, "What does his company need?" and if this proposal answers that need.

NEED-BASED PROPOSALS

Well-written proposals are need-based. The proposer determines
through research what the prospect's needs are before a word is
ever put on paper. In some cases, determining needs is much easier
than in others. A company may be growing and it needs additional
computer terminals and new software. Another firm may find it
needs expanded health or pension plans for its executives, or perhaps a communications system for its field workers, or coordinated
designs for its housewares line.

Those needs are straightforward, others are not. The company
that has trouble getting timely sales information from its data processing department may or may not have a computer (hardware)
problem. It could be a time management problem, such as the head
of the department may not want to distribute the information until
he has seen and analyzed it. The proposal company that does sufficient research will know the problem before the proposal is written.

REPLACING COMPETITORS

Some proposal companies interview a prospect and discover there
is already a firm in place but management wants a new company
to handle its business. The proposer's job is not easy in this case.
Not only does he or she have to analyze the job that must be done,
but they also must determine why the present firm has failed. Why
is management displeased with the current vendor?

Raelene Arrington's firm faces that problem constantly. They
are asked to prepare proposals for clients who are unhappy with
their current CPA firm. The client's needs may not, at first, be obvious. Management may be dissatisfied with its current firm because it is not "getting enough creative tax information" or perhaps
it feels it is not getting sufficient attention from its present vendor.

Clients who have a firm doing work for them do not decide to
change overnight. The need for change has been brewing. Why? Is
this a firm that has not received the service promised in the proposal, or is this a firm that plays musical chairs with its outside
consultants?

In some industries, changing consultants frequently is a way of doing business. This is sometimes true in the advertising field. An automobile manufacturer always has the opportunity to compare his agency's work with that of others in the industry—because the ads are usually on TV. Others with mass-marketed products have the same comparison opportunity. Comparisons are not as obvious when it comes to a firm that is replacing a client's manufacturing equipment or altering its computer operation.

To determine the reasons why a client is replacing a firm, research is necessary. The president of a large company may be unhappy with his outside auditors, and is replacing them because "he dislikes the way the audit was done." In reality, he may be unhappy with the lack of attention the firm gave his company. It could be one of the proposers sold the client on his firm's services and his ability, but they never saw him again.

Some firms utilize super salespeople to present the proposal. The client is enamored with the representative's ability and signs. They never see him again. Private sector firms find that one way to alleviate the client's concern is to make sure everyone's services (and the fees for those services) are contained in the proposal. Thus if the client is sold on a partner and not enthralled with staff doing the work, he can also see that he will be paying a premium for that partner's services if he asks for them specifically.

Hourly fees will vary, of course, depending upon the skills and experience of the person who works for the proposal submitter. There are other price variables that go beyond labor rates. A company may propose an idea, but it will cost $X, while another will cost $XX. It is up to the client to decide whether he wants one or both, and which one.

Consultants selling services often prepare a menu of possible services with fees for each. Kracke is one consultant who practices this laundry-list approach. If the company asks for a proposal revolving around a new design, Kracke may end up presenting not only a plan for a design but a marketing plan as well. His proposals contain a great deal of what is commonly called "what if . . . ." "What if we slanted the design in this manner, then you could do this . . ."

He will give ideas far and above what the client expects. By the time he is finished, there is a long list of concepts that the client can pick and choose from. Each has a price tag.

BUDGET- OR TASK-ORIENTED FEES

Proposals may be task- or budget-oriented. A task-oriented proposal is prepared when the client has given the proposer a specific task without any dollar amount specified. The proposer solves the task within the proposal and comes up with a dollar figure. The client may be able to pick and choose what he wants, or he may have to take the entire proposal at the given task price or leave it.

A budget-oriented proposal means the proposer starts with a specific dollar amount and builds the proposal around that figure. The burden is on the proposal writer to create a program within the given figure.

Psychology plays an important role in a firm's expenditures. Some clients may not want to set a dollar amount because they have no idea what it will take to get the job done. They may never have used a consultant before. When no budget is specified, it is important for the proposal to detail and justify each task. The client should not have to guess the cost of each element in the proposal.

Some clients prefer to leave out the budget because they want to see if their planned budget is realistic. In this case, if the proposer comes in with a figure higher than what the client had in mind, the client may reveal the "hidden" budget figures.

Whereas few consultants get paid for their pre-proposal time and the proposal itself, Bill Johnson's firm does. This is because of the way the firm approaches a prospect and his problems. Johnson will completely analyze the company and its problems, and he will develop a solution and a course of action. The client has the option of buying Johnson's plan and using his company to implement the solution, or going somewhere else. Johnson's compensation is based upon hourly rates for his staff (and himself).

Johnson wants to be sure the client understands what he or she is getting for the money. Clients have become more sophisticated— and suspicious. Many feel they have been "burned" previously. They are anxious to know exactly what they are going to get for their money.

"Many [clients] prefer a fixed fee. They want us to price the entire job. That may be okay for the firm that is selling a product, but the service company can have difficulty. What happens is that you may end up in a situation where you have an idea how many hours it will take but you are not sure. Then let's say you get into the project and suddenly discover that the job is changing, it's growing. You could lose money on it if you are dealing with a fixed fee."

Experienced firms know the client has to be educated. The client must be aware of what could change within the proposal. Consultants sit down with top management before the job is underway and outline the areas they foresee as possible problems. They give the client their rationale based upon past experience. Laying everything out beforehand eliminates unwelcome surprises that could develop later.

Paul Hackett utilizes a "cost/benefit" approach. For each benefit he outlines the cost in simple terms so that the client can understand. "Price," he says, "does not make or break a proposal."

CLIENT'S GOALS AND PRICE

"The client's goals and objectives overwhelm price. A client wants a problem solved. In relation to the problem, the price may be miniscule," says Hackett.

If price is going to be a consideration, consultants should ask the prospect about their budget or how much has been allocated. What do they hope to accomplish? Sometimes by having the client explain his or her goals, the fees become easier to explain. A specific task—and its cost—can be tied together. The client begins to understand that the task is more time consuming. He also begins to see the justification of the fees, and why it is impossible for the consultant to do it for less than the stated amount. Evaluating the price of services is more difficult for a prospect than weighing the cost of two similar products. With product proposals, the prospect can often compare apples to apples.

With services, there are many intangible elements, such as the personality of the proposers, their track record, and the rapport that does or does not exist between the proposal company and prospect.

In the minds of most clients, pricing can always be negotiated. They would prefer not to commit themselves to any specific amount and therefore the proposing company often finds itself in a position where the prospect is asking "how much." That's when the laundry-list approach can be effective.

Giving a prospect more than they ask for also shows creativity on the part of the proposer. There is, of course, always the fear of having good ideas stolen, with the prospect of either giving it to another firm or doing it themselves. The protection for ideas is with the execution, procedure, and process. Proposals present the ideas but they do not detail how they will be carried out. Even by leaving out the procedure, there is no guarantee ideas will not be stolen.

Hackett has some fears about theft but remains an optimist. "I believe people will deal straight most of the time, and they do. During an oral presentation, you also have the opportunity to point out the originality of the idea. It is an added selling point.

"If you do a good job, and you have done your homework, I think theft is the last thing on a client's mind. I believe they may look at original ideas and say, 'Yes, I could steal it but who will do my thinking next time if I don't use this firm now?'"

Abraham looks upon the theft of new ideas as a positive. "If someone tries something I suggest and they make an extra $10,000, it is an affirmation of my skills. I want them to see my ability. The possibility they may steal the idea has never bothered me."

THE ORAL PRESENTATION

Few companies can win business with a proposal in the private sector without interfacing with top management through an oral presentation. The oral presentation usually occurs after management has had a week or so to digest the written document. There are times, however, when the oral presentation will be given at the same time the proposal is presented.

If management has had a chance to read the document, the oral presentation should not be used as reiteration of the written. In a 30-minute session (oral presentations should not be longer), consultants have the opportunity to impress management with their track record, understanding of the problem, solution, and knowledge.

The consultant's track record should be the first item on the oral agenda. Within 5 to 10 minutes (at most), a firm can review its history and accomplishments.

The next 10 to 15 minutes should consist of an interpretation of the problem and the solution. Presenters should always save an idea or two for this section that may not be in the proposal. They should also pluck one or two ideas from the proposal that are original and present them at this time.

Keep in mind that the oral presentation is similar to the written in that it must always address the prospect's needs. It should never turn into a bragging session about the proposal company, nor should it drift from the subject at hand.

The meeting is used as a sounding board, a vehicle to not only explain any points that might confuse management, but to also bring in other service aspects that are not present in the proposal or that need clarification.

New ideas are explained, but the process of how they will be carried out is still not detailed. Between the ideas and the oral presentation, bids are won and lost. It is crucial that a company presenting a proposal prepare as well for the oral session as it did for the proposal itself. There is nothing worse than a group of decision-makers being bored by a disorganized dissertation.

Slides and/or viewgraphs are a must. It is difficult to hold your audience's attention without them. The visuals keep your audience involved.

If the prospect has numerous questions and wants to extend the time allowed with questions and answers, fine. That is up to them. Make every statement and sentence count.

The presenters should also know who is going to be in the room. Will all the decision-makers be there? If the proposal has been presented in advance, prepare a brief (written) outline for the oral presentation.

If there are three people in the room, talk to all three. Look from one to the other. Never ignore someone in attendance even though it may require you to turn in order to see them. Some additional pointers include:

- Make eye contact.
- Smile.
- Avoid "ahs" and "ands."

Above all, do not assume that those in attendance remember what was in the written document. Tackle the oral as if it was the one chance for your firm to win. That's one way to ensure that you will win.

CHAPTER 6

Winners in the Private Sector

Few firms in the private sector have been more successful in generating business from proposals than Joe Izzo's JIA Management Group, Inc. Izzo, author of a data processing book, *The Embattled Fortress,* writes proposals (including the one in Figure 6–1) that illustrate the key selling points in such a document. (The actual client's name has been removed to provide anonymity.)

First, a proposal is customized. The name of the prospect is clearly indicated on the cover and throughout the document. Izzo's business is one that deals with computers, and it can be technical. To clarify terms and concepts, Izzo graphically illustrates every section so that the reader understands the important points whether he goes through the text or consults the charts.

The type is large and double-spaced to make it easy to read. Headings and many paragraph lead-ins are boldfaced.

He also uses "bullets" (page 154–155) to make important points easier to read.

Izzo's proposal is printed horizontally, as opposed to most others which have a vertical configuration, usually on an $8\frac{1}{2} \times 11$ inch paper. Izzo prefers the horizontal format because it enables him to display his graphics more fully, and "it makes our proposal stand out from the rest."

The six-page introduction and objective section is the summary. Management can read this and get an overview of what elements Izzo proposes along with his ideas. He follows with methodology, a timeline (work plan), and résumés of those who will be working on the project. Notice that the timeline on page 179 includes everything from additional research through program development.

Izzo's approach to the problem is objective. He never says how great his firm is although the résumés included show many years of experience.

One of the most impressive things to a prospect is the consultant's understanding of the problem—does he understand it? Izzo's analysis is evidence that he does.

There are no prices included in the proposal. The dollars are in a separate letter sent to the CEO, or to whomever is the decision-maker. The decision-maker has the option of sending the price around with the proposal or holding onto it. If the decision-maker is looking for an objective opinion, he generally holds the prices back from others in management so they can compare proposal to proposal and not price to price.

According to those who judged this proposal, it was the most thorough document presented. The client was well-researched, and the problem was covered completely in the proposal. The physical appearance of the presentation was another plus.

After reading through the proposal, can you determine which parts are boilerplate? The résumés may be but is there anything else?

Bill Johnson's private sector proposals (Figures 6-2, 6-3, and 6-4) are unique documents that prospects pay to have presented. Johnson spent hours analyzing the problem and he developed a solution that can either be used by his firm (if it is retained to implement the proposal), management, or even another firm.

Why was it accepted? No other firm had taken the time to so completely analyze the problem and develop a solution. In doing so, Johnson's firm also became acquainted with all of top management as well as numerous employees throughout the company with whom they would be working. Johnson built rapport and confidence in his ability through the time he took.

The proposal is completely individualized with no boilerplating. It has several interesting features within it. One is that management can buy either the entire proposal or a part of it. There is a laundry list of programs.

Johnson's fees are based upon hourly rates for different personnel within his firm. They are outlined in advance to the client with a separate letter that usually does not run more than a page or two.

MANAGEMENT SUMMARY

The cover letter in Figure 6–2 is the typical executive or management summary that accompanies a proposal.

The proposal itself (Figure 6–3) is exceptionally well organized. It tells what was examined and when and which personnel were interviewed. This not only demonstrates Johnson's thoroughness, but it also shows the client that the fee he is paying for the proposal represented many hours of interviews and analysis.

The last document (Figure 6–4) is the "engagement letter." It reiterates what Johnson and the prospect have agreed upon in terms of the duties that Johnson's firm will perform. The engagement letter is written after the proposal has been studied and agreed to by the prospect.

WINNING LETTER PROPOSALS

Jay Abraham's "winning letter" is, at the very least, daring, unorthodox, and brash (Figure 6–5). But Abraham is a marketing consultant who fits the description of all those terms.

His letter/proposals are anything but conservative, as illustrated in Figure 6–5. The unsolicited letter was sent to franchisors and master distributors.

The results? Phenomenal. This approach would not "fly" if it were used to pursue a firm's banking, accounting, or insurance business, but it fits in with marketing.

Firms searching for marketing help are looking for creative, innovative people and ideas. They are willing to read the long, brash prose put together by Abraham. Abraham has researched his market well.

The layout of the letter makes it easy to read. Even before the salutation, he gets to the point with a paragraph that tells the reader what the subject is going to be. He uses numerous visual devices. His paragraphs are short—one-sentence structures for the most part.

He uses "I" but he is selling *his*—and no one else's—services. In Abraham's view, it also makes the document more personal, more "one-on-one" and conversational.

Abraham's philosophy is "grab them at the beginning" or you never will. And he does. The executive or management summary that is at the front of most proposals is designed with the same idea in mind. Summarize everything and see if the prospect is interested. If they are, they will go on and read the rest.

The remainder of page 1 (page 200) is nearly all questions posed to the client. Since he has not spoken to the prospect, he is hoping that one of the questions will hit home, causing the reader to say, "Yes, that's what I need."

He hits the prospect with a statement they may question—his earnings. But he gives himself the needed credibility with references to *USA Today* and the other publications.

Abraham also gives the client five possible ways they can work together, from a fee to a trade. The trade represents a low-cost way a client can engage Abraham.

If his brashness has caused the reader to question his ability, he comes right back at the prospect with the statement that refers to his "audacity and either he is uniquely qualified or the biggest b.s.'er around."

He closes by giving them options. They can call him (if they are daring) or contact him through the mail (if they are less).

He does not offer to call them—and for good reason. Abraham sent out more than 500 of these letters, all individualized. His response: 10 percent or nearly 50 of the people answered, and that's an excellent response in any marketer's book.

PROPOSAL

TO DEVELOP A PERSONNEL TRANSITIONAL

CHANGE PROGRAM

FOR

INFORMATION SYSTEMS

OCTOBER, 19

The JIA Management Group, Inc.
1299 Ocean Avenue
Suite 333
Santa Monica, California 90401

FIGURE 6–1. Sample proposal for private sector.

TRANSITIONAL CHANGE PROGRAM

TABLE OF CONTENTS

FIGURE 6–1. *(continued)*

SECTION I. INTRODUCTION AND OBJECTIVES

INTRODUCTION

The JIA Management Group, Inc. (JIA) is pleased to propose our services to assist in positioning its information systems function to meet its future business needs.

We have worked with many companies whose industries were experiencing dramatic change. Economic and regulatory changes in the marketplace frequently result in a re-examination of business practices and objectives. Such a re-examination increasingly involves the use of technology. Progressive company management recognizes that technology can be a powerful tool when it is used as an enabling mechanism to satisfy business needs. To those in the information systems business, the replacement of the computer they have worked with for much of their career with another technology is a traumatic experience. Few companies have given the requirement for personnel change a high priority. Even fewer have established comprehensive plans for employee education and training to accommodate this change. To have the opportunity to carefully evaluate the needs of the individual and to satisfy these needs to achieve company objectives, is a rewarding challenge.   is to be congratulated on its foresight in this endeavor, and JIA is excited for the opportunity to be a participant.

Since JIA's first engagement in 1976, we have successfully completed assignments for more than 100 major corporations. We have approached each assignment as partners, working with the business in determining the most effective means for exploiting the assets of computer technology toward the goals of the business. Since the inception of the company, JIA has uniquely positioned itself to address the major challenges that corporations face in using this technology. We have assisted corporations in developing future strategies for the use of computer technology, have evaluated and corrected operations performance within the information systems organization, and have been responsible for managing information systems organizations on a turnaround basis.

JIA's staff is also unique in its breadth and scope. The staff has a blend of business and computer technology expertise with a minimum of fifteen years' experience in information systems management. This management experience ensures a results orientation that is sensitive to the needs of the individual and the organization. JIA's turnaround management assignments demand that JIA consultants are well versed in dealing pragmatically with personnel issues, while demonstrating respect for the client staff at all times. This staff experience enables JIA to become a true partner in working with both the business executive and information systems executive. JIA services are summarized in the following four major categories:

I/S Operational Review—The review encompasses all aspects of the information systems function and the impact of performance related to business requirements. It is oriented to highlighting key problem areas from both an information system organization and user environment perspective. The objective of the review is designed to be constructive rather than critical and is oriented toward achieving a more effective information systems organization.

System of Management—JIA implements professional management practices within the information systems function. Included are application development methodology, quality assurance practices, resource and performance management, project management, business systems planning, staff development, and capacity planning.

Strategic Planning—This is the development of an information systems strategic plan which aligns information systems resources with the accomplishment of company objectives. The ultimate strategic plan is the development of a **Future System Architecture**. Working with a group of key user managers and information system staff members, JIA facilitates the use of technology as an enabling mechanism in defining the business of the future.

Management Contract—JIA contracts to manage, for a limited duration, the information systems function, which includes implementation of required change, enhancement of performance, and repositioning the organization with a focus toward the company's business needs. Professional practices are implemented, and a strategic plan is developed. User and executive management become the controlling mechanism for the application of information systems resources toward business objectives. JIA management processes are established to ensure user and executive management visibility and direction into key decision activities related to the utilization of the information systems resource.

In order to provide   with the most comprehensive program possible, JIA will be supplementing our staff with those of Jorgensen and Associates, Inc. Jorgensen is a Human Relations consulting firm specializing in personnel consulting for companies in transition. They are included in our proposed work plan and resumes of the principals are included with our selected staff resumes.

FIGURE 6–1. (continued)

151

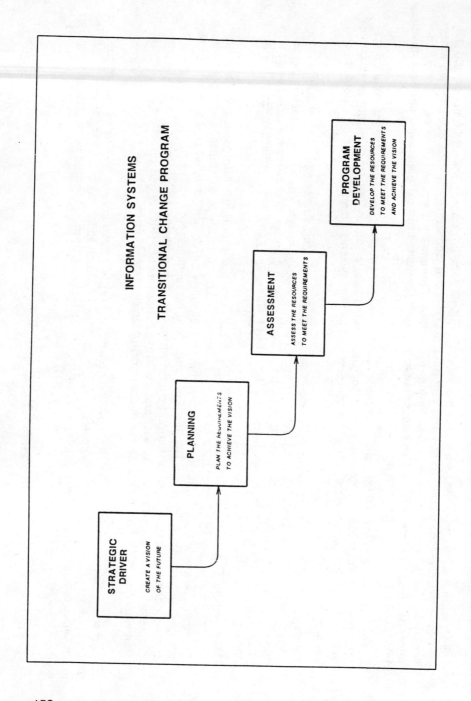

INFORMATION SYSTEMS

TRANSITIONAL CHANGE PROGRAM

STRATEGIC DRIVER

CREATE A VISION
OF THE FUTURE

PLANNING

PLAN THE REQUIREMENTS
TO ACHIEVE THE VISION

ASSESSMENT

ASSESS THE RESOURCES
TO MEET THE REQUIREMENTS

PROGRAM DEVELOPMENT

DEVELOP THE RESOURCES
TO MEET THE REQUIREMENTS
AND ACHIEVE THE VISION

OBJECTIVES AND APPROACH

We are proposing a staff development program which will result in a plan to organize and enhance the capabilities of the internal staff to become a positive force in accomplishing the planned changes. This effort will identify how existing skills can be channeled into the change program, as well as the education and training that will be required to provide each employee an opportunity for growth and accomplishment. Maintaining an effective staff to support current systems, while developing a quality staff to implement and maintain new systems, will be a high priority.

The proposed work plan contains four distinct phases. As depicted above, each phase has individual objectives which establish a framework for the following phase:

Strategic Driver—This phase creates a vision of how technology will be applied to meet business needs in the future, and identifies the organization that will be required to achieve it. Differences in the current and future roles of technology will be explored, as well as the underlying requirements for changing skills and experience. The impact of these differences on personnel will be analyzed and strategies for dealing with them developed.

Planning—Detailed personnel requirements to support the proposed organization will be developed and documented in this phase. These requirements will form the basis for a salary survey to develop recommended salary ranges for each new position. Educational requirements will be defined and sources of training will be compiled. Alternative methods of providing training will be explored.

Assessment—This phase will assess the current information systems staff to meet the technical and leadership requirements of the future organization. Staff needs for training and growth will be identified, as well as required capabilities not available in the current staff.

Program Development—A phased implementation plan will be developed to implement the required organizational changes and train personnel for their new assignments. An education and training function will be established to administer the training program and ensure prerequisite training is complete, and that required skills are in place. The primary objective of this phase, and the program as a whole, is to create a self-sufficient environment, fully capable of continuing the change program.

FIGURE 6-1. (*continued*)

DELIVERABLES

The following section describes our proposed methodology which will result in the deliverables shown below:

- **Future Organizational Requirements**—Statements of the functions required to meet future business needs.

- **Future Organizational Structure**—The placement of functional responsibility within the framework of an appropriate organizational structure, including estimated staffing levels.

- **Transitional Organizational Structure**—The interim organizational structure(s) which will be required at major change points to ensure current systems are supported until the new systems are operational.

- **Human Resource Impact Analysis and Strategy**—An examination of the impact of the planned changes on the current information systems culture, and strategies and contingencies for accommodating it.

- **Position Descriptions**—Functional responsibilities and required skills for each position within the proposed information systems function. Required education and experience is included, as well as personal attributes. Prerequisites for the position, to grow in the position and beyond the position, will be included.

- **Recommended Salary Ranges**—The salary range of each position described above, including the methodology and rationale used to develop it.

- **Education Requirements and Sources**—An evaluation of educational sources and recommended course content, which will include professional management practices for information systems, as well as technical skills. Internally developed courses and other alternatives will be recommended when appropriate.

- **Career Paths**—An outline of primary and secondary promotional routes and the prerequisites for achieving them.

- **Individual Assessments**—As assessment of each individual's(1) skills and experience, and the applicability of current skills to the planned environment. Inadequate skills and/or skill levels will be identified.

- **Individual Development Plans**—The educational and training requirements for each current position to effectively make the transition to the new environment.

- **Analysis of Required Skills and Experience**—An evaluation of the need for skills and experience which cannot be internally developed within the planning period, and recommendations for acquiring them.

- **Cultural Change Strategy**—An examination of the cultural issues, and strategies and contingencies for dealing with them. In its final form, this document validates the earlier H/R impact analysis with the results of the completed process.

- **Training Function**—A charter, responsibilities, and authorities for an internal function to administer the training program. It is hoped this function can be put in place during the course of the JIA engagement.

- **Migration, Implementation, and Training Plans**—A schedule of the events, and the responsibilities for accomplishing them, to complete the transition of personnel to support the new environment.

Note (1)—There may be current job classifications that can be assessed based on a representative sample of individuals.

FIGURE 6-1.   (*continued*)

155

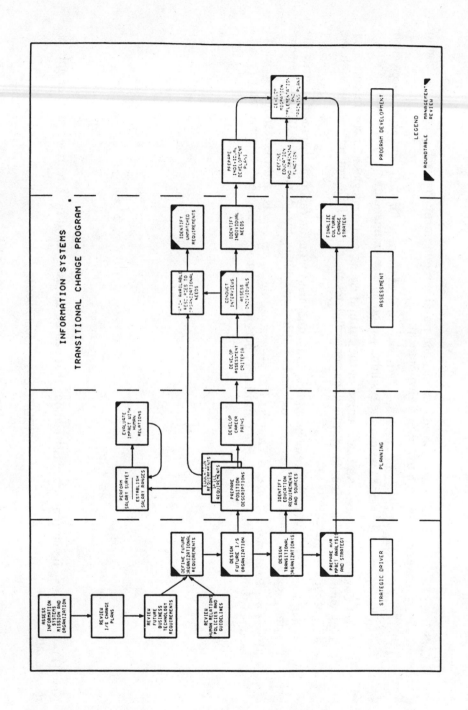

INFORMATION SYSTEMS
TRANSITIONAL CHANGE PROGRAM

STRATEGIC DRIVER

PLANNING

ASSESSMENT

PROGRAM DEVELOPMENT

ASSESS INFORMATION SYSTEMS MISSION AND ORGANIZATION

REVIEW I/S CHANGE PLANS

REVIEW FUTURE BUSINESS TECHNOLOGY REQUIREMENTS

REVIEW HUMAN RELATIONS POLICIES AND GUIDELINES

DEFINE FUTURE ORGANIZATIONAL REQUIREMENTS

DESIGN FUTURE I/S ORGANIZATION

DESIGN TRANSITIONAL ORGANIZATIONS

PREPARE H/R IMPACT ANALYSIS AND STRATEGY

PERFORM SALARY SURVEY

ESTABLISH SALARY RANGES

EVALUATE IMPACT WITH HUMAN RELATIONS

EDUCATION SKILLS REQUIREMENTS

PREPARE POSITION DESCRIPTIONS

DEVELOP CAREER PATHS

IDENTIFY EDUCATION REQUIREMENTS AND SOURCES

DEVELOP ASSESSMENT CRITERIA

IS AVAILABLE RESOURCES TO ORGANIZATIONAL NEEDS

CONDUCT INTERVIEWS ASSESS INDIVIDUALS

IDENTIFY UNMATCHED REQUIREMENTS

IDENTIFY INDIVIDUAL NEEDS

FINALIZE CULTURAL CHANGE STRATEGY

PREPARE INDIVIDUAL DEVELOPMENT PLANS

DEFINE EDUCATION AND TRAINING FUNCTION

DEVELOP MIGRATION IMPLEMENTATION AND TRAINING PLANS

LEGEND

ROUNDTABLE

MANAGEMENT REVIEW

SECTION II. METHODOLOGY

STRATEGY

JIA has had the responsibility of repositioning many computer installations and understands the difficulty and resentment that major change can cause in an organization. Some employees cannot accept change. Others may be anticipating retirement during the planning horizon, and will find it difficult to relate the need for change to their career. A relatively few will greet the changes with enthusiasm and look forward to the opportunity that they provide.

Our objective on completion of the assignment is to have the plans and responsibilities in place for   to continue the change program with a minimum of outside assistance In order to accomplish this, it is important that information systems personnel participate and "own" the results to the greatest extent possible. The work plan, therefore, contains several "roundtable" activities. These roundtables are identified in the work plan above by a shaded upper left corner. Although JIA will present proposed recommendations and the rationale used to reach them, the participation of the members could alter the conclusions. Membership in each roundtable activity may vary. It is suggested that the Executive Director of Information Systems be involved in each roundtable and be responsible for the selection of other members.

The management reviews are identified by a shaded upper right corner and will be a review of the progress to date and conclusions for management concurrence. Management reviews, therefore, will include interrelated conclusions from all preceding activities, and may address issues not specifically outlined in the work plan.

ACTIVITIES

Strategic Driver Phase

- **Assess the current information systems mission and organization**

  —Review functional composition, mission, and objectives of the current I/S organization.
  —Review structure, staffing, and skills of the current organization

FIGURE 6–1. (*continued*)

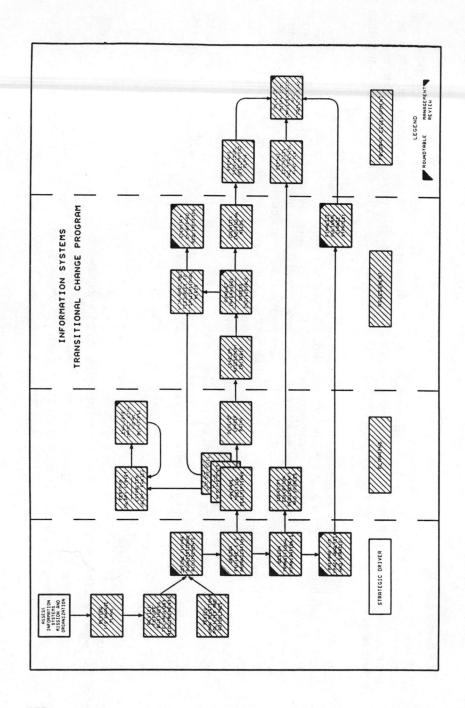

Methodology . . . .

—Review the available documentation supporting personnel activities, i.e., job descriptions, training plans, salary ranges, performance reviews, turnover statistics, etc.

—Review the installed delivery mechanisms for providing services (hardware, software, communications)

—Review the use of professional management practices in the system life cycle (decision process, development methodology, project management, labor management service level reporting, capacity planning, etc.)

—Interview key I/S managers and gain their perspective on the quality of current systems to meet business objectives

- **Review information systems change plans**

—Review stated future system needs (RFP) and accepted vendor proposal

—Review plans and schedules for implementation

—Define the planned changes in user functionality and access, from both a development and processing view

—Determine major differences in the planned deployment of technology and the method of delivering services. Review I/S plans for supporting the new environment

—Evaluate key I/S management views of the planned changes and their value in supporting the business needs

- **Review future business technology requirements**

—Review current company organization and functional responsibilities that are being, or will be, supported by information systems.

—Gain an understanding of the current role of technology in meeting business needs

- **Review future business technology requirements . . .**

—Interview key user management to gain insight into their perspective of the role of technology in supporting the business in the future

FIGURE 6-1. (*continued*)

159

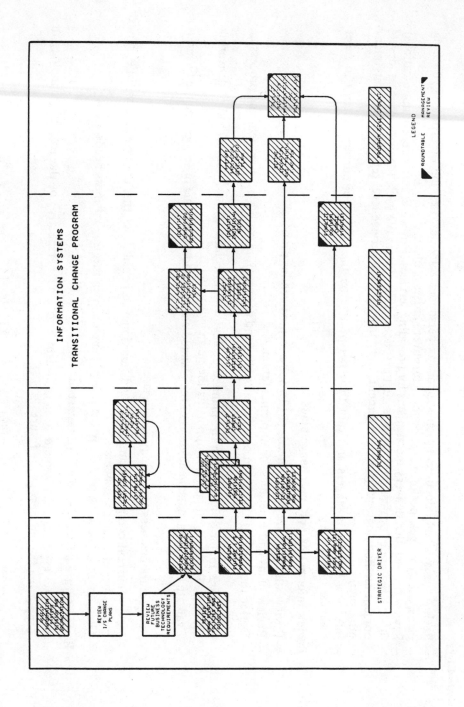

INFORMATION SYSTEMS
TRANSITIONAL CHANGE PROGRAM

LEGEND

ROUNDTABLE

MANAGEMENT REVIEW

STRATEGIC DRIVER

160

Methodology . . . .

—Review key business issues and industry changes which should be addressed by information systems
—Review planned changes in company focus, work content, and objectives

• **Review current Human Relations policies and guidelines**

—Review Human Relations policies and guidelines and identify any major constraints to the proposed approach
—Review Human Relations procedures and resolve any major inconsistencies with JIA deliverables
—Identify major personnel issues to be considered in the change program

• **Define future organizational requirements**

—Develop a preliminary set of organization and skill requirements to support the planned use of technology
—Conduct roundtable discussions. Validate, expand, and finalize the future organization requirements

• **Design future information systems organization**

—Develop a preliminary organization structure to satisfy the requirements
—Conduct roundtable discussions. Validate, expand, and finalize the future organization structure
—Develop estimated staffing levels and skill requirements
—Evaluate required changes in information systems professional management practices

• **Design transitional organization(s)**

—Identify key events in the implementation plans that create a need for significant changes in organizational structure or skill mix
—Develop interim organization structures and staffing requirements to support the changing environment
—Conduct roundtable discussions. Validate and finalize interim organization

FIGURE 6-1. (*continued*)

161

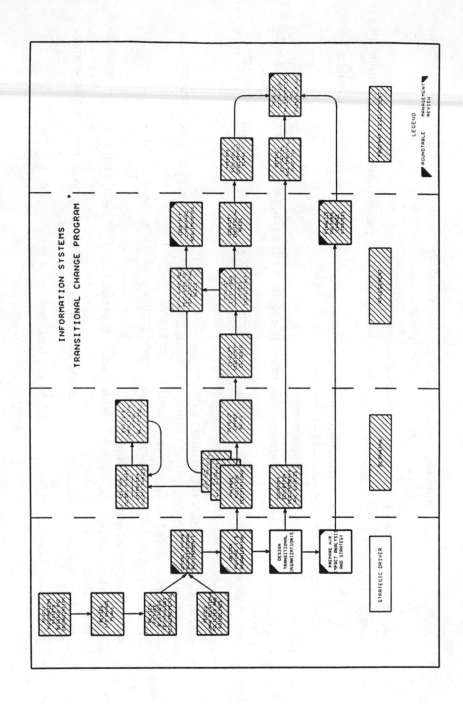

INFORMATION SYSTEMS

TRANSITIONAL CHANGE PROGRAM

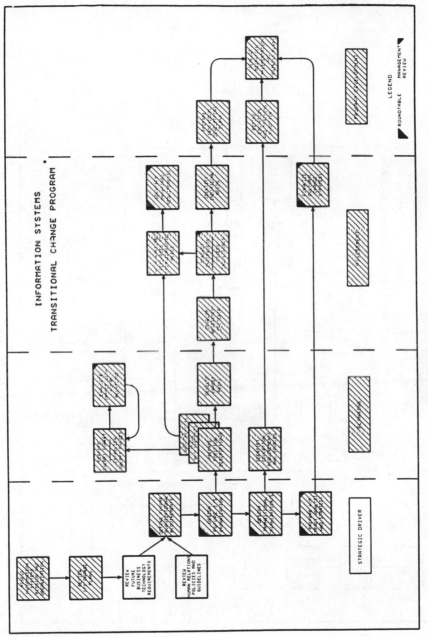

FIGURE 6-1. (continued)

163

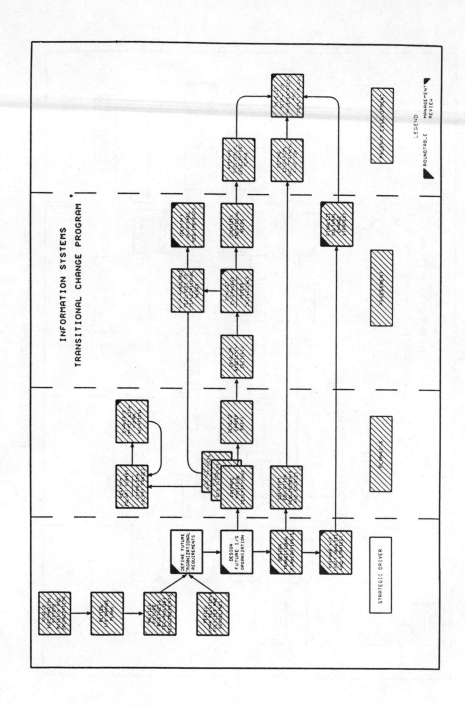

INFORMATION SYSTEMS
TRANSITIONAL CHANGE PROGRAM

Methodology . . . .

- **Prepare Human Relations impact analysis and strategy**

  —Based on previous roundtable discussions and meetings with information systems and user management, identify individual and group attitudinal issues

  —Identify current skills with little or no applicability to the new environment (if any)

  —Identify major constraints to the change program inherent in the current organization and recommend solutions

  —Conduct roundtable discussions and management reviews and develop strategies to effectively deal with the identified issues. Develop contingency plans to ensure adequate support of required functions now and in the future

Planning Phase

- **Prepare position descriptions for each new position in the interim and final organization, including:**

  —Duties and responsibilities

  —Prerequisite education, experience, and skills

  —Normal and alternate promotional paths

  —Mandatory training (or equivalent experience)

  —Required training for growth within the position

  —Required training for advancement (promotion) to the next position

- **Develop career paths**

  —Prepare a graphic representation of the normal and alternate career paths overlaid on the final organizational structure

FIGURE 6–1. (continued)

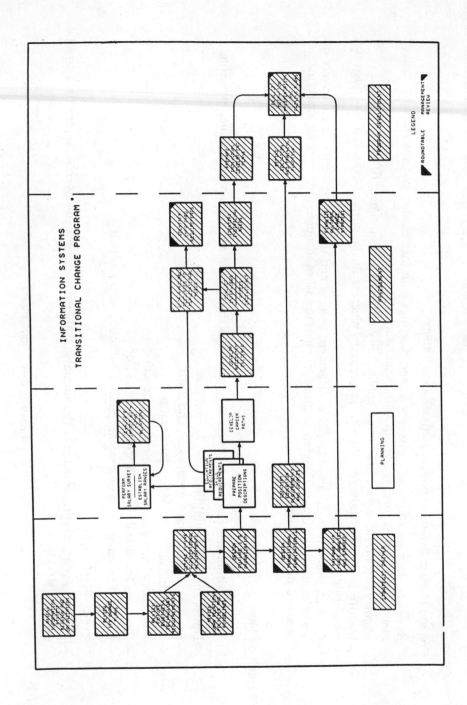

INFORMATION SYSTEMS
TRANSITIONAL CHANGE PROGRAM

- **Perform salary survey and establish salary ranges**

  —Review published salary survey material for information systems personnel, e.g. Hansen Survey

  —Evaluate position descriptions and identify comparable survey positions and salary ranges

  —Modify published ranges based on geography, industry, installation, and local labor market characteristics

  —Initiate sample survey comparison with "friendly" (labor) competitors

  —Prepare recommended salary ranges for each new position

- **Evaluate impact with the Executive Director of I/S and Human Relations**

  —Modify recommended ranges based on Human Relations objectives, i.e., lowest cost versus least turnover, considering the strategic value of salaries from the Human Relations impact analysis

  —Develop economic/budgeting impact of recommended staffing levels and salary ranges

- **Identify education requirements and sources**

  —Coordinating with the preparation of position descriptions, identify educational prerequisites for each position

  —Review software implementation plans and identify required supporting skills

  —Assemble course schedules and contents from hardware and software suppliers and evaluate the appropriateness of available classes to educational requirements

  —Assemble and evaluate commercial course schedules and contents

  —Evaluate the use of internal staff and/or educational companiesto develop unavailable (or uneconomical) educational programs

  —Evaluate the applicability of computer-based instruction, audio-visual, and/or self administered program instruction

  —Recommend an appropriate schedule of education including on-the-job training

FIGURE 6-1. (*continued*)

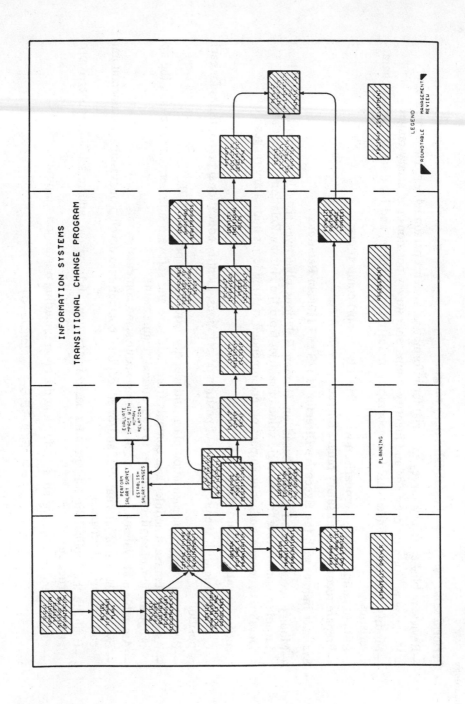

INFORMATION SYSTEMS
TRANSITIONAL CHANGE PROGRAM

Assessment Phase

- **Develop assessment criteria**

  —Modify JIA skills inventory worksheets, as appropriate, and prepare and distribute advance questionnaire to all information systems employees

  —We recommend that testing of Potential Development be given to 25–35 key I/S employees. The results of the testing should be shared with the employees. These tests could provide valuable insight into personal and vocational attributes. The selection of tests should be made at the start of the engagement. Processing the test results would cost $7,500–$10,000.

  —Review completed questionnaires and develop interview schedules

  —Modify JIA career development methodology, as appropriate, to isolate personnel related data

- **Conduct interviews and assess individuals**

  —Using modified career development methodology, interview all scheduled personnel

  —Complete a skills inventory worksheet on all interviewed personnel, noting relevant aptitude and attitude considerations and conduct a management review of findings.

- **Match available resources to organizational needs**

  —Identify a probable position in the future organization for each employee and/or current position

  —Identify skills and experience that would be particularly helpful in the transition

- **Identify unmatched requirements**

  —Identify requirements in the future organization that cannot be met by the current staff in the time imposed by the implementation schedule

FIGURE 6–1. *(continued)*

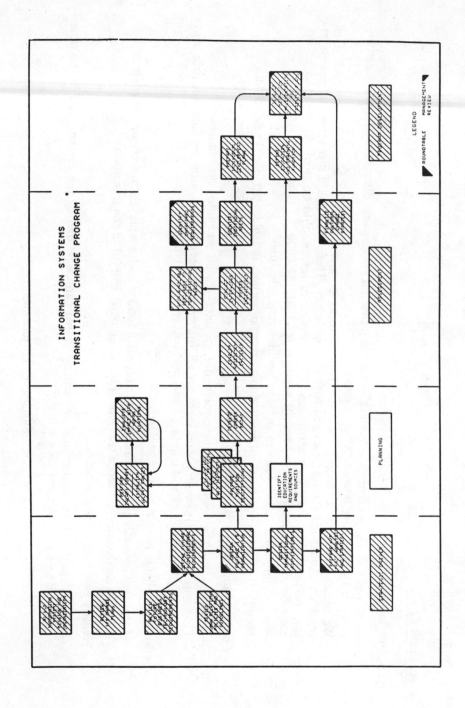

170

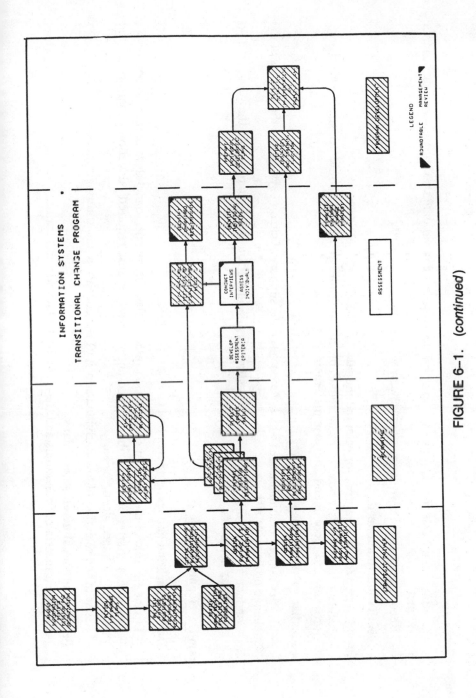

FIGURE 6-1. (continued)

171

— Conduct roundtable discussions with appropriate managers and validate that the requirements cannot be met

— Recommend alternative sources and review with management

• **Identify individual needs**

— Identify required training for each individual

— Identify individuals whose training requirements, aptitude, or attitude could constrain the change program and recommend alternate placement

• **Finalize culture change strategy**

— Identify major personnel issues which would place the support of current systems or the success of the change program at risk

— Conduct a roundtable and validate the strategies developed in the first phase of the program and modify as necessary

Program Development Phase

• **Define education and training function**

— Define the role of the internal organization in administering the personnel development programs

— Establish a charter of responsibilities and authorities to ensure required education is performed and skills are in place when needed

— Assist in the selection of key individuals to staff the education and training function

• **Prepare individual development plans**

— Prepare a matrix of individuals and their required education and training

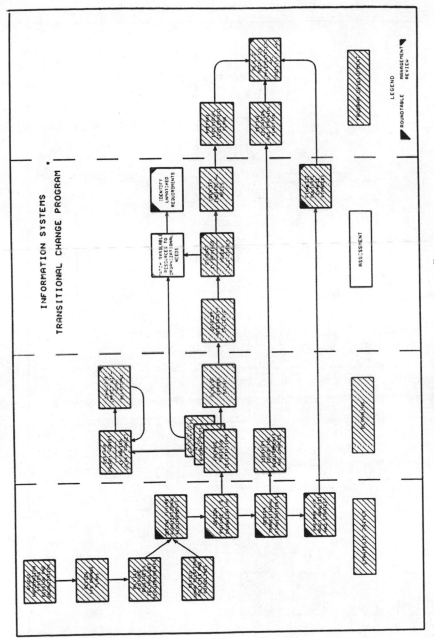

FIGURE 6-1. (continued)

173

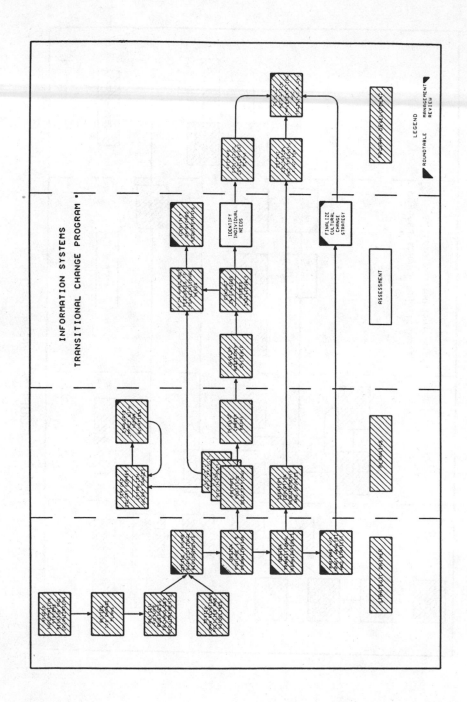

INFORMATION SYSTEMS
TRANSITIONAL CHANGE PROGRAM

LEGEND
◣ ROUNDTABLE
MANAGEMENT REVIEW

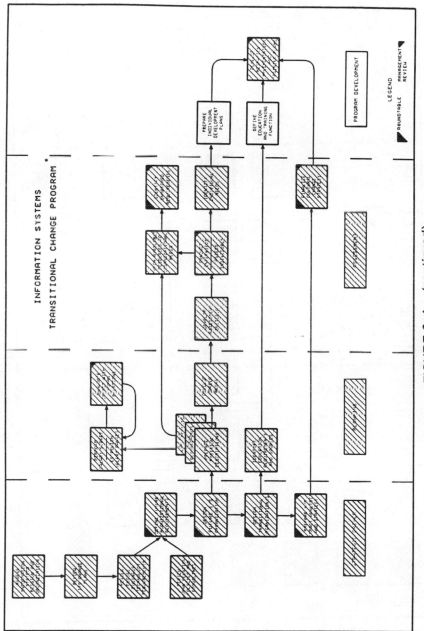

FIGURE 6-1. *(continued)*

175

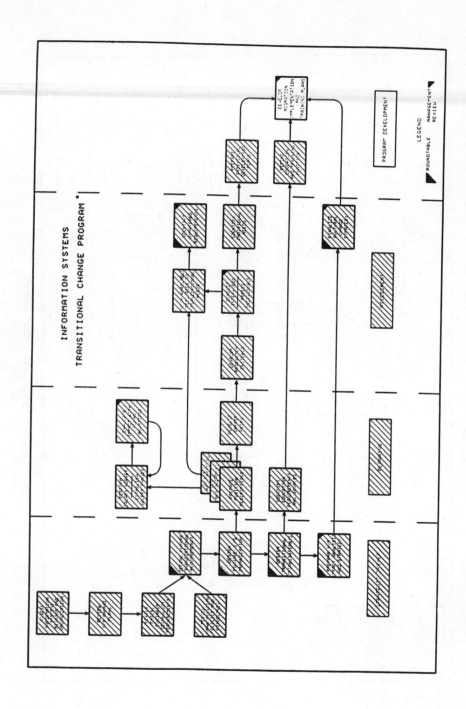

INFORMATION SYSTEMS
TRANSITIONAL CHANGE PROGRAM

LEGEND

PROGRAM DEVELOPMENT

ROUNDTABLE

MANAGEMENT
REVIEW

176

Methodology . . . .

—Prepare a recommended development plan for each individual (or position, if appropriate)
—Meet with I/S managers and review individual staff needs

- **Develop migration, implementation, and training plans**

—Formalize and schedule all required activities
—Identify Pacific Bell responsibilities for continuing the program
—Develop overall economic impact of incremental staffing and training costs
—Conduct final management review and evaluate identified personnel risks and issues

FIGURE 6–1. (*continued*)

177

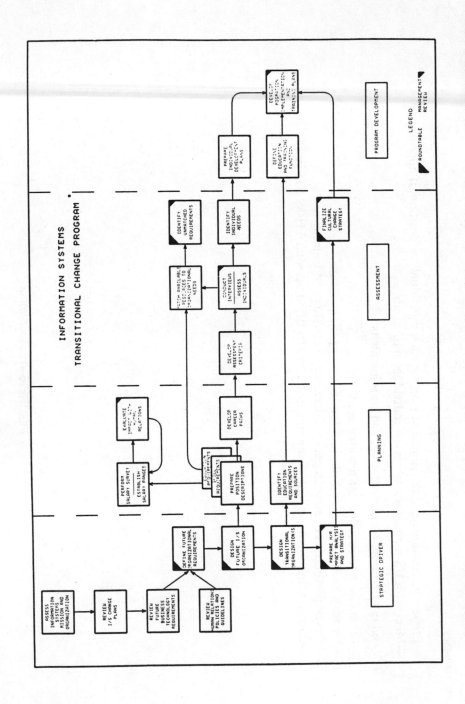

INFORMATION SYSTEMS
TRANSITIONAL CHANGE PROGRAM

STRATEGIC DRIVER   PLANNING   ASSESSMENT   PROGRAM DEVELOPMENT

LEGEND

ROUNDTABLE   MANAGEMENT REVIEW

178

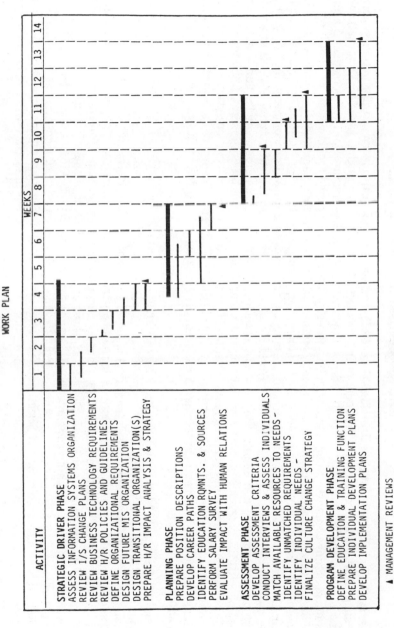

INFORMATION SYSTEMS
TRANSITIONAL CHANGE PROGRAM
WORK PLAN

FIGURE 6-1. *(continued)*

SECTION IV. SAMPLE RESUMES

Larry R. DeJarnett, Managing Principal—Mr. DeJarnett has 25 years' experience in information systems and management. As Corporate Vice President of Information Systems for Lear Siegler, Inc., Mr. DeJarnett initiated and directed the decentralization of the corporation's information systems functions to more than 50 business units, matching computer architecture with business structure. He completed the four year, $12 million program 15 months ahead of schedule, and subsequently restructured the corporate organization into mobile, value-added consulting teams, emphasizing the use of information technology to solve business problems. Previously, Mr. DeJarnett held a variety of systems management positions with Ford Motor Company, including directing company-wide consulting teams for Ford's World Headquarters, and managing information systems groups for the automotive assembly and engine divisions. Mr. DeJarnett is author of numerous articles and a noted speaker and panelist for corporate seminars and symposiums, including IBM, Digital Equipment, McDonnell Douglas, AT&T, and the American Management Association. He is a member of the information systems advisory board of Claremont Graduate School and past chairman of the Southern California Chapter of the Society for Information Management. Mr. DeJarnett earned his BS in Personnel Management and MS in Business Administration from Southern Illinois University.

Frank J. Devonald, Managing Principal—Mr. Devonald has over 25 years' experience in MIS managing and consulting. Prior to joining JIA, Mr. Devonald was Associate Director of Consulting Services for Hughes Aircraft Company. There, he managed the development of an MIS and communication plan for a billion dollar division; he also managed the design of a closed-loop shop floor control system; and he developed comprehensive information systems, including manufacturing (MRP), finance, and program management. Prior to that, he was Director of the MIS Consulting Group with Deloitte, Haskins & Sells, where he managed major information systems reviews and strategic planning assignments for Nissan Motors Corporation, AIRCO, Inc., The New York Times, and McCormick Spice Company, among others. Previously, he was on the technical staff at IBM Corporation, where he was responsible for the design and implementation of computerized systems to support the financial, order processing, and manufacturing requirements of companies in various industries with emphasis on manufacturing (MRP) systems. Mr. Devonald received his BS in Industrial Engineering from Rutgers University and attended New York University Graduate School of Engineering.

Karen Jorgensen, President, Jorgensen, Jorgensen and Associates, Inc.—Ms. Jorgensen is founder of Jorgensen and Associates, a firm which specializes in providing Human Resources consulting services to companies in transition. Ms. Jorgensen has twenty years of Human Resources management experience. As Personnel Director for Golden West Broadcasting, she worked for Gene Autry and assisted in the divestiture of several divisions, and closures of the company's radio and telephone affiliates. Prior to Golden West, Ms. Jorgensen was Vice President and Personnel Director of a major California bank. Ms. Jorgensen has trained over 2,000 personnel managers. She is a noted speaker and educator, having participated in the White House Conference and the MIT/UCLA Venture Forum, as well as serving on the faculty of Loyola Marymount. Ms. Jorgensen is a past member of the Executive Board of the Personnel Industrial Relations Association, where she remains active. Ms. Jorgensen earned her MBA from UCLA and is a theoretical mathematician who graduated number one in her class from the University of Illinois.

James T. Lewis, Principal Consultant—Mr. Lewis has 25 years of experience in data processing and communications-based systems management. Prior to joining JIA, Mr. Lewis was the System Director for AVCO Financial Services and held senior technical positions with Computer Sciences Corporation, Comress, and IBM Corporation. Mr. Lewis has managed major JIA assignments in data management, capacity planning, and network design. He received his BS degree in Mathematics from the University of California at Santa Barbara.

Norman D. McCue, Managing Principal—Mr. McCue has 30 years' experience in information systems, including almost 20 years as the senior MIS executive with several firms. In this capacity with Braniff International, he improved systems availability of more than 4,000 interactive computer terminals supporting passenger activities, enabling the carrier to improve on-time departure performance from sixth to second place nationally. As the senior MIS executive for The Garrett Corporation, Norton Simon, Inc., and a major division of Litton Industries, Mr. McCue turned around ailing installations. Behind-schedule and over-budget projects were brought into line with company objectives. Earlier he managed the manufacturing and engineering systems group for Rocketdyne and pioneered factory data collection and on-line inquiry systems supporting the space program. In his five years with JIA, he has held the senior MIS position in several turnaround management engagements, directing client staffs of more than 500 personnel, establishing business systems planning functions, performing operational audits, and managing the development of a future systems architecture for a major aerospace company.

FIGURE 6-1. (*continued*)

181

Gwynda J. Myers, Managing Principal—Dr. Myers has an extensive background in management and consulting. As an independent consultant she advised several major software companies in the development of systems for inventory control, transportation, and mortgage accounting, and also developed operating standards for a major bank. As Associate Professor, Director of the Computer Center, and Vice President of Student Affairs for Rio Hondo College, she established the school's data processing function and was a key participant in the design and implementation of an information system for the State of California, supporting more than 100 community colleges. In her nine years with JIA, Dr. Myers has held key client management positions in turnaround engagements, led several operational audits, and developed future system architectures. Dr. Myers earned her BS and MS degrees in Education and an MBA in Quantitative Analysis at the University of Southern California. She earned her PhD in Management at Claremont Graduate School.

Ross F. Penne, Managing Principal—Mr. Penne has 30 years' experience in the data processing industry, with emphasis on management, consulting, and system analysis. Mr. Penne held senior technical positions with Burroughs, TRW, Inc., and IBM Corporation before participating in the establishment and subsequently managing the Computing Center for the University of Southern California. While at Computer Sciences Corporation he was a member of the advisory staff and directed the facilities management contract for the County of Orange (California), managing a staff of 150. In his five years with JIA, Mr. Penne has directed effectiveness reviews, hardware planning, quality assurance reviews, and system design efforts for JIA clients. Mr. Penne received a BA in Business Administration from Coe College and an MA in Economics from Ohio State University.

James H. Reesing, Managing Principal—Mr. Reesing has 20 years' experience in information systems management and consulting. As Senior Vice President and Director MIS for First Interstate Services Company, he was responsible for the overall management of several data centers supporting the California banks. In this capacity, he managed a technical staff of 600 and a $70 million operating budget. He was credited with a $3 million annual savings, while achieving a substantial increase in the overall quality of operations and improved customer service. Previously, he held several technical and management positions with IBM Corporation where, as marketing man-

182

ager, he was responsible for sales and technical support for clients in the financial services industry in the Western United States. Mr. Reesing earned his BS in Business Administration from Xavier University.

Martha L. Ryan, Principal Consultant—Ms. Ryan has more than 20 years' experience in data processing management and consulting. She held senior systems management positions with Digital Equipment Corporation and a major division of General Electric, before forming her own consulting firm. As president of Martha Ryan Consultants for five years, her firm developed data processing strategies and project plans to focus on project oriented business goals. She was also Vice President of Operations for Computer Composition International, where she was responsible for the development, manufacturing, service, training, and user support of the company's composition/typesetting system. Ms. Ryan is APICS certified in production and inventory control. She received her BA degree in Mathematics from George Washington University.

James K. Zimmerman, Vice President, Jorgensen and Associates—Mr. Zimmerman is a human resources professional specializing in organizational development. While Vice President of Human Resources for First Interstate Services Company, he was responsible for the human resources activities of the firm's data processing company and managed the compensation function for First Interstate Bancorp's 22 non-banking subsidiaries. Mr. Zimmerman has lectured extensively on human resources issues and is on the staff of California Polytechnic Institute, Pomona, where he teaches human resources classes in the School of Business. Mr. Zimmerman is a licensed psychotherapist, specializing in interpersonal conflict resolution.

FIGURE 6–1. (*continued*)

Ms. _____
Senior Vice President and
Chief Accounting Officer
_____ Corporation
_____ Boulevard
Long Beach, California 90801-5630

Re: Tenant Receivables; reconciliation and proceduralization

Dear Ms.

We have completed our initial study of the tenant receivable accounting and related areas. A copy of our report is attached for your review. Our study indicates five areas where we feel action programs should be initiated; 1) receivable reconciliation and tenant billing, 2) internal control, 3) system, 4) policy and procedure and 5) organization. Only the action plan for the receivable reconciliation and tenant billings is being set forth here as per our engagement letter. Other plans should be developed on in conjunction with the reconciliation/billing program to attain and retain a high degree of system and accounting integrity. For example, Mark _____ should be officer in charge of the system side of our recommendations so as to insure proper and timely integration into the MBA and in-house computer system. Much of the data we will create during the implementation of the receivable action plan will be needed by Mark for his conversion.

We can prepare the other action plans as you request.

Our receivable reconciliation/billing review plan is as follows:

1. Review all current in-house prepared reconciliations where a write off or adjustment was made in excess of $2,500. Correct as required.

2. Reconcile all tenant receivables not currently reconciled with delinquencies in the 90 day and over category. Reconciliations would be prioritized first to those where the over 90 day balance exceeded $10,000. Second, over $5,000, third, over $1,500. We would not reconcile receivable balances where the over 90 day balance was less than $1,500 unless requested by you.

3. All write offs or adjustments in excess of $2,500 not considered in the item (1) above which occurred during the past 18 months will

FIGURE 6–2. Sample cover letter.

be reviewed. Such reviews will be of both current and vacated tenants. All write offs or adjustments which cannot be properly documented or justified will be brought to your attention including adjustments due to "previous owner lease interpretations" and AMI lease interpretation differences. Such items, if material, possibly should be brought to the attention of your legal department.

4. We will review lease contracts or other documentation available to determine tenants subject to rent escalations, CAM's/BOCI, percentage rent, etc. including the amount, percent and payment frequency thereof. Such information will be entered into the tenant billing system as possible or if not possible a manual tickler control system will be established to ensure such billings are made on a timely and accurate basis.

5. Utilizing the information gathered in item number (4) we will, for all current tenants and all tenants which have vacated during the last 18 months, verify that they have been properly billed for such charges. All discrepancies will be brought to your attention for a determination of further action.

We suggest that temporary personnel be utilized to minimize disruption to the accounting department in the performance of its day to day duties. We will assist you in locating the temporary staff required to complete this engagement. These temporary personnel will be your employees or independent contractors and accordingly you will be responsible for all payroll taxes and insurance coverage and reporting, etc. We will supplement these temporary employees with members of your staff as you may deem appropriate.

It is our current intention to utilize 3–4 such temporary employees, a full time William J. Johnson manager, and a part time review principal. Given the condition of the records and systems observed, we are unable at this time, to estimate the time required to complete this program. We will, however, give you weekly oral progress reports as to its status.

We recommend utilizing the August 31, 1987 tenant balance for all tenants whose account were not reconciled at July 31, 1987.

We suggest that all tenants with problem balances be notified of your effort to identify and resolve the differences. It should be made clear that they are expected to pay all current charges and that you are not waiving any right as to past due amounts.

It is our belief that the above program will generate amounts of cash flow to your projects substantially in excess of its cost.

Very truly yours,

James L. Miller

FIGURE 6–2. (*continued*)   185

STUDY: Tenant receivable accounting and related areas

BY: William J. Johnson, An Accountancy Corporation

FOR:

The following sets forth various conditions we have observed during our study of the tenant receivable accounting department and the tenant receivable balances at _____ Financial Corporation/ _____ Management, Inc.

PROCEDURES PERFORMED

Interviews were conducted with Company personnel in the following departments:

> Tenant Accounting
> Property Management
> Accounting Administration
> Leasing Administration
> Selected Senior Management

Whenever possible, accounting procedures that were perceived to be in place in the past and present, were confirmed or denied within departments or between departments. The past procedure confirmation was sometimes limited because of turnover in personnel, especially in Tenant Accounting.

Copies of input documents and the related print outs from the service bureau were obtained and reviewed to aid in documenting the procedures in place and currently being followed. This did not include the interface to the general ledger system, although we did attend an overview session of the general ledger interface relating to tenant accounts receivable.

We selected one tenant accounts receivable reconciliation to review in detail. The review included reading the lease and amendments, reading the correspondence file, reviewing the supporting workpapers, talking to the property manager and tenant accounting personnel. Several more reconciliations with adjustments to receivable balances were reviewed to obtain an understanding of the procedures that were being performed.

FIGURE 6–3. Sample proposal for private sector.

Flow charts were prepared for cash receipts, master file set up, charges and move outs, in order to identify strengths or weaknesses of the accounting procedure.

SUMMARY OF OBSERVATIONS

The majority perception as to the genesis of the tenant-receivable problem at _____ is the MBA system. This perception is shared by senior managers both on the property management and accounting side of the organization and filters down through most of the organization. The second most frequently stated reason for the problem is the lack of training and management of the tenant accountants. Many employees are also of the opinion that there exists too many projects per accountant for an effective and efficient maintenance of the tenant receivables and billing system. The tenant accountants complaint is too many errors in data entry.

Our observations lead us to the conclusion that the tenant receivables evolved to their current state due to the previous lack of responsible management. The tenant accounting function for this substantial amount of cash flow appears to have been relegated to a junior status within the established priorities. The responsibility for tenant accounting has been transferred throughout the organization three or four times during the last several years.

No one has accepted full responsibility for the tenant accounting function. Multiple departments had been permitted to affect the automated billing system, adjust tenant receivable records through the posting of cash receipts and in other ways determining what may or may not be billed to tenants. The application of cash receipts to tenant balances was assigned to a department with no understanding or responsibility for tenant accounting. No one was given the authority and responsibility for the tenant accounting and billing system.

It appears that the MBA service bureau system may be capable of performing billing tasks needed by the _____ organization. It has not been utilized. The MBA Accounting System is not utilized for percentage rent billings, cost of living adjustments or for rent escalations all of which appears to be currently deficient outside of the system. Such delinquencies are the result of the lack of accountability for actions or non-actions. It is our belief that whether the tenant accounting system

FIGURE 6–3. (*continued*)

was on an in-house system or with a service bureau, the problems currently being experienced would still exist. The lack of organization, policies, procedures, appropriate forms and training can cause any system to falter.

On the positive side, you have recently implemented numerous changes to the handling and recording of cash receipts. Such changes appear to have corrected the cash application procedures resolving what appears to have been one of the major problem areas. Also, tenant accounting has recently been given the responsibility for setting up the tenant master files and recurring charges.

Tenant accounting believes that the tenant receivable reconciliations are 45 to 50% complete. At this time we cannot concur. The reconciliations we reviewed eliminated significant amounts from the receivables balances without satisfactory documentation. Accountants appeared to rely heavily, if not totally, on data provided by property management and the tenant and did not document a standard independent reconciliation approach.

SPECIFIC FINDINGS

Internal Control

Throughout the course of our study of the tenant receivable activity, we have observed conditions within the organization not totally tenant receivable related, which should be brought to your attention. It is quite possible that you may already be aware of many of the following items.

Cash Receipts:

— Cash is being received from tenants by two departments within the organization—accounts receivable and tenant accounting. Centralized receipt of all cash should be implemented to the extent possible.

— Checks received by the accounts receivable clerk should not be forwarded to tenant accounting when the clerk is unable to code the receipt, rather, xerox copies should be utilized.

FIGURE 6–3. (*continued*)

— All checks should be deposited on a daily basis. We have observed a check for $26,000+ held for almost 3 months prior to deposit.

Tenant Billing/Receivables:

— Tenant receivables are being written off or adjusted by substantial amounts without senior financial officer approval. Such adjustments in several situations observed appears to have been based on analysis prepared by the regional office and the applicable tenant and not by independent verification by the tenant accounting department. It also appears that in one specific instance substantial amounts of money were written off which may remain due to the project.

— The review of the financial viability of prospective tenants prior to a least being consummated is not being conducted by the finance and accounting department. Subject to specific limitations, the finance and accounting department should review the financial viability of tenants prior to lease execution, tenant improvements and move in.

— Tenants who are, by the terms of their lease, to pay common area maintenance charges on a quarterly, semi-annual or annual basis are not being billed during the course of a year on an estimated basis and not until the year end adjustment analysis is complete. In those cases where the 1986 year end adjustments are not complete, amounts of money that may be substantial are due the organization possibly for as long as a year and one half. Given the possible operating deficit positions of certain projects, this condition should be addressed immediately.

— All request for journal entries, adjustments, write offs or reclassifications within the general ledger or tenant accounting system must be approved by a responsible financial officer of the organization.

— The ability of the fund accountants or tenant accountants to bypass either the general ledger or the tenant receivable sub-ledger when making entries should be eliminated or otherwise be controlled.

— Security deposit checks should not be issued to vacated tenants without the approval of the tenant accounting supervisor or manager.

FIGURE 6–3. *(continued)*

— Internal notification systems and procedures must be strengthened for move ins and move out. Such data many times is received several months late by the tenant accountants, causing a delay of rent receipts or a continuation of erroneous billings. In addition, tenant accountants many times do not input the required data on a timely basis when received causing similar problems.

Other:

— Accounting administration appears to be responsible for accounts payable, cash receipts, data entry and cash control functions. Such duties should be separated to the extent possible.

— All data input documents are not being stamped when entered into the system especially the tenant information file report possibly resulting in duplicate input. Currently most edits are within the data entry department and again checked in tenant accounting after information is entered. Batch and edit functions should be performed for all system input and should be performed outside of the data entry department prior to system entry to the extent possible.

— All policies and procedures affecting the finance and accounting departments must be approved by a senior financial officer. Recent policies have been issued by other departments requiring the accounting departments to perform certain functions. These policies had no senior financial manager approval.

— The opening of all cash accounts, including petty cash authorizations, should be approved by a senior financial officer of the corporation.

— Approval and authorization for commitment and expenditure limits should not be established by individual departments, but by corporate policy.

System

It is understood that it is the intention of _____ management to bring its entire financial, accounting and reporting system in-house. Such

FIGURE 6–3. (*continued*)

a process cannot be accomplished in a short period of time. Therefore the continuation and expanded utilization of the MBA System would be deemed prudent during the in-house conversion process.

— No changes should be made to the MBA System unless approved by the vice president of management information systems and the senior vice president–chief accounting officer. No one should contact the MBA Service Bureau direct without the express approval of the vice president of the management information systems. Such contacts with the MBA personnel in the past have been uncontrolled.

— The MBA Service Bureau should be requested immediately to provide documentation behind the automatic cost of living percentage rent and step-up rents features of the system. When received, and if acceptable to senior management, the automated system should be utilized immediately. If not acceptable, a manual control system should be designed and implemented.

— Consideration should be given to the utilization of the MBA tenant lease abstract form versus the forms currently being utilized. Current forms do not capture the data needed and require certain departments to insert data in an unorthodox manner into the system. It is assumed that current input screens conform to the MBA form. Few differences were noted between the MBA form and the AMI form.

— Existing MBA data input screens should not be changed or adjusted at this time, if possible. The MBA System should be utilized as is until the company has converted to its new system, if possible. The constant changing has created ambiguity and uncertainty within the organization.

— A data entry control desk should be established to control all input and output. Strict documentation approval requirements with strong batch and edit controls should be implemented. I would propose this function report outside of the data entry function, if possible.

— MBA should be requested to ensure that sub-ledgers and/or general ledgers cannot be bypassed through the data entry function or, given their inability to change the system, provide an exception report, detailing those entries processed which bypass one or the other reports.

FIGURE 6-3. (*continued*)

Policies and Procedures

— Broad corporate policies should be established from the top of the organizational structure providing for delegations and limitations of authority levels to the various senior officers and their subordinates. Such policy would include, but not be limited to, dollar limitations as to the commitment of funds without presidential or board approval, authority to open bank accounts, check signatories, capital expenditure authorization, etc.

— Detailed job descriptions should be developed for each position within the company, but more importantly, within the financial and accounting department. In a well controlled environment, it is mandatory that each employee fully understand those duties and responsibilities for which he is charged.

— An accounting manual should be developed for each control area within the finance and accounting department. Procedures should be established beginning with cash receipts, bank reconciliation and cash disbursements, establishing step-by-step requirements to properly discharge these functions. Thereafter the accounting manual should be expanded to include other policies and procedures as needed.

— Data entry and training procedures should be developed for the MBA System as it applies to tenant billings and accounting. This element should take a top priority to ensure that tenants are billed timely and accurately in accordance with the terms and conditions of the various lease agreements. The development of new procedures within the MBA Service Bureau System might not be cost effective in as much as the conversion to an in-house system has been approved.

— Policy should be established requiring at a minimum that security deposits be received from all tenants prior to the lease being executed, occupancy permitted, or construction of improvements.

— Any and all policies and procedures issued by _____ Financial and any of its various departments should be approved and signed by the senior responsible officer. In the event that a policy directly affects the operation of more than one department, the senior officer in each of the affected departments should approve and sign. Such a policy has not been followed in the past.

FIGURE 6–3. (*continued*)

Organization

— Monthly accounting calendars should be established for each area of responsibility within the finance and accounting departments of _____ Financial group. In this way each management employee knows, in advance, what is expected of them and when and accordingly can be held responsible for the completion of various duties by the applicable manager.

— The tenant accounting function must be brought under the direction and control of a strong financial manager reporting directly to the senior vice president and chief accounting officer. Without total delegation of responsibility and authority to a hands-on manager, the company will be faced with a continual need of clean up and lost dollars. It would be suggested that in addition to this senior position, a supervisor remain in the department.

— Atypical of all organizations of the size and complexity of _____ is the tendency to finger-point and place blame for problems which arise within the company. Then tenant accounting situation is not an exception. Efforts should be made by the senior managers involved from both a property management and financial stand point to ensure a free flow of communication as to the existing status of any problems which may arise throughout the course of business. An example of the failure of such communication was when all data entry into the Service Bureau was stopped during June, 1987, which precluded timely reporting, billing, reporting. Our interview indicated that this fact was never communicated to the regional and area property managers.

RECOMMENDATIONS

_____ has attempted to address its tenant accounting and billing problems over a long period of time and under the direction of various department and various degrees of management involvement. It appears that much of this work has been expended without substantial benefits to the company. To resolve the billing and collections problems, strong and experienced management must be placed "in charge" of specific problems to be resolved and provide the organization supervision and follow through to its resolution. It appears that

FIGURE 6–3. (continued)

substantial amounts of the data collection process have been completed and hopefully can be utilized. We believe that the benefits to _____ Financial of a formal clean up program would substantially exceed any costs expended during the problem solving and reconciliation process. This would include the ability to invoice current and vacated tenants for previously unbilled cost recoveries, escalations, or rents, as well as a significantly improved operating and control systems. Specific areas of needed attention would be as follows:

— Accounts Receivable Reconciliation

Step one in the reconciliation process would be to review all current reconciliations prepared by the tenant accounting department where the adjustments or write offs to the receivable balance exceeded $2,500. In these cases we would ensure that the adjustment was proper and that adequate documentation was provided. Throughout this process we would verify that proper adjustments to the recurring billing system had been made as required to insure correct future billings to tenants.

Other tenant accounts receivable not currently reconciled would be analyzed in detail in the following sequence:

Priority One: All tenants with $10,000 balance in the over 90 category.

Priority Two: All tenant receivables with account balances in excess of $5,000 in the over 90 category.

Priority Three: All tenant account balances with $1,500 in the over 90 category.

We would utilize as our basis for analysis, the August 31, 1987 tenant receivable balances. Staffing for this analysis would utilize temporary personnel in the $15–25 per hour range, not your existing tenant accountants unless excess AMI staff was available. It would be our recommendation that your tenant accounting department be left free to keep all day to day activities on a current and smooth running basis. Specific fund and/or project priorities would be set by you.

— Unbilled Items

We propose a planned, managed effort be immediately commenced to determine the uninvoiced amounts to tenants as authorized per their lease contract; this would include percentage rents, graduated and stepped-up rents, cost of living adjustments and in certain cases CAM's and BOCI's. Although sporadic

FIGURE 6-3. (*continued*)

attempts have been and are being made to determine these unbilled items, the organization, planning and control of this effort is not being provided. We would first direct our efforts in this matter towards current tenants; however, given what appears to be a significant problem, we would also direct our analysis to those tenants who may have vacated during the past 12 to 18 months. We believe that substantial amounts of unbilled revenue and cash flow may be generated from a well managed, planned, and supervised effort in this area. From this analysis will come the data to automate the billing process of these items or, in the alternative, a manual control systems.

— Write offs/Adjustments

Our review has indicated that substantial reductions have been made to tenant receivables as adjustment to previous billings rather than "write offs." As we understand your policy and procedures, write offs require the approval of the senior financial officer of the corporation, whereas adjustments do not. We propose that all such adjustment and write offs which have been made during the last two years, in an amount which exceeds $2,500, be examined for propriety. As in the above, we would first address current tenants. This analysis would also be extended to any tenants who have vacated, whose write off falls within the scope of the review. We have been informed that many of these adjustments relate to leases where the previous owner billed tenants differently than AMI. We would suggest that such differences, if noted, should be brought to the attention of the legal department. We would make the assumption that the tenant has the obligation to conform to the lease or in the alternative, the previous owner is responsible if he guaranteed the validity of the lease.

— Policies and Procedures

We propose that specific corporate policies and procedures be drafted immediately for senior managements review, approval and implementation. These procedures would include the establishment of authority levels for all levels of management. These would include: the commitment of expenditures, execution of contracts, signing of checks, credit review of prospective tenants or others to be indebted to the corporation, etc. We also recommend that the skeleton of an accounting manual be developed within the _____ Financial group. Such a project would first entail the preparation of a broad table of contents by control

FIGURE 6–3. (continued)

195

function, and then building detailed procedures within that skeleton to enhance the controls and reliability of the accounting function. It would be our suggestion that the first policies revolve around the control areas, more specifically, cash receipts, disbursements, bank reconciliations, receivable collections, etc. Once these basic procedures are in place your department can fill in the remaining procedural requirements on a scheduled but less urgent basis.

In conjunction with the above and as previously noted, it is recommended that a senior accounting person be hired to take direct control over the tenant accounting organization. This individual must be mature, experienced, and be able to deal effectively with the members of the property management group and tenants of the various projects. This individual should report directly to the senior vice president-chief accounting officer and most importantly, this individual must be given the responsibility and the authority to say NO to requests made of him, if required and bump the request to a higher financial authority. It is also suggested that the existing supervisor be retained and trained to create a stronger tenant accounting group.

If possible it is suggested that _____ be assigned the task of training the tenant accounting group in the use of the MBA tenant receivable system. In conjunction with this training, standard input and output policies and procedures should be developed.

Copies of all tenant accounting receivable reports including edits, batch controls, aging and ledgers should be given to the tenant accounting department on a timely basis.

The transfer of all tenant cash receipts activities to the regional offices should be recommended. Perhaps one of the biggest problems affecting the tenant billings and receivables appears to be that of mis-applied cash receipts. Current management has reorganized and substantially reduced the occurrence of these errors. Cash management and cash applications are best handled and controlled from a central location. Secondly, the multiple handling of cash prior to its deposit and recording enhances the risks of loss, fraud and delays the investment or use of funds.

It is also recommended that a review be made of the specific internal control points heretofore set forth above in this letter, and that

FIGURE 6–3. (continued)

management's attention be directed towards the elimination or mitigation of these conditions.

The use of exception reports should be developed and used by financial managers. As an example, a monthly report of all (credits) to tenant receivables excepting code 5 cash receipts. Such a report highlights "adjustments" or write offs which may not have been approved.

It should be noted that substantial amounts of data gathering and adjustments will be required by the above activity. Specifically, the purification of the system as it applies to base rent, cost of living adjustments, percentage rents, escalations and step-ups. All this will give your management information department a leg-up when the time arrives for the conversion to your in-house data processing system.

The above recommendations are not based on or intended to be a detailed audit or review program. The scopes and parameters recommended should be carefully reviewed and expanded or contracted as deemed required by _____.

Should you need to discuss this report further, please advise.

FIGURE 6–3. (*continued*)

William J. Johnson
An Accountancy Corporation

Member of the American Institute of
Certified Public Accountants

August 11, 19

Ms.
Senior Vice President
Chief Accounting Officer
    Financial Corporation
    Long Beach Boulevard
Long Beach, California 90801-5630

Dear Ms.

This letter is to confirm our understanding of the terms and objectives of our engagement and the nature and limitations of the services we will provide.

We will perform the following services:

1. We will review the books, records, reports and other underlying documentation supporting your commercial real estate tenant receivables.

   —Based on said review we will recommend to you accounting and operational procedures required to verify material amounts payable to you.

   —We will estimate the amount of time necessary to perform the procedures outlined above and the personnel required.

   —We will not review individual tenant leases or verify the accuracy of company calculations of expense and allocation billings to tenants unless directed by you to do so.

2. Upon your approval of the procedures submitted in accordance with number 1 above, we will undertake to organize, implement and supervise the required analysis, reconciliations, and study, to verify the propriety of your commercial real estate tenant receivables.

3. We will assist you in locating the temporary staff required to complete this engagement. These temporary personnel will be your employees or independent contractors and accordingly you will be responsible for all payroll taxes and insurance coverage and reporting, etc. We will supplement these temporary employees with members of our staff as you deem appropriate.

FIGURE 6–4. Sample "engagement letter."

198

It is our understanding that these commercial real estate tenant receivables have not been reconciled, verified or confirmed for several years. We can give no assurance whatsoever that these receivables can be reconciled, verified, confirmed or collected or that any projected completion deadlines can be achieved as estimated.

Our engagement cannot be relied upon to disclose errors, irregularities, or illegal acts, including fraud or other defalcations that may exist. However, we will inform you of any such matters that come to our attention.

Our fees for these services will be based on the time expended at our standard rates and will be billed to you monthly, payable upon receipt. Out-of-pocket expenses, including travel, meals or lodging will be charged to you at our expense. We shall be pleased to discussed this letter with you at any time.

If the foregoing is in accordance with your understanding, please sign the copy of this letter in the space provided and return to us.

Sincerely,

William J. Johnson, An Accountancy Corporation

Acknowledgment:

_____
Name

_____
Title

_____
Date

FIGURE 6–4. (*continued*)

(date)

(name)
(company)
(address)
(city/state/zip)

I'm told you're interested in vastly improving the effectiveness (and efficiencies) of the marketing your franchise company does—without increasing your overhead.

Dear (name):

Perhaps we can help each other.

I perform very extraordinary types of marketing enhancement for companies who aren't maximizing their marketing.

I increase the results of ads my clients run.

I increase the conversions of leads they generate.

I develop direct mail, display advertising, and telemarketing programming.

I leverage the dollars my clients spend—and the dollars they've already spent—many times over.

I construct master marketing strategies that are founded (or built) on solidly diversified, broadly stable "pylons" of on going programming that will endure.

My programming endures long term. It pays sustaining residual effect. All programming interrelates to each other so maximum leverage is achieved.

I was not told exactly what kind of marketing you wanted to improve upon.

Is it lead generating efforts for your distributorship/franchises?

Is it better conversion of leads into sales?

Is it developing more effective and profitable ads or sales letters?

Is it enhancing the marketing for your operating franchises?

FIGURE 6–5. Sample proposal for private sector.

Is it developing broader ways to build added profits off your customer base?

Is it understanding and capitalizing on ancillary marketing opportunities?

Whatever the specific marketing-related improvement you wish to effect, I could prove invaluable.

I'm actually not a consultant—though I consult, administer and advise my clients.

Nor am I an agency. I don't take commissions or place advertising or printing.

Actually, I'm more of an "entrepreneur's entrepreneur" who understands expansive (and overlooked) loopholes of marketing opportunities most people in your business aren't aware of.

It is not, for example, uncommon for me to increase the pulling power of an ad by 3–5 times.

Or increase conversion of leads to sales by 10–25% or more. Occasionally, a lot more.

Or develop ways to profitably exploit leads you've given up on.

Or construct wonderful back-end, residual-based, ancillary marketing programming to add to your existing operation.

But don't take my word on it.

I've got credentials coming out of the woodwork.

Full page articles in USA Today. An article in the New York Times. OTC Stock Journal. American Underwriter. Automotive News. Success Magazine. Interviews on 30 radio stations.

Perhaps better credentials than press are dollar denominated results.

I've earned $2,000,000 a year more than twice. Seven figures three years in a row—all on a percentage of increased profits I produced for my clients.

I write a $500 a year newsletter that 5,000 people subscribe to.

I do $2,000 an hour—that's correct, two thousand dollars per hour—consultations for smaller entrepreneurial clients who can't justify my minimum contingency value limit. And occasionally, when I'm anxious for a short-term challenge, I'll do 100 or so one hour, half-priced, $1,000 an hour consultations on a 100% money back basis.

No one has ever asked for a refund.

My clients over the years have ranged from a 500 million dollar a year investment firm to dozens of famous newsletters to Howard Ruff

FIGURE 6–5. (continued)

to insurance companies to retailers to distribution firms to service companies.

I've been successful in over 165 unrelated fields. It's given me an extremely broad focal perspective.

One that might help you.

If you are interested in improving your current marketing results—for either franchise or distributorship expansion—or the marketing you develop for your distributors to use, I can probably help. At least we should talk.

I work one of four ways (and possibly a fifth).

1. If you are large enough and promising enough, I'll perform all the marketing for zero fixed fee and only get paid a reasonable percentage of the increased profit my proprietary concepts and programming procedures produce.

Usually I get 25% of the increased profits if you pay the marketing expense—50% if I pay for it.

2. Fee against percentage. If you're not large enough yet to make me six figures on percentage, but you could be if you better husbanded your marketing assets, I'll take you on for a modest fixed fee (just enough to force you to get your money's worth out of me by acting on my advice) and/or a percentage of sales or profits. This is negotiable.

3. Marketing insurance. For a fee ranging between $25,000 and $75,000 a year, I provide regular weekly advice, review, overview, administration and masterminding by phone of all relevant marketing required. However, for this fee, I do not actively interact with anyone other than you or your designate.

4. One shot, day-long, week-end crash course and private seminar re-working your complete master strategy—complete with all corresponding programming.

This is individually negotiated.

5. Trade. If your product/service/franchise is desirable, I'll entertain exchanging services.

Can I really perform?

Obviously to have the audacity of writing a letter this brash, I'm either the biggest, most obnoxious B.S.er around or I'm uniquely qualified to actually handle your marketing requirements for you.

I humbly submit, it is the letter.

FIGURE 6-5. (continued)

I can furnish more references attesting to my performance than your directors can call in a day.

I'm writing you for one reason. I need underutilized marketing companies to play off of. It appears you have marketing opportunities I could lavishly enhance.

If the opportunities are substantial, I'd willingly work strictly on a "pay-on-results" percentage basis.

If the underdeveloped assets are lucrative but not lucrative enough, I'll consider some partial fee, partial percentage, hybrid corporation. I am flexible.

It seems reasonable and prudent for us to at least talk.

Your time is, admittedly, valuable.

My time goes for $2,000 an hour.

I'd like to buy you and your marketing director $1,000 of my time. No cost. No obligation.

We'll talk for 30 minutes. All discussions will be confidential.

We'll explore and probe your current marketing and examine its effectiveness in achieving the goals you desire.

Since I work mostly on percentage, I'm extremely covetous about my time. So I won't patronize or dance around.

If I think I can help you, I'll tell you and I'll tell you precisely how.

If I don't, I'll tell you so.

I'm looking for a challenging and lucrative client in your field.

If you'd like to make the marketing efforts and monies you spend go many times farther, it seems worthwhile for us both to talk.

My number is 213-541-5901. I'm there from 10 A.M. to 3 P.M.

Call me. Or write me.

Please, initially at least, don't relegate or subordinate this call to an underling. I prefer dealing with owners, principals, COO's or CEO's.

I think you'll enjoy thoroughly any conversation we share.

By the way, much of what I do is non-traditional. It's totally ethical, unusually desirable stuff—but programming most people don't understand how to commandeer.

For example:

Endorsed promotions where other people recommend you to their audience.

30 to 60 minute infomercials where we run wonderful ads on your business, nationwide on cable, and solicit franchise requests.

Direct mail to other people's prospect lists. Etc.

FIGURE 6–5. *(continued)*

I could go on for pages, but you get the general idea. I think we can benefit one another on a basis that's inordinately equitable all around.
If you agree, call or write me.
Send me anything you'd like me to review before we talk.
I'll wait to hear from you.

Warmly,

Jay L. Abraham

FIGURE 6–5. (*continued*)

CHAPTER 7

Making Internal Presentations & Proposals

A young, aggressive, new product manager stood in front of five top managers in the New York offices of a major record company. His job was to sell them on the marketability of the tape he held in his hands.

He had spent nearly a month gathering information on a rising young star, and his hopes were to convince those in the room to sign the singer to a long-term contract. The five executives had never heard the young woman sing, nor did they know much about her. At the time, female singers had a poor sales history, and when the product manager suddenly announced his "new find" was a young woman, there was an immediate drop in enthusiasm.

Only one of the executives seemed to have any interest. The product manager directed his presentation to his one supporter and ignored the others. Even when he played a tape of the young lady's voice, his attention was directed to his supporter.

When it was over, the five executives had voted unanimously— they would not sign the singer. . . . Barbra Streisand was passed over by one of the most prestigious record labels in the country.

Within a year, Ms. Streisand would sign with Columbia Records, and a career of nonstop hits would begin.

The Streisand case illustrates factors that should be kept in mind when presenting new products or developmental ideas internally.

1. Never ignore anyone in the room.
2. Never ignore opposition.

3. Never surprise anyone with information.

4. Make sure your case covers cost, benefits, and needs.

5. Lobby beforehand.

6. Be aware that those in the room may know more than you do.

When making an *external* presentation, there seldom is going to be anyone on hand who knows as much about the product, service, and so on, as the presenter. An engineer from one company talking to management from another is going to know more about some new technology he has developed than the managers. It stands to reason—he developed it.

An insurance salesman making a presentation to management for a new pension plan is going to know the intricate workings of the plan better than anyone else in the room because it is his business; he developed it. The managers, for instance, might be in the toy business and have absolutely no knowledge of insurance.

Internal presentations, however, are different. The record company management knew just as much (if not more) about their business as the producer. There was no chance for him to make a statement that was not completely accurate and get away with it. Management is sold by facts, not emotion.

INTERNAL ADVANTAGES/DISADVANTAGES

Trying to sell your company on a new idea, product, and so on, takes as much—if not more—preparation than an external proposal.

The internal proposer has advantages and disadvantages. The fact that those who are listening are familiar with the product or idea is a benefit because they have an understanding of (1) the company, if it is a product or idea for use within, or (2) the industry, if it is a product or idea for sale.

The disadvantage is the presenter has to be extremely accurate. There is no room for generalizations. If he or she makes a mistake in facts or figures, or glosses over an important element, his credibility among those in the room will be questioned. If one statement in an internal presentation is not completely accurate, it will usually ruin the rest because of the doubts that suddenly pop into everyone's mind.

Internal presenters are usually talking to their superiors or upper management. These managers are familiar with the presenter's duties and qualifications. They may have even worked in the same position at one time. They are authorities on the subject, even if it happens to be a new technology. They can ask the pointed, penetrating questions that poke holes in a presentation.

The product manager for the record company found that to be the case. Three of those in the room had previously been responsible for new product development. They had made hundreds of presentations themselves, and they were looking for certain facts, figures, and information that the product manager never presented—what makes this female singer a more marketable commodity than others?

Management also looks for a "cost/benefit" analysis. How is it going to benefit the company (projected sales of the singer's records translated into revenue), and what is the cost (the amount it will cost to record the artist and promote her)?

Whether it is a record or new idea, every internal proposal has cost/benefit implications.

THE SIGNIFICANT DIFFERENCES

There are two significant differences between internal/external presentations aside from the familiarity the internal audience has with the company. The burden of the internal presentation is on the speaker and his abilities as a communicator. If he or she stammers, hesitates, or is not well-rehearsed, the idea can be blown.

The second important difference is "support." The external presenter has a written proposal that is handed to management. He may only have to amplify what is written or explain a section.

Internally, the speaker may only have an outline or copies of viewgraphs (slides that can be written upon with colored pencil) as an aid. There is no concise written document, and lengthy proposals are not appropriate. In fact, a drawn-out proposal explaining the pros and cons of the internal project is a drawback. Management does not want to waste time reading; they want to hear it from the presenter.

TYPES OF COSTS

Karl Brennan, who heads the proposal division of a large defense contractor, cautions internal presenters to keep in mind that there are two different kinds of costs—new product/technology development vs. new machinery and/or plants—and each is viewed differently by management. The former is easier to sell because it is going to result in sales and profits for the company. It is revenue enhancing and might be an idea for a new widget, part, and so on.

The new machinery and/or plant does not generate revenue. It is designed to save costs. It might be the purchase of a new and faster machine that will crank out widgets in half the time and at half the labor cost. Management does not have to buy this proposal. They can continue to roll along with the old machine and stay in business.

The same division exists within nondefense-oriented and service firms. In a service organization, new products may relate to the creation of a new marketing division that will go out and pursue additional business. New machinery, on the other hand, could be anything from a new typewriter, computer, or private jet, to expanded office space.

Reorganization of departments, divisions, and so on falls into the nonrevenue-producing sector. A reorganization may help the company run better but it does not necessarily bring in more dollars—unless the presenter can prove it with facts and figures. It is, however, not a tough sell. If a company is going to run more efficiently, and it does not cost (or costs little) to reorganize a department, why not?

The factor management examines closely in this area is the "human factor." If a presenter wants to merge the accounting and data processing departments, there is going to be a "human cost." Perhaps the accounting supervisor will end up reporting to the data processing supervisor. How will that be accepted in the organization? Is it going to hinder production in the long run? If not, can you demonstrate it won't? Have the different departments been consulted as to the merger? What do they think?

New product/technology is easier to sell because it is going to result in sales and profits for the company. Investing in new technology and products is the lifeblood of a company. Some may have a fixed percentage allocated to research and development. Others may allocate funds as Brennan's company does. There is a separate research and development (R&D) budget. The funds are apportioned yearly according to the revenues that a particular division brings to the company. A company may have five product lines, with four bringing in 50 percent of the sales, and the fifth bringing in the other 50 percent. The first four will share 50 percent of the R&D funds, and the fifth will get the other 50 percent.

COMPETING FOR R&D FUNDS

Splitting research and development (R&D) funds is commonplace in defense. Still, the various divisions must compete for the dollars and prove their project is worthwhile. They must convince management that their idea, product, and so on is going to produce for the firm. That comes down to the presentation and the preparation that goes into it.

R&D is part of what is commonly called "strategic planning." Much has been made on the business pages of major U.S. newspapers about industry's failure in this country to plan for more than next week. In some industries, this is true. The corporations are pressured by shareholders and directors to show profits—now.

But within companies that have vision, there are usually several different strategic planning time cycles. There is a long-, medium-, and short-range. In real time, this could break down into one year (short-range), one to five years (medium), and five to 15 years long-range.

Time is an element that must be addressed in presentations. Is your product or idea going to bear fruit in one year, two, or when? Will it take a year (or how much time) in the development stage before it is ready for production? More? These are important questions that management must know the answers to if they are going to invest funds in a project.

Planning differs in every industry. In defense and aerospace industries—those that specialize in government and agency contracts—the products and ideas that get the most planning attention are those that will give the firm "technical superiority" or a "proprietary" product. Both terms mean almost the same thing. The technically superior product is exactly what it says—a product that will perform better than any other competitor's on the market. Proprietary products are those in which the firm can obtain a patent. It belongs exclusively to them. Either way, these two are the most important, and if funds are available, companies do not hesitate to invest in these areas.

SALES IN THE PRESENTATION

Management has to be sold. Those allocating the monies know that R&D is only step one. Down the line is the eventual manufacture and sales of the product. How much revenue will the product bring to the company? Often that is difficult to project, but if it comes down to a battle between one product and another, management will attempt to determine those figures.

At many firms, representatives from both sales and engineering are on hand for evaluation of the idea. Engineers have a grasp on the technology and its feasibility. Sales has an idea of the potential of the end-product. Management utilizes these two departments to help make difficult decisions.

Suppose, for instance, management finds itself with two new R&D ideas. One relates to "Star Wars" which is a rapidly growing field; the second relates to a new steering mechanism for an existing commercial aircraft that is being currently sold. On the surface, the new steering mechanism may have an immediate market. After all, the airplane is on the market and is being sold. Marketing of the mechanism, however, poses problems. The airplane is already being sold. That means the prime manufacturer has subcontracted (or is making) the steering mechanism. If the current mechanism is satisfactory, there is no reason to change. In addition, a change may force the manufacturer to change other parts and fittings and to do additional testing. This could be a bad investment unless the proposer knows that the manufacturer is having trouble with the present steering and plans to replace it. This information is necessary before an internal presentation.

The "Star Wars" (SDI) product may not have an immediate application but there could be utilization for it in areas other than space. Some of the new laser technology originally developed for SDI is being used in medicine. Another SDI product may have similar potential.

The astute proposer keeps both sales and engineering in mind when making a case for their product and/or idea. If it comes down to management choosing between two, there may be sales projections required.

Companies monitor the progress of every project. An R&D project that has been funded goes through the following stages:

1. Study
2. Plan
3. Develop prototype
4. Test prototype
5. Production

The progress of each phase is reviewed yearly and additional funding decisions made at that time.

SYNERGISM IN PRESENTATIONS

Companies prefer products and/or ideas that "tie together." A computer company looks more favorably upon the development of a proprietary keyboard that must be used with its new computer than the development of a computer stand for the new computer.

With the stand, the customer has an option, he may or may not buy. He can use his desk or someone else's stand. But if he buys the computer, he must purchase the keyboard. Both products must be sold together.

This approach is akin to the thinking that goes on in another seemingly unrelated industry—fast food. McDonalds may have started out with a hamburger, french fries, and soda as its basic menu. Then someone suggested a dessert. Someone else mentioned coffee, sweet rolls, a double-cheeseburger—all add-ons or combined items that "swell" or make the sale larger.

Instead of just X, companies want to sell X plus X plus X. They want 3X, and that is true of every industry. The key to acceptance behind many of these products is that they will enable the firm to increase sales, but the marketing cost will not be proportionately higher. With the new product, an average sale may go from $2 to $3, but the cost of marketing the products may not rise at all. Management likes those ideas.

This approach gets the same acceptance in the service sector. A company that provides temporary secretarial help may discover that its clients need temporary accountants as well. They may add the "product" (accountants) to their line and sell both at the same time, hardly increasing their marketing costs.

PROPOSALS FOR NEW PLANTS/EQUIPMENT

Building a plant, purchasing new equipment, and making similar investments are judged primarily on their internal rate of return, the return on investment.

"When you spend your own money," says Brennan, "and it does not show a return in sales, you are looking at a hard cost and it is going to be scrutinized more thoroughly."

The presenter has to convince management that this investment is going to reduce costs. They also have to show why the present equipment is not doing the job. If, for instance, there is a piece of equipment on the line that requires abnormal maintenance and supervision, it may be a prime candidate for replacement by a machine that requires half the supervision and has twice the reliability.

Engineers and product line managers encounter this situation frequently. They may know of an improved, faster piece of machinery, or they may even develop one internally that does the job. Either way, it has to be sold to management.

Internal replacement proposals are not confined to machinery that produces parts for a company. The same thing happens in the office environment when a copy machine can no longer handle the volume a company requires. The office manager has to convince management that a new copy machine with sufficient capacity and twice the speed is worth buying.

Some of these proposals are no more than a verbal request from secretary to boss. Others develop into full-blown presentations between the proposer and top management. Behind both are the same questions: How much? Why? Can we get along without it? If we do not buy it now, what does that mean to our future?

Managers do not want to expend funds for equipment that does not bring in revenue. The presenter has to prove the old machine is not doing the job, it is costing too much production time and wasted manhours, and it may not last long based upon repair records.

None of these factors can be ignored when making a presentation. Too many times a manager loses his case for a new idea, piece of equipment, or R&D funds because of a lack of research. Never "wing" it or try selling something off-the-cuff. The key to selling management is to have a well-researched, fact-filled presentation. Emotion never sells.

OPINIONS FROM DECISION-MAKERS

Research involves more than putting together facts and figures on costs. It also means sounding out fellow managers and decision-makers and finding out what their attitude is towards the idea.

One reason the product manager for the record company failed was that he did not find out what the decision-makers thought in advance. Were they interested in a female singer? If not, why? He failed to accurately assess their objections *before* the presentation. There is no greater mistake than failing to get the opinion of others who will be involved in the decision.

Bounce ideas off managers. Find out their opinions. Revolutionary ideas do not make good fodder for internal presentations. Most successes are evolutionary. French fries are a natural adjunct for a hamburger stand. It's evolutionary. Fried chicken would be revolutionary.

If a presenter runs into opposition when bouncing an idea off a manager, it is wise to get a second opinion. If the second opinion puts down the idea, the presenter should scrutinize his thinking and go through his research data once more. He may have missed something. It is not wise to forge ahead with a presentation if two out of two surveyed are down on the concept. At best the presenter is wasting his time and management's. There is no question that sticking to it is a marvelous trait, but not when you are wrong.

On the other hand, do not always look for an enthusiastic "yes" when sounding out others with a new idea. Some managers may not want to make a commitment until they hear the opinion of others. That may sound indecisive but it is actually a cautious approach. The presenter has had weeks, perhaps months, to research his case. In five or ten minutes, he outlines it to a manager. It is unreasonable to expect the manager to offer an unqualified yes without having a chance to study the facts and figures.

Dr. Sam Schauerman says he always looks for the "noncommittal response" when sounding out people beforehand. "That usually means the person is not opposed and you can develop and present your idea."

In getting opinions from others, internal proposers often use the "fish" method. That is, they ask decision- and opinion-makers within a firm the question "what if . . . " and go from there. They are "fishing" for an opinion and suggestions. They leave the door open by asking a hypothetical question instead of making a statement.

Statements such as "I'm going to propose that we . . . " do not generate an exchange of opinions and ideas. Telling someone something is far different from asking their opinion. The flat statement seldom generates a suggestion. And the person who is being "told" may save his objections and opposition for the proposal meeting, at which time they might be an unwelcome surprise for the proposer.

FINDING OPINION-MAKERS

Surveying and obtaining opinions does something else for the proposer, says Dan McClain. "You find out if someone has a pet project or interest. Sometimes you may want to propose something that someone else has a special interest in. They may know more about it than you do, and they could be opinionated about it. Those are things you want to find out beforehand."

Within every company are managers who are opinion-makers. They have the ability to sway others, and these are the people the presenter needs to get on his or her side before the presentation.

Formal approval and opinions help every idea. When management gives its blessing to an idea, project, or whatever, they are as involved and as committed as the presenter. If they are committed they may feel obligated to see that it comes off well.

McClain, who has the power to implement ideas without getting formal approval, seldom does so because of the lack of cooperation that he will receive. Once, he says, he adopted an idea and implemented it without the approval of his executive board. When they heard about the project, they did not object, "nor would they had I presented it to them beforehand. I should have done this because they would have become more involved. They would have felt obligated and perhaps they might have helped by working on the project. Instead they had no interest and the project failed."

RISK ASSESSMENT

"One common reason for internal proposals failing," says Joe Izzo, "is because the proposer did not do an accurate 'risk assessment'." What do we stand to lose if we attempt this project? What do we stand to gain? What happens if we do not attempt it? What happens to our sales? Production? Employee morale? Those are all questions of risk and reward that relate to presentations.

If a thorough risk analysis is done, it will alleviate the concerns of management. Risk assessment, however, may require the aid of the sales manager, personnel director, vice president of finance and of manufacturing. As a rule, Izzo adds, "the more original the idea, the greater the probability of failure with your proposal regardless of the risk."

Originality, unfortunately, is the hardest commodity to sell to management. Most people prefer the status quo, particularly if it is working.

Within companies, management is conservative as well. A new idea calls for a convincing, well-researched argument. It also calls for proposers to present their concepts so they do not appear to be radical.

Whether an idea is good or bad, one thing is always true: Everyone would like to have credit for a success and no one wants to touch a failure. By surveying opinions beforehand, the presenter cannot only determine who is for and who is against, but who wants the credit.

Internal proposals can be particularly touchy when it comes to credit. Bob Ritchie, who was an executive with a large aluminum company before opening his communications firm, says his proposals usually went to the supervisory level, and if it was received with some degree of "warmth" it went to higher management where vice presidents of various divisions were on hand.

Problems emerged when proposals were well-accepted. Some supervisors, who had employees beneath them originating the ideas, were anxious for the credit. On several occasions, the supervisor would take the proposal and present it to the vice presidents without the employee present.

"If you had a supervisor who is primarily interested in furthering his or her career, you could count on your participation being minimized at the next meeting," recalls Ritchie.

In large corporations, the ambitious supervisor is found too frequently. He or she sees proposals for new ideas and products as a way up the corporate ladder. There are ways, however, to get around the ambitious supervisor, although they do have an element of risk. One way is to tell as many people as possible about your idea before it is presented to the supervisor. That way, it becomes a well-known fact that it is your idea. The supervisor cannot take the glory, but he or she could be upset that you spread the word.

An alternative is to talk to the supervisor before the presentation stage and get his opinion. If he likes it, share the credit, and suggest both of you present it to the other supervisors.

Too political? Internal presentations are loaded with politics, and the successful presenter cannot get away from them, but he or she can prepare.

"They must," says Izzo, "be extremely well-prepared. The internal presentation demands you know more about the proposed idea than anyone else and be prepared for pointed, subjective questions." "That's the importance of preparation," advises Dr. Schauerman. "Talking to your peers can be tougher than being in front of a bunch of strangers."

The way you speak is important, too, says John Hamond. "You're selling to people in-house. A dry, flat monotone does not make it. Successful proposers have some pizzaz. They're dynamic."

They also have a grasp on the amount of time they should take. "Never go over that half hour," cautions Brennan. "Don't ever forget that the managers in the room are busy, too. Brevity is one of the keys. Ramble and you will never sell the idea."

ORGANIZATION

Be organized. Internal proposers do not fly by the seat of their pants for a half-hour, either. Successful ones utilize an outline and viewgraph. They have a beginning, middle, and end to the presentation. They also stress three things:

1. Need
2. Solution
3. Benefits

Why do we need this product or idea? What will it do for us? How do we get it or develop it? What does it cost? What (profits, prestige, and so on) do we get?

There is no need for a formal proposal handout, but it is a good idea to give those in attendance copies of the viewgraph slides. Successful presenters advise against giving viewgraph handouts in advance for the following reason. "The people in the room," says Minor, "can't help but get ahead of you and the presentation. They'll end up not even listening. Hold the handouts until the end, and don't detail everything on them, either. The viewgraph should be short, concise, and to the point. It should be nothing more than an outline. It is the presenter's job to 'fill in' between the lines."

Brennan advises an "executive or management summary. The summary would cover the idea, rationale, or a statement of need, cost, and benefits. It would not be detailed."

Ritchie says there is "a need for some sizzle with the steak." By sizzle, Ritchie means a presenter does not just talk about the end product of his or her idea, but he stresses the benefits (the sizzle) to the company.

Consumers, for example, do not buy new clothing, insurance, or automobiles because they want to help the salesperson. They buy because the products provide benefits.

Management is similar. "You have to put on a show to sell them," Ritchie says. "Just because it is your own company does not mean it requires less effort than the external presentation."

WHERE GRAPHICS FIT

Graphics are more than for show. There could be a variety of department heads in the room, and graphics help to display the relationship between each. Sales, manufacturing, and financial vice presidents could be on-hand. A graphic, showing projected sales and units, enables all three to relate to each other. The sales vice president can see his goals, the financial vice president sees the dollars generated, and the manufacturing vice president can see the expanded production he may need.

STEPS IN THE NARRATIVE

The four steps in the internal presentation that should be covered in the narrative are:

1. *Objective*.   The development of widget x which will enable us to increase sales by 30 percent and profits by 15 percent because of the buyers in the marketplace.
2. *Approach*.   Appropriate funds for prototype. Plans already drawn. Manufacture prototype, test, make additional market revisions if needed.
3. *Cost*.   Prototype will cost $X. Testing $X.
4. *Schedule*.   Approximately 90 days for prototype; development based upon existing plans; 30 days for testing; 60 for revised testing; and 14 days for final approval and manufacturing to gear up.

After that comes the most difficult phase of the internal presentation—questions and answers. If the proposer has done his or her homework, the objections in the room will not be a surprise. They know if there is opposition.

Opposition should never be ignored. If a proposer has the capability of cooling off those who disagree, he or she should do so by addressing them. The opposition is usually well aware of the weaknesses, and if the presenter does not mention them, they will. If there is someone in the room in total disagreement, avoid arguments. The speaker who is standing can never win when he or she argues with someone in the audience who is seated. It is as though the speaker is a bully because he towers above the seated person.

If the person asks a controversial, inflammatory question in a negative tone of voice, do not argue. Minor tries to make something positive out of it. "I will say 'that's a good question.' Then I give my version of the answer. By recognizing the validity of the question, you diffuse the situation."

Astute presenters know "who the players are." They know what kind of questions and from whom they will come. They also know the tone of the queries if they have done their homework and there will be few objections that will take them by surprise.

WHY PEOPLE OBJECT

Reasons behind objections are varied and not always obvious. Suppose there is an internal proposal for a new program that has a chance of doubling production. The presenter may feel that the objections will all be centered around the feasibility of the program and how effective the sales plan happens to be. This may not be the case. For example, an objection could come from the vice president of manufacturing, only three years away from retirement, who says to himself, "If we get into this program and it goes, I will have to change our plants all around. It may involve weekend work. I'm against it. I will not work weekends when I am just three years away from retirement."

That scenario comes from an actual case. Some years ago, the vice president of a division within a major recording company turned down the opportunity to sign and release records by a group that was destined to become one of the biggest-selling acts in history.

His reasoning had nothing to do with his ability to see the sales potential of the group. He opposed the signing because he did not believe the company could actually manufacture enough records to keep up with demand. If they were unable to do so, they would have to go to other companies and subcontract manufacturing. This would have taken many hours of additional time from the executive's schedule. His company passed up the opportunity.

How do you prevent a program from being killed because of personal reasons? There is no magic remedy. It is difficult, especially in a large company where the presenter may not intimately know all the personalities involved in a decision-making process. But by sounding out objections beforehand, the doubts could surface.

Internal proposals are more subjective and generate more disagreements than external ones. Subjectivity also includes jealousy. Dr. Schauerman, who has seen jealousy enter numerous academic situations involving proposals, says "that it is one of the most difficult objections to force out in the open. Most of the time the presenter will never know."

The presenter may want to approach the person he or she suspects is jealous. Outline the proposal, and get a reaction. From that reaction, it is sometimes possible to determine if jealousy is going to play a role in the decision-making. By knowing, the presenter has a chance to devise a strategy to combat the jealousy at the time of the presentation.

There is no foolproof technique to overcome jealousy. Sharing the credit is an alternative, but no guarantee. Some of the best internal proposal ideas ever devised have been killed because of jealousy. It is not a good idea to avoid those who are in opposition, regardless of their reason. Many presenters confine their remarks and concentrate on the faces of those who will support them. That does not eliminate the opposition. It may infuriate them, however.

Opposition can be effective even if it is in the minority, says Izzo. "If there is a management team of five and two are opposed, the idea has a good chance of losing. Few management teams will let themselves be torn apart, and it is much easier to turn the proposal down than to live with two disgruntled fellow managers."

Minor adds, "If the voices are loud, you can lose easily. Even if three out of five favor your proposal, if those three are softspoken you will probably lose because the others are so vocal."

THE CEO AND THE PRESENTATION

Vocal opposition can be surmounted, however. "If you gradually warm them up, and slowly build your case," says Izzo, "you have an excellent chance of overcoming opposition. It is only when you hit people over the head that you will firm their opposition and lose. Most people in management are flexible. They can be swayed."

While there is a divergence of opinion as to how flexible the decision-makers might be in a room, there is unanimous agreement on how to treat the CEO if he or she should be in the room.

Never argue with anyone, especially the CEO. There is a difference between arguing and exchanging ideas, however. A presenter can cite facts and evidence, but never raise your voice. Make sure everyone understands what you are saying before moving on. If data is being used that was previously used, and someone does not remember it, do not embarrass them by saying, "I showed you this before." There is no quicker way to turn off a manager and possibly turn the tide against the presentation.

The preferred method is to say something such as, "Let me review this with you." Bring the person in the room who has doubts up to speed. Do not act as if they should know. Never put them down "or the game's over," emphasizes Minor.

How to Write Winning Proposals

Proposal writing has nothing to do with creative writing, nor does it have anything to do with stringing together descriptive adjectives and superlatives.

Universities hire professional grant writers, but it is not for their ability to write polished prose. Rather it is because the professional has contacts, and he knows who to call and talk to in order to make his written grant more saleable.

Proposal writing can be learned; it does not require the skills of an English professor or a polished writer. In fact, most defense contractors use a team of engineers and managers to answer RFPs. Despite the improbable pairing, it works.

Successful RFP proposal writers are astute gatherers of facts. Particularly in the private sector, they have excellent intuition and insight added to that fact-gathering ability. Whether writing to answer an RFP or going after a contract with a proposal in the private sector, four things should be kept in mind by the proposal writer:

1. No generalizations
2. No hyperbole
3. No adjectives
4. Keep it simple

As Sgt. Friday of the old *Dragnet* TV series used to say, "Just the facts, ma'am, just the facts." That does not mean a proposal has to be written in dry, unimaginative terms. On the contrary, the proposal *is* creative. It has ideas and solutions to a problem and/or need. Those ideas in themselves should be exciting enough to keep the interested reader on the edge of his or her seat.

- *Generalizations.* The cardinal sin—A statement with no backup, analysis, or proof. A proposal loaded with generalizations is a sure loser. Typically, the proposer sees the problem and writes something to the effect that "our firm has handled problems similar to this on many occasions. We feel confident we can do the same for XYZ company." To the person reading the proposal, that says nothing. Avoid generalizations and stick to the specifics. Proposals get down to details. The proposal writer could have rephrased that sentence and given the details of an actual situation without naming the firm.

- *Hyperbole.* Bragging and exaggerating about a firm's ability are another turnoff. Muhammad Ali always said, "I am the greatest" but no one believed him until he performed. It is the performance that convinces prospects your firm is the greatest. Citing past successes is one way for proposers to say, "I am the greatest." If a firm has rendered a "knockout" for a previous client, there is nothing wrong with mentioning it and the circumstances in the proposal. However, saying, "We are the greatest" without proper backup is not a way to win the business.

- *Adjectives.* Creative writers love them, but writers of proposals should avoid them at all cost. There is no need to describe the procedures outline in a proposal in glowing terms. The prospect is primarily interested in how you see his problem (do you see it), how you are going to solve it, and how much is it going to cost.

- *Simplicity.* Keep out the technological jargon. There is a tendency on the part of some firms, when making a proposal to a company in another industry, to try and knock the prospect off his feet with buzzwords, inside terminology, and acronyms. Avoid this temptation at all costs. There are few things more disturbing to a client than trying to read through something he cannot understand.

Those dealing in high-tech industries are going to have terms within a proposal that may be difficult to understand. If so, define them without going into detail. For example, "The X widget, which enables computer operators to catch spelling mistakes without consulting a dictionary, is one of the new advances a firm can have when they purchase our system."

By itself, X widget may not mean a thing, but with the explanatory phrase, the prospect can keep reading without getting lost or wondering what X widget means. A proposer can explain without talking down, even if there are engineers or others among the readers who understand an X widget.

Certain proposals will, of course, deal with a great amount of technology. This is particularly true of companies that submit answers to RFPs. An entire volume may be about the technology. Where there is a separate technological volume, it is advisable to stick to the high-tech terms because companies understand that volumes labeled "technology" are meant for engineers or others who have the ability to read and understand the terminology. This situation is usually found only in answers to RFPs.

Equally as important as these four rules is the need to design and write a proposal so it is readable. Double-space proposals, use headlines, indents, underlining, and boldface. This same approach should be used in RFPs, unless otherwise specified.

RFP FORMAT

One type of format for an answer to an RFP follows. This approach is utilized by one of the most successful proposal writers in the aerospace and defense field whenever he answers an RFP that does not provide a *specific* format.

Table of Contents

1. *Introduction and Summary.* This may run anywhere from two to ten pages. It is a condensed overview. The Summary is written in simple terms so that anyone can read it.
2. *Program Plan.* Detailed statement of work. Specifics as to what is required. It outlines what the firm will do, the type of testing, and evaluation points. A milestone schedule (each month or report period the winning bidder reports to the agency and is graded on

the work reported. The milestone schedule indicates when this is done). This is written in the same style as the Introduction and Summary.

3. *Technical Discussion.* Usually the largest portion of an RFP where most defense industry firms are concerned. Talks about the specific technology, how it works, how it will be changed or modified (if that is planned) to fit the agency's needs, and how the contractor is going to do what the agency wants. A combination of simple and technical is how this section is written. Use technical terms when it comes to describing equipment or a subject that requires technical language because this section is usually read by a project engineer who understands the concepts and technology.

4. *Management (Plan).* Describes the organization, who they are, shows an organization chart, lines of responsibility, personal résumés, key people, levels of effort of these people and what percentage of their time will be spent on the project. Simple, understandable language. Under this section there is usually a subsection:

   a. *Related Experience.* Do we know what we are doing? People and hardware capability.

   b. *Facilities and Capabilities.* Section on the company, the specific plant or division, its background, awards, and so on.

5. *Cost.* All costs have to be justified, and forms filled out completely. Usually a summary chart in tabular form shows labor and material costs. Then there is a detailed rationale of labor and material costs.

GRANT FORMAT

The structure for a grant is similar. When a grant does not specify a particular format, the following can be utilized:

1. Program need/needs analysis
2. Program goals
3. Program objectives (measurable)
4. Methodology—how it will be done
5. Evaluation
6. Sponsoring organization capability
7. Work plan

8. Budget and budget narrative
9. Letters of endorsement/support
10. Attachments (which could include affirmative action plans, compliance with certain laws, and so on)

STRUCTURAL TOOLS

Whether it is an RFP, a grant, or a private industry proposal that is being answered, there are certain structural tools that enhance the readability of a proposal.

Few people can read 30–40-page documents without getting sleepy. With some RFPs, the proposal can run up to 4,000 or more pages. Make the reader's job easier and he or she becomes more interested in the proposal. Paragraphing breaks up the body copy and helps the eye flow down the page. Headlines spaced within the body copy make the document more readable. For example:

Five Keys To Writing a Good Proposal

Notice that the headline has a specific number. Be specific whenever possible. Readers (and others) are intrigued by numbers. Secondly, when writing headlines try to avoid using all capitals if the headline goes beyond five words. Lengthy headlines in all-capitals are difficult to read; compare to:

FIVE KEYS TO WRITING A GOOD PROPOSAL

Boldface type or italic can be used in headlines or in the body copy to highlight certain terms. Avoid overuse of underlining or boldface—too much and the effect is lost.

Proposals should avoid long, drawn-out sentences such as this one, which make it difficult for the reader to pause, and digest a thought when it is important for him or her to do so, in order to keep the flow and idea behind the proposal in mind.

Don Kracke and Jay Abraham use ellipses . . . and parenthetical dashes—to make the proposal less formal and easier to read. It also enables the writer to make the proposal more conversational. Both believe that a proposal should sound as if one person is talking to another.

Paragraphs should not be lengthy. If a reader is going through a lengthy document, and he turns a page and finds a paragraph that runs nearly the full-length of the page, the tendency will be to give it only a superficial reading.

Use a variety of short and long sentences, but do not follow one long sentence or paragraph with another. The reader gets bored and lost.

Avoid first-person writing. The proposal should be a third-person narrative that shows the strength of the firm, not of any one individual writer.

Be positive. There is nothing more damaging to a proposer's case than writing, "*I think* we can do the job" rather than, "*We can* do the job." When an outside firm is called in to prepare a proposal, the company making the request is searching for expertise. If they could do the job themselves, they would never hire a consultant. They are going to rely on the consultant and they expect certainty. For a proposal to say "we will try" conveys lack of confidence to the potential client and is usually enough to cripple the relationship before it starts.

A manufacturer may call in an outside accounting firm because he needs help with his tax return and inventory evaluation. If the CPA says we have never done accounting work for a company in your industry, nor have we ever done an inventory evaluation—but we will try—that does not instill confidence in the prospect. There may not be superlatives or adjectives in a proposal, but there should definitely be positive statements.

Positive statements are what Jim Baxter calls "proposalmanship." Without superlatives about the proposer's company, proposals sell the company by citing a track record, résumés of key personnel, and knowledge of the field and industry. Proposalmanship also includes a description of the facilities (if it is a manufacturing or development project).

A buyer, whether it is a government agency or an independent company, has to have full confidence in the ability of the proposer's firm to do the job. Confidence is built in the client's mind when the proposal covers areas such as:

1. Showing a clear understanding of the client's need and/or problem
2. Detailing the solution

3. Experience in a similar industry or with a similar client
4. Significant accomplishments of the proposal firm
5. Background of the principals who will handle the project
6. Awards the firm has earned

The list constitutes a typical outline a consultant should follow in *gathering information* for the proposal. To answer these questions, the consultant/writer must do considerable research. In the private sector, that research is usually done through interviews with the prospective client (and his or her staff), studying trade papers which carry industry news, and talking to the prospect's competitors.

Everyone gathers information in a different manner. Bob Ritchie obtains his on the telephone, as does Jay Abraham. Don Kracke uses the telephone but also does a great deal of industry studies before he formulates his solutions.

Paul Hackett conducts a fact-finding interview that ends in determining a client's goals and objectives. After investigating and interviewing management, Joe Izzo's technique is to sit down with top management once again, and reiterate the problems he has found. It is only after they agree that Izzo's findings are correct, that he goes back and prepares the formal proposal.

If part of the solution is going to involve new ideas, Izzo will "present the ideas before I ever put them in writing. I do not want to surprise anyone. Surprises will lose you a point. If you have something original to present, ask them beforehand about it. It's relatively easy. All I usually ask is 'what would you think if . . . ' and I wait for their answer."

With RFPs, Jim Baxter puts together a proposal team with a project manager. A clear, concise outline of exactly what the RFP calls for is written. This is done by someone going through *every* page of the RFP and, on a separate sheet of paper, listing every question that is asked.

Later the proposal team works from this checklist to gather its data. The RFP may be consulted later, but most of the work is done from the information gathered on the checklist. Many RFPs are too long and complex to continually refer back to.

Listed on the checklist is the "point schedule." With every RFP, regardless of the size, each section has a point value. Some proposal writers feel that the most important part of the proposal is the section with the most points. That is not necessarily the case. Although one section can account for 50 percent of the scoring, the other 50 percent should not be taken lightly.

When preparing the answer to the RFP, some companies use a detailed, formal structure. That is, they structure the content before they write by going almost page by page.

They plan a "story" on every page or section, and each story is analyzed to make sure it fits. "Story" is a term utilized in the industry, however, the material referred to is not fiction. It can be, for instance, a detailed description of the facilities (describing them, where they are located, what advantages they may have), followed by a "story" on management (who will handle the project, their expertise).

Beginning with a Summary

Regardless of the information-gathering techniques, when a private proposal is written, the first portion the prospect will see and read is the "executive summary" or "management summary." The summary is a brief statement of the problem and the solution as seen by the proposer.

"It is an introduction or a summary. It talks about us, too. It goes into our objectives and what we expect to deliver. I avoid putting the price in the summary or in any part of the proposal. That is usually in a cover letter," says Izzo.

The price or cost is seldom in the summary and for good reason. Top management may want others in the firm to read the proposal, but that does not mean they want them to see the price.

Raelene Arrington says Coopers & Lybrand prefers a two- or three-page cover letter that it places in front of the proposal. The letter describes what Coopers & Lybrand will do, who will be on the engagement team (the people who will work on the project), what the services will be, and reiterates the problem that was found.

The cover letter and executive or management summary is designed to "grab the reader" from the beginning. Think of cover letters/summaries as advertisements. They have to attract and keep the reader interested. Lose the reader in the cover letter, and they may never get to the proposal.

To grab a prospect, the proposal firm must know exactly what the prospect's concerns are. In one case, Arrington says, a prospect had two concerns they wanted addressed. "They were concerned about our size, we were big. Would they get the service they wanted? They were also concerned about a smooth transition between our firm and the old one. The first paragraph in our summary addressed and answered both those questions. It enabled us to get the account."

Abraham, who specializes in letter proposals, maintains that whether it is a letter or bound proposal, proposal writers should keep in mind that "they are competing against other distractions." The client picks up the proposal and the telephone rings. Bam, down goes the proposal, and unless it has a provocative lead, summary, and other elements, the client may never pick it up again.

Abraham uses headlines and underlining throughout his proposals. He hits the client with a provocative headline that promises a benefit for the client at the very beginning.

"But make sure you can deliver the promise," he cautions. "Never promise something that you cannot deliver. My promises are always part of the lead or summary. They are benefits for the clients, and they cannot help but attract the reader."

Grant writers start proposals with a summary as well. In the case of the grant, the writer should always say something about what the grant recipient "hopes to accomplish. It is a conclusion that summarizes the value of the project," explains Dr. Schauerman.

Summary Formula

Nowhere, however, is there greater evidence of the importance of a summary than with RFPs. Karl Brennan says that "as you get higher in management, your proposals should be shorter." Naturally, that is not always possible with RFPs. Brennan gets around the voluminous material that must go into an RFP with a formula he has developed for executive summaries.

He will boil a 200-page technical document down to two pages. Then he adds two pages for cost, two pages for schedule, two pages for management, and two pages for "selling the company and management." If possible, there might also be one photo included of the system if it exists.

Brennan believes there is no reason to go beyond 10 pages in the executive summary. If the presenter can keep it that short "he will probably have an advantage over his competitors." RFP summaries usually do not contain costs because agencies do not want "others to be contaminated by dollar figures," laughs Sam Brownell of Boeing. The cost is thoroughly detailed in a separate volume.

The summary is the key. It indicates to the prospect whether or not to go on reading the document or if the proposer missed the problem. Every summary, whether it is written for someone in the private sector or a government agency, addresses the client's needs and outlines a solution. In the private sector, those needs should be clarified through questioning and probing, long before the proposal is written.

With RFPs, the need is not always obvious. Government documents have a tendency to ramble and use obscure language. If the proposal firm has done its job, however, they will know the need before the RFP is issued.

With local and regional agencies that issue RFPs, it is advisable to develop a checklist even though the RFP may only be 10 or 20 pages. Even though the local agency has fewer requirements, the wording at times is less clear. The bidder's conference can resolve the vagueness, however.

As RFPs get thicker and more complex, the agencies issuing them usually ask for a summary along with the proposal broken into the following three volumes of material:

1. Technology
2. Management
3. Cost

Companies form proposal teams consisting of authorities in each area before they attempt to answer the RFP. Organizational meetings are held, and each member is given an assignment that must be researched and written. There may be 20 or more people working on these lengthy proposals, and when they finish their written portion it is brought back to the proposal manager for review.

The RFP has a time limitation. Writers seldom have more than 60 or 90 days to complete the proposal, which means the competing company has to move rapidly. John Hamond's firm examines the RFP, sets up a table of contents, checklist, and appoints a proposal manager. The manager is responsible for assuring that everyone turns in their section early enough so that it can be put together in a readable form.

Most defense firms operate in the same manner, but there are weaknesses in the system. The proposal or project manager is usually technically oriented so that he or she can understand the complex engineering involved. Problems develop if the project manager overlooks the preparation of the management portion of the RFP. Although there would not be a program without the technology, the program will not run without the business—or management—end. When this unintentional "slighting" occurs, the proposal usually ends up with a weakness. The engineers may be satisfied, but management—the people who play a significant role in overseeing the project—may suffer in the eyes of the agency that is evaluating the proposal.

Contrast this approach with the typical private sector proposal outline:

1. *Summary.* An overview of the problem and solution.
2. *In-depth analysis of the problem.* This should show a thorough understanding of the prospect's company and its needs.
3. *Description of solution.* Based upon the previous section, here is what we are going to do and why. Here are the techniques we will be utilizing. New ideas are in this section as well.
4. *Timetable.* This is how long it will take. In this section, different tasks are broken down to show the length of each.
5. *Staffing.* Here are the résumés of those who will be overseeing the project.
6. *Firm's qualifications.* This gives the past history of clients we have dealt with and our notable successes, awards, and so on.
7. *Cost and/or hourly rates.* This may be in a separate document depending upon the prospect's preferences and the proposer's policy.

EFFECTIVE PROPOSALMANSHIP

Every proposal has to demonstrate a confidence level high enough so the buyer has no doubts. Remember, proposalmanship is not attained through the use of superlatives, but rather with examples, case histories, a firm background. None of these require adjectives—just the facts.

When writing a private sector proposal, the reader seldom knows if something was left out, unless it is a serious error where the writer fails to address the problem or solution. The private sector document requires checking and re-checking because there is no thorough checklist, usually only an outline. There is more guesswork involved.

Seemingly, RFPs and RFQs leave little guesswork. There are numbered questions that must be answered. One of the most common mistakes made when answering an RFP is the proposer fails to answer *every* question. The most common reason for the oversight is because of the length and complexity of some RFPs. They may run hundreds of pages, and there are usually "questions within questions."

In long, detailed RFPs that defense industry contractors face, there may be subsections within sections. "Let's say," explains Baxter, "that item number one is management. It may have 10 subsections within it, and you must respond to all 10. RFPs are detail-oriented, and it is easy to miss something extremely minute unless you have a checklist. And if you miss one, you may be out of the ballgame."

Details can determine whether a proposal will be won or not. In fact, some agencies count upon missed details to help eliminate proposals and narrow the list they have to consider.

The answers supplied should be "written in the same style as the RFP is written," advises Pat Unangst. "The greater the amount of the contract, the more closely it should follow the RFP style."

"Agencies," says Unangst, "are not looking for creativity within the answer." They want to know "did you fill out all the forms, did you answer all the questions in the subsections. If there is something technically wrong, it is easy to throw out the proposal. The theory is that the person or company that is careless in answering an RFP, is usually the person who will not do the job well, either."

Some agencies insist that every paragraph/question have an answer even if it does not apply to the proposer's company. These should always be answered, even if the answer is nothing more than "yes, we will comply."

Carol Geisbauer calls this all part of the "technical portion" of the proposal. Together with the proper grammar, spelling, facts, and figures, this portion of the RFP (or grant or RFQ) is worth 50 percent, in Geisbauer's estimation.

Spelling, for example, can have a tremendous impact with both RFPs and private sector proposals. If the reader sees a spelling error, it is not just a matter of a misspelled word. The error reflects on the company presenting the proposal. If they do not care enough to spell correctly, how much do they care about "our company"? Errors reflect carelessness in the prospect's eyes.

Negative language should not be part of a proposal, either. If there is competition between two or more companies, avoid making any disparaging remarks about the competitor in the proposal. This does nothing more than damage the proposer's chances.

The Place for Graphics

Graphics enhance the technical portion of the proposal. Regardless of a person's ability to visualize, graphics are going to be an aid. They should be used with anything that is hard to understand, especially technological sections, timetables, and schedules.

Ed Pearson is an engineer who deals extensively with planners. Although the planners are responsible for putting their stamp of approval on his drawings, Pearson has found that few can visualize, especially when it comes to three-dimensional plans.

"Don't ever assume that someone can read plans, or see the outcome," cautions Pearson, "even if they hold an engineering or planning degree. Many cannot. What is on a flat piece of paper does not have any relationship in a person's mind to the actual product or structure. If I have difficulty, and they cannot understand the graphics on the piece of paper, I try to bring in a three-dimensional model so that nothing is left to the imagination."

Graphics should be kept simple. A fancy pie chart with 18 segments, each in a different color with a dozen different patterns, does not simplify the message. Among the graphics that are helpful and enhance readership are:

Flowcharts
Bar charts
Pie charts
Matrix
Organization charts
Time and schedule

Graphics should be effectively used. That is, if there are five things the proposer's company is going to do, the five should be shown graphically (if possible). They help shorten the reading time, illustrate what is written, and clarify the message. "As much of the written material as possible should be illustrated graphically," recommends Izzo. "If graphics are used in this manner, they give an elegance to the proposal. Remember, if you do not use them, your competitors certainly will."

Proposals should be bound, and there should be a customized title or cover page. The page should have the prospect's name (the customized portion) on it. Do not use a boilerplate title page. It takes away from the personalization that is so important in a proposal. And it gives the prospect the impression that everyone gets the same "pitch." The prospective client wants to believe he or she is unique; that the consulting firm will treat them in a special way. Here is a typical title page:

Proposal of
Marketing Services
for
XYZ Corporation

February 22, 19XX

The cover page and binding gives the prospect his or her first impression of the proposer's company image. Izzo always binds his 8½ × 11 proposals sideways. The graphics are placed horizontally, enabling him to get more detail into them. It also sets his proposal "apart from the rest. Either they love you or they hate you," he says smiling. "They must have some emotion about you, and the proposal has to help create it. You do not just want to be one of the pack that they cannot remember."

Image means a great deal and is certainly part of proposalmanship. The proposal should have a uniform, neat look, and the proposal company's logo should be evident.

The logo need not be used on *every* page of the proposal. Colored paper, unless it is being used to emphasize a graphic, should be avoided. Proposals are best printed on plain white paper with black ink. Do not get too fancy, it can destroy the readability of the proposal.

To Customize or Not

The cover page, as well as the management summary, and problem/ solution are customized, but there are portions of the document that can be boilerplated, or copied verbatim from previous proposals.

Boilerplating should be handled with care. Too much and it becomes obvious to the client that this is something everyone gets. Boilerplated sections should be examined for updating each time they are used.

The résumé or management background section is usually boilerplated except for updating. Accomplishments of managers change. If, for instance, John Jones is the account supervisor, and he has just completed handling a similar job for another company in the same industry, this should be included in his résumé as well as in the executive summary. It is an important selling tool.

Carol Geisbauer restricts boilerplating to 25 percent of the proposal. "I try to be fresh, because you have a tendency to get stale if you do too much boilerplating. If you are serious about going after a client, try to think of ways you can improve the boilerplated section. You would be amazed at what pops into your mind."

Karl Brennan's RFPs contain boilerplating of facilities, policies, rules, and law. Management résumés are updated for each presentation, and of course the cost section of the proposal changes.

Written Proposal Strategy

Just as consultants strategize before interviewing prospective clients, the written portion has strategy, too. Strategies range from how the information will be gathered to how the proposal will be written and presented. Who will present it? What is really the problem?

The initial strategy consists of:

1. What will be an acceptable proposal approach for this company? Who(m) do we talk to?
2. What kind of company is this? Formal? Informal?
3. What kind of personality does it have?
4. Who is our competition? What approach will they use?
5. What are the strengths we should be emphasizing?
6. Who will be at the presentation? What will they expect?
7. How long will our presentation be? Who will make it?
8. How much risk should we take when making the proposal?

The greater the risk, the higher the reward, and "the greater chance you have of losing," says Izzo. When deciding how much risk to take, proposal companies are saying "how many new ideas shall we present . . . how orthodox or unorthodox should our approach be?"

Companies answering RFPs take risk in outlining their new ideas, often in the form of detailed descriptions of new technology. Those with new technology stamp pages "proprietary information." In most cases, the government recognizes the confidentiality of the information and it will keep the proposal information confidential even if the page is not stamped. It is, however, always advisable to stamp the pages.

With some RFPs, particularly those that are for services rather than products or technology, confidentiality is not possible. The proposal becomes the property of the agency and it can do anything with it—including giving a copy to another presenter who happens to win.

In heated competition for private companies, consultants must be prepared to take risks with their proposals. That may be the only thing that sets them apart from the competition. Companies should differentiate themselves from the competition, but they should avoid being "too different or far out." Being radical may scare the prospect. Everyone admires originality, but when a company gets too original, people back off. Too much can lose a bid for the proposer.

Every consultant should determine his company's unique selling proposition (USP). A USP differentiates one consultant from another. What does his or her company do that others do not? How do we differ, and why would it be a benefit to the client?

When it comes to proposals, the consultant's company may have some special experience in the field that none of the other candidates can claim. An accountant may have handled the installation of a computer system for a clothing manufacturer, and now he or she may be preparing a proposal for another clothing manufacturer. A defense contractor may have utilized the technology for a radar system. Now, an agency wants the same technology for an updated system.

Avoid the mention of competitors in proposals. This is particularly important when a competitor lacks expertise in an area. Never criticize or "put down" the competition. Instead, the proposal company should play up its strength. By doing so, it makes the prospect aware of its attributes and it can cause them to question competitors about their ability in the same area. When that is done, the competitor's weakness is brought out—by the prospective client.

Avoid comparisons. Automobile companies that compare their vehicles to others during 30-second TV commercials succeed in only confusing the consumers. When it is over, at best the consumer only remembers the names of both companies. He or she does not remember which had the better widget or leather upholstery. It is a common mistake made over and over again by many who market products to consumers.

Strategy includes more than finding a USP. Dan McClain's chamber recently went after a large contract with the city for a visitors' and convention bureau. The need for a bureau was known among council members, but whether or not the chamber should run it and be involved was the question.

Before McClain turned in a written proposal, a strategy session was held. The chamber members realized they were not influential enough by themselves to capture the backing of councilpeople. To compensate for the lack of influence, they developed a strategy that consisted of soliciting support of influential people in the community—people who were important to council members.

The chamber gathered its supporters, and McClain made appointments to see each of the councilmembers. Each time he visited a member to explain the program, he took someone with him who had "pull" with the particular councilmember. When the written proposal was submitted, it had letters of endorsement from each of the influencers. The chamber won its bid.

Following an initial prospect meeting in which both he and his staff are present, Bill Johnson holds a session with his people and they decide the best way to get from "point a to b. Oftentimes if we just accepted what the client said without really doing our homework, all parties would be disappointed in the proposal. The main part of our strategy is to dig out the truth."

Oral Presentation Tips

Strategy also determines how an oral presentation will be structured. In the private sector, when proposers are narrowed to the finalists, there is almost always an oral session held in front of the decision-makers.

There is no guarantee the proposal is going to be presented orally. "That's one reason I make my proposal personal," explains Kracke. "I want them to sound as if they are being made one-on-one in a room."

Oral presentations should not be a reiteration of the written. Instead the proposers should pluck out those elements which set their company apart from the competitors.

In oral presentations, time is usually limited to 30 minutes or less. Despite the relative shortness of the time, there should be visual aids. Visual aids enhance anyone's talk, and if the speaker is less than dynamic, they will help make up for that deficiency.

Much attention should be paid to the visual portion. They can be presented in several different formats. Slides (35mm) enable the presenter to utilize color.

Viewgraphs are sufficient. These inexpensive charts allow for graphics. Copies of the graphs should be made and handed out to those in attendance. A short outline of the oral presentation should also be prepared. This should not go beyond a page in length. The outline can be given out at the beginning of the session, but the viewgraphs should be held until the end. Viewgraphs spark too much curiosity, and those seated may end up looking ahead at the graphs and not paying attention to what is being said.

There is much subjectivity in an oral presentation. The audience is going to get two distinct impressions which will weigh heavily in its decision-making: (1) The appearance of the speaker and (2) the speaker's ability.

Every speaker can be equal in appearance; all it takes is grooming, but not everyone speaks equally. The wise presenter must also be conscious of not only what they are saying but how they say it. A talk littered with "uhms" and "ahs" is distracting. It seldom gets the message across. The presenter should be smooth, have exactly what he or she is going to say memorized, and do it without notes. A two-hour presentation may require notes, but not a brief, 30-minute or less talk.

The talk should follow the format of the written proposal. That is, there should be a statement of the firm's need which shows understanding by the proposal company. That should be followed by the solution. The remainder of the written document can be touched upon, and the presenter should make sure that ample time is left for the USP.

The viewgraphs should be used to illustrate any difficult or technical areas. They should show timelines or graphs, and there should be time (five minutes) left at the end of the talk for questions and answers.

In contrast to the private sector oral interview, many of those going through RFP interviews may face an entire day of proposal examination and analysis. Regardless of the time allotted and the depth of the proposal, the organization should always be the same. A statement of need followed by the solution, and then into the qualifications and other pros of the presenter.

The key to a winning oral presentation is the same as the one that is the secret of a winning written proposal—preparation. No one should "wing" a talk, regardless of how well they know the material. It seldom comes off. There is no substitute for preparation.

Pricing

Where does the bottom line belong? With most RFPs there is either a budget section or a cost volume. Either way the fees are explained in detail. Agencies are picky about where the money goes, who gets it, and exactly how much.

In the private sector, fees are not as precise. Coopers & Lybrand spells out the fees for services in the "executive summary." Bill Johnson gives prospects an engagement letter which spells out his firm's hourly fees depending upon who is doing the work. If the client goes for the proposal, he signs the engagement letter which includes everything that is in the proposal. It is similar to a contract.

Izzo's fees are in a separate cover letter, and they are estimates based upon a rate schedule he includes. Izzo, Johnson, and others avoid being pinned down to specific amounts because their time is billed primarily on an hourly basis, and the firm's needs may change.

In Kracke's proposals there are line items, each with a dollar value. The customer can turn to the end of the proposal and see the total dollars, and he can go back and begin chopping if he just wants part of the program.

Kracke always goes beyond what is asked, and supplies more programs than he is asked to submit. Psychologically this has an interesting effect on the buyer. He sees the expanded presentation with all the additional ideas and appreciates the extra work that Kracke has put into it.

With all the extras, the price may be too high. There is nothing to prevent the prospect from cutting back and spending only what his original budget allowed. Or he could spend somewhere between the original and total package.

What normally happens is if the buyer goes for the proposal, he will try and take the entire package, even if it is more than he planned to spend. Car salesmen use a similar ploy. When a prospect comes in to buy a used car, and they ask for a $3,000 auto, the salesman usually ends up putting them in a $4,000 or $5,000 car first, and then he takes them to the $3,000 model.

The prospect has had a taste of "more" and "better." The $3,000 model usually pales in comparison to the $5,000 one, and if the buyer can afford the more expensive car, he certainly will buy it. Kracke presents the same opportunity to his buyers.

CHAPTER 9

Public/Private
Winners Combined

What type of opportunities are there for private agencies to tie in with public agencies in order to generate proposals and contracts at the local or regional level?

One is through the local chamber of commerce. Every community has a chamber (a private organization). These groups are supported by the dues paid by private businesses, but they do work for the public as well as the private sector. They not only represent businesses in the community, they also promote and publicize the city in which they are located.

With costs rising every year, many local chambers are looking to cities for increased revenue. They promote the city so why not do a few additional projects for the city and earn added revenue at the same time?

That is where a visitors' and convention bureau enters the picture. Visitors' and convention bureaus try to bring in additional business and tourism. They actively market the city with letters, brochures, and other techniques in order to increase visits to the city by outsiders. The visitors' bureau usually obtains its financing through a bed tax that is paid by local hotels to the city. It is left up to the discretion of the city as to whether it will use the revenues for a bureau.

For years the City of Torrance (the third largest city in Los Angeles County) had been pondering one. The bed tax revenue was substantial, and there was grumbling among hotel owners that not enough was being done to foster tourism.

The thinking among councilpeople was to have the tourism bureau run through the city and staffed by city personnel. The local chamber had other ideas. They wanted to run and staff the bureau and be compensated for their efforts by the city. They had only one obstacle. They had to convince the city the chamber was the correct vehicle to use for a bureau.

The proposal in Figure 9–1 contains all the arguments the chamber was able to put together. It is a document that was well researched and covers all the bases.

Notice the facts and figures that are cited throughout the proposal. Aside from the "mission statement," there are few generalizations.

The proposal contains no boilerplating, and all original material was researched during a three- to four-month period. It not only plays upon the city's needs (the economic impact through more visitors), but shows the city how it can save money by running the bureau through the chamber.

It also points out that competition for the dollar is growing, and that the city without a bureau is going to be left out in the cold.

The arguments were well-researched and convincing. It won because it was thorough and addressed, in the opinion of those who made the decision, all the "doubts and questions" the city council had. It did not leave one question unresolved.

In addition, before it was written, the chamber personnel made a personal visit to each councilperson and questioned them to as to the problems they might have with a chamber-controlled bureau. One frequently mentioned objection was a lack of control and input by the city. The organization chart in Figure 9–1 answers that completely.

In the next chapter, the opportunities for tie-ins between the public and private sector is explored more fully.

**PROPOSAL TO ESTABLISH
THE
TORRANCE VISITORS BUREAU
SUBMITTED TO
TORRANCE CITY COUNCIL
BY
THE TORRANCE AREA
CHAMBER OF COMMERCE**

FIGURE 9–1. Sample proposal for private/public agency tie-in. Used with permission of the City of Torrance, Employment and Training Division.

PROPOSAL TO ESTABLISH A
TORRANCE VISITORS BUREAU

TABLE OF CONTENTS

FIGURE 9–1. (*continued*)

I. MISSION STATEMENT

The mission of the Torrance Visitors Bureau is to enhance the quality of life in the City of Torrance through the controlled activities and outreach that attract quality business, and therefore, income to support the community goals.

The Torrance hospitality market has changed dramatically in the past three to five years, resulting in a viable marketplace for the tourism or visitors industry. The visitors bureau would take advantage of the growth in the hospitality industry to accomplish greater benefits for the economy as a whole.

An increase in visitors to Torrance would mean greater retail sales, increased patronage at restaurants, growth in transportation services, more jobs for residents, and increased revenues for the City of Torrance.

Increased revenues allow the City government to continue to provide superior services to its residents, thus enhancing the quality of life for all.

FIGURE 9-1. *(continued)*

II. WHY THE CHAMBER OF COMMERCE

Of the many options available to the City of Torrance in the establishment of a Visitors Bureau, the Chamber of Commerce has the greatest background and experience in serving visitors in Torrance and has the support of the Visitors industry in Torrance. The following points are but a few of the reasons why the City Council would be interested in the Chamber's proposal to operate a Torrance Visitors Bureau:

—The Chamber can offer the active participation of the Torrance business leaders—especially those who work every day in the visitors industry and who are *the community's best experts in the field of travel marketing.*

—The city's major source of visitors is from the business community. The Chamber has ties to business in Torrance and to business groups across the nation. Through the national network of chambers of commerce and visitors and convention bureaus, the Chamber has the connections needed to get the message to business travelers about the benefits of visiting Torrance.

—The Chamber offer a business base from which membership dues to a visitors bureau could be collected, if the bureau is structured as a membership organization.

—The Chamber has been involved in some aspects of the visitor marketing area for many years. We currently provide the following services to visitors or potential visitors:

—Publish a City Map and distribute it to visitors.

—Distribute demographic information to potential visitors.

—Maintain a visitor information center in our lobby to assist visitors that are looking for local attractions or other information.

—Respond to inquiries from all over the world about Torrance.

—Distribute Torrance Magazine to chambers of commerce across the nation.

—Assist small groups wishing to hold meetings or conferences in Torrance.

—The Chamber has recently restructured Torrance Magazine by adding a Visitors Guide that will assist those staying in Torrance hotels and motels. This guide has been supported by local hotels who are planning to provide copies for each of their guests. This guide will be available in mid-April.

FIGURE 9–1. *(continued)*

—The Chamber is the only organization in the City of Torrance that has researched, planned and proposed the visitors bureau. We have conducted dozens of meetings with those in the hospitality community who provide the visitor services. We have also met with City Staff to discuss our plans and worked together with them to clarify our previous proposal.

CHAMBER'S DIRECT COMMITMENT TO VISITORS BUREAU

In addition to the visitors services that the Chamber currently provides, the Chamber would subsidize the following costs in the Visitors Bureau's first year of operation to ensure that the bureau can get a healthy start:

CONTRIBUTION	ESTIMATED VALUE OR COST
OFFICE SPACE	$ 8,000
TELEPHONE CHARGES	$ 2,700
VISITORS GUIDE (Supported by Chamber members' ads.)	$12,800
ADMINISTRATIVE EXPENSES (Office supplies, postage, etc.)	$ 3,000
STAFF SUPPORT (Reception, Accounting, Visitors Guide production, Supervision)	$10,000
MINIMUM INVESTMENT	$36,500

The Chamber also anticipates other costs associated with setting up office for two employees, but do not have cost analyses at this time.

III. ECONOMIC IMPACT

The motivation behind any community that supports a visitors bureau is economic development. Visitors bureaus are community resources that are designed to bring money into a local economy which would not otherwise be spent in the community. This additional

FIGURE 9–1. (continued)

money provides the support for jobs that are filled by local people, businesses owned by local merchants and tax revenues paid to the local government.

The Torrance Visitors Bureau would endeavor to enhance the local economy by promoting Torrance as a destination for visitors who would otherwise not visit Torrance. It is important to recognize that the impact of increased visitors is not limited to the hotel or hospitality industry. Millions of dollars are spent in Torrance already by guests in our hotels and motels. The following is just a brief list of some of the businesses that are impacted by additional visitors in Torrance:

> Advertising and Public Relations Agencies
> Attorneys
> Accountants
> Audio Visual Equipment and Services
> Auto Rental Agencies
> Banks, Savings and Loans
> Beauty Salons
> Catering Services
> Communication Equipment and Services
> Data Processing Services
> Decorators
> Delivery, Paging and Message Services
> Display Builders and Rentals
> Electrical Contractors
> Electronic Sales and Service
> Entertainment Businesses
> Florists
> Foreign Currency Exchanges
> Formal Wear Rentals
> Gift Shops
> Golf, Tennis Clubs and Shops
> Guard Services
> Hotels and Motels
> Health Clubs
> Insurance
> Medical, Dental, and Health Facilities
> Office Machine Rentals and Services
> Personnel Agencies
> Photofinishing
> Photographers

FIGURE 9–1. (*continued*)

Plumbing
Printing and Copying
Publishing
Restaurant and Hotel Suppliers
Restaurants and Other Food Services
Shopping Centers and Other Retail Businesses
Transportation Services
Typesetting Services
Utilities

IMPACT OF VISITOR SPENDING ON
LOCAL ECONOMY

According to the 1986 Corporate Travel Index Annual Survey, prepared by Laventhol and Horwath, the average Los Angeles area visitors receives $185 per diem per day. The report also showed that of all money spent by travelers in Southern California in 1986, 37.8% was spent on lodging, while 62.2% was spent on meals and other items. Of the money spent on meals, one local hotel estimates that only 15% of its guests eat dinner in the hotel restaurant, with the other 85% eating in local restaurants.

As a demonstration of the impact of visitor spending for the local economy, there is currently an international airline which provides lodging for all of its flight crew employees in one of Torrance's hotels. These employees stay in Torrance for only a few days at a time, and would probably have never heard of Torrance except for their employer's arrangements. This group of visitors spends $2.6 million each year in per diem funds that are distributed by the hotel on behalf of the airline. That money is received by the employees upon arrival in Torrance. This $2.6 million figure is in addition to the amount spent by the airline for the hotel rooms.

This airline account is indicative of the value of marketing Torrance as a destination for business travel. The account was brought to Torrance through cooperative efforts of the hotel, the City of Torrance, the Chamber and other interested parties. A visitors bureau would greatly increase the opportunity for marketing efforts such as this one which would bring additional revenues into our economy.

FIGURE 9–1. (*continued*)

ECONOMIC IMPACT AS IT RELATES TO THE TAX BASE

The two most direct benefits from visitors to the local tax base are the collection of Torrance's Transient Occupancy Tax and sales taxes from purchases in Torrance's retail businesses, or meals taken in Torrance restaurants. In the simplest analysis, these sources of revenue are the most evident benefits of increased visitors in Torrance. Taking into account the impact of visitors on the economy as a whole, however, there are other benefits which are more difficult to identify.

These include the sales made by businesses that serve the front-line visitors industry, purchases made by the additional employees needed to serve the visitors, businesses that exist solely to serve the visitors (such as auto rental, tour companies, etc.) and the overall increased business activities of the community. These increases in business will result in increases in other taxes such as utility users tax, property taxes, construction fees, business licenses, etc.

Another indirect benefit of The Chamber of Commerce marketing Torrance to visitors is that business people are the type of visitors likely to visit Torrance. These same people are targets for the office and industrial parks which currently are seeking tenants, as well as those projects that are being planned and built. These projects are much more profitable as tax sources when occupied. Lodging these business travelers in Torrance provides them with an opportunity to experience the benefits that our city offers a business which is considering a move.

IMPACT OF A DIMINISHING MARKET SHARE ON THE LOCAL TAX BASE

Although the bulk of this proposal focuses on the advantages of adding visitors to the current visitors market in Torrance, a review of the construction plans in the South Bay area would indicate that competition for visitors is growing at an alarming rate and that without an increased marketing effort, Torrance may find the occupancy rate of its hotels actually decreasing, with an accompanying decrease in revenues from transient occupancy sales and other taxes. The following is a review of major hotel activity in and around Torrance:

—Based on a survey of the ten major hotels in the South Bay, average occupancy is just below 62%. We estimate that the major Torrance hotels are about 5% higher, but smaller motels about the same.

FIGURE 9–1. (*continued*)

—Hotels in the City of Redondo Beach in 1986 included 570 guest rooms with an occupancy rate of approximately 65%.

—Torrance hotels include 1,770 rooms (not including Downtown residential hotels).

—Proposed hotel rooms include:
Redondo Beach—379 rooms (Sheraton and Pier Inn)
400 rooms proposed for next two years
Torrance—583 rooms (Madison Park, Marriott expansion, Marriott Courtyard)
600 rooms (Gascon Mar Development)
Carson/Harbor Gateway—1,150 rooms
(Holiday Inn, Radisson, Embassy Suites, Compton Plaza)

—Additional hotel construction is also occurring in the Long Beach and El Segundo/LAX area.

The Torrance area hotel market, if all of the proposed projects are indeed constructed, would increase by more than 2,000 rooms. Considering the current occupancy rates in the area, 60–65%, it would appear that Torrance will have to prepare for a decline in occupancy or make efforts to draw additional visitors to its hotels.

According to leaders in the Torrance hotel industry, a significant downturn in the current occupancy rate would lead to price-cutting measures. This price-cutting would results in tremendous pressure on the smaller motels in the area, forced to compete with the larger hotels. Depending on the severity of the downturn, operating small motels could become unprofitable.

Transient Occupancy Tax collection would fall-off in three ways:

—Room rates would be lower, therefore, lowering the dollar amount of tax collection.

—Less visitors staying in Torrance would result in less rooms occupied and less transients paying the tax.

—If small motels are forced out of the market, the City would lose a potential source for TOT revenues.

IV. TARGET MARKETS

It is clear that Torrance's largest target market consists of business travelers, both domestic and foreign. Additional markets which are appropriate for Torrance are small associations and other groups and some leisure travelers.

FIGURE 9-1. (*continued*)

253

Torrance's strong business community has naturally drawn business travelers, especially from Japan. There are literally millions of business travelers who would just as soon stay in Torrance as in the LAX area, Pasadena, Anaheim or other places in Southern California, if Torrance was a known destination for them.

With its two main hotels, the Holiday Inn and Marriott, and its soon-to-be-completed Fine Arts Center and Theater, Torrance can successfully recruit and serve small associations, business meetings, and other groups of 800 to 900 participants. Without a major convention center, Torrance is not in a position to compete for major conferences, but regional and statewide conferences for many groups would be ideal for Torrance.

Leisure travelers wishing to visit Southern California in general would be better served staying in Torrance with its pleasant weather, safe environs, beach access and convenient location than in a lot of locations that currently ply the leisure trade in Southern California. While this type of tourism would not be the top priority of a visitors bureau, Torrance could expand this area of tourism in some significant way.

The main task of the visitors bureau will be to create an image among these groups, especially among business travel arrangers, that Torrance is a new and better place to stay if you're doing business or planning a small conference in Southern California.

V.   PROPOSED ORGANIZATIONAL STRUCTURE

The Torrance Visitors Bureau would be a division of the Torrance Area Chamber of Commerce. It would be operated by a staff manager who would report to the Visitors Bureau Advisory Board. The chairperson of this board would be the Vice President of the Visitors Bureau Division.

The majority of the funding of the bureau would come from the City's Transient Occupancy Tax Collection. A specific contract would be negotiated by the City and Chamber for the expenditure of these funds. We would not recommend that these funds be administered as an amendment to the existing contract between the City and Chamber. All funds which are contracted or collected for visitors bureau purposes would be placed in a separate account and not in the Chamber's general fund.

Other funds would be collected as membership dues from companies which participate in the visitors bureau activities. These funds and

FIGURE 9–1.   (continued)

any other funds collected would also be placed in the special visitors bureau account.

The Visitors Bureau Advisory Board would oversee the operation of the bureau and would approve all expenditures. The chairman of this board would serve as a vice president of the Torrance Area Chamber of Commerce, and the Board of Directors of the Torrance Area Chamber of Commerce would also have to approve all expenditures by the bureau. The City of Torrance, through its contract administration, would also approve any expenditure of City funds, either through a quarterly accounting or another approved method.

The chart below describes the Advisory Board:

City of Torrance (Contracting Agency)

+

Torrance Area Chamber of Commerce (Contractor)

+

Visitors Bureau Advisory Board V.P. of Visitors Bureau Division, Chairperson

+

Hotel City	Hotel Chmb.	Rest-aurant VB	Retail VB	Media VB	Open VB	City Manager Ex-Officio	Chamber Manager Ex-Officio

The Chairperson would be appointed by the Board of Directors of the Chamber, as would one of the hotel representatives.

The other hotel representative would be appointed by the Torrance City Council.

The other members would be elected from among the membership of the Visitors Bureau.

We believe that this board would be representative of the industries that are directly involved in visitors service, leaving one open seat for other individuals that may be involved in the visitors industry or in an indirect, but supportive, business.

This board would also assure that the best travel marketing experts in the community are guiding the visitors bureau efforts. Promoting

FIGURE 9-1. (continued)

travel is a business. It takes skill, imagination, energy and money to do it properly. Like any successful business, many factors must be balanced and woven together to develop a package worthy of a consumer's investment.

VI. FUNCTIONAL RESPONSIBILITIES

The visitors bureau, once staffed, must work with local businesses, community leaders, residents and educational leaders to determine the community's needs with regards to visitors. Once these needs are determined, the visitors bureau would inventory the City and its amenities to develop materials for a marketing plan. This plan would define a program for outreach to key feeder cities in the U.S. and other nations that would lead desirable visitors to Torrance.

Details of the marketing plan would depend on the results of the study, however, the bureau will likely make use of the following resources to accomplish its goals:

—Development of an attractive brochure, logo and other printed material (visitors guide) which can be distributed to interested travel planners.

—Joint participation in the activities of existing tourism agencies such as the California Office of Tourism, Travel Association of Southern California, Western Association of Convention and Visitors Bureaus and all other agencies that promote domestic and international travel to Southern California. Sharing costs stretches budgets and being associated with a known entity gives credibility and saves time, effort and dollars.

—Trade show participation. It is the most economical way to reach a wide marketplace. Therefore, development of collateral material is critical and must receive a high priority in terms of quality and thoroughness. The cost of some material might be assisted through the advertisement of Visitors Bureau members.

—Local visitors services and information. An important and often overlooked marketing tool is word of mouth. The visitors bureau will likely produce and use materials which assist visitors once they have arrived in Torrance. These materials would likely be in conjunction with the local retail community and other groups in the community which would cater to visitors.

FIGURE 9–1. *(continued)*

VII. STAFFING AND BUDGET EXPECTATIONS

In order to properly administer the visitors bureau, two staff persons would be required, a staff manager and secretary/assistant. Based on this level of staffing, a simple budget is proposed below:

REVENUE SOURCE	
$43,700	City of Torrance 1986/87 allocation carryover
$43,700	City of Torrance 1987/88 allocation
$87,400	

EXPENSES	
Rent	Provided by Chamber
Telephone	Provided by Chamber
Supplies and Equipment	Provided by Chamber
Additional Staff Support	Provided by Chamber
Salaries and Benefits	$52,300
Marketing, Promotions, Operations	$35,100

**It should be noted that this budget calls for a City allocation in 1987/88 equal to the 1986/87 allocation. The 1986/87 allocation would be carried over and funding of the visitors bureau would not begin prior to July, 1987.

It should also be noted that in order to retain status-quo funding in 1988/1989, the City would have to double its allocation for that fiscal year, to a level of $87,400.

We believe that $87,400 is a minimal amount for start-up of a visitors bureau, which is the reason for the Chamber's desire to subsidize part of the first year costs. It should be recognized, however, that $87,400 is not an adequate budget amount for the ongoing success of the visitors bureau. As can be seen in the attached Redondo Beach city staff report, only one of 19 California visitors bureaus had a budget of less than $160,000 in 1984. The smallest bureau, in Bakersfield, has a $120,000 annual budget.

FIGURE 9-1. (continued)

CHAPTER 10

The 10 Hottest Proposal Opportunities

A short time ago, in the Gulf of Mexico, a crew of workers on an offshore oil platform were frantically running back and forth trying to loosen a drill that was stuck deep beneath the surface in mud and refused to move.

The workers tried everything including a special mud lubricant designed to keep the pipes clear. Unfortunately, the lubricant was too thick. The crew had a problem—there was no specialist around to give them advice as to what they might do to free the jammed piece of equipment.

Enter a desktop computer and a special program called "Mudman" which was created by NL Baroid, the world's leading supplier of mud lubricants, and John McDermott, professor at Carnegie-Mellon University.

"Mudman" is an artificial expert. It contains all the knowledge that a trained mud engineer has in his head, plus a great deal more. "Mudman" is also a problem-solver. It offers advice to someone seeking it, and it thinks only about mud and its effect on oil drilling. "Mudman" is a specialist, and it solved the problem for the drillers more rapidly than a mud engineer could.

"Mudman" is typical of the new expertise that is developing in the computer field. Single-purpose programs are being designed to solve problems in a variety of fields ranging from medicine and law to soup* and mud.

Knowledge-based systems, where the information and logic of a person is put into a computer program, is one of the hottest new growth areas of the future. "The computer," explains Joe Izzo, "makes the judgment and calls the shots."

The difference in the logic computer and those we are accustomed to is that the computer makes the decision based upon the data and facts presented to it. There is no guesswork.

In the medical area, this decision-making capability is already being utilized by physicians, and it is radically altering the accuracy of a doctor's diagnosis, as well as solving a dilemma when a physician is faced with a patient who may have one of two possible diseases.

The computer is fed all the data possible on both diseases. Should a physician then examine a patient suspected of having one of the two, the medical information on the patient is fed into the computer as well. The question posed to the computer is which disease does the patient have: a or b?

The computer examines the information from the patient, and if necessary, comes back with a question for the doctor pertaining to the patient's data. The physician answers and enters it. The computer comes back again with another question which is answered as well.

Within minutes after the second answer, a probable diagnosis as to which disease the patient has is printed out.

"It takes extraordinary power to duplicate the mind," says Izzo, "and it is now feasible. The famed October, 1987 selloff in the stock market was generated by computers. It is an example of simple decision-making, but the computer can certainly do more complex calculations."

Decision-makers in every industry are going to be looking towards the computer for help in the future. Izzo believes the

* The soup refers to Campbell's and the steps it took when its expert on can sterilization was about to retire. For seven months, the sterilization professional fed his information into a computer with the aid of an engineer. By the time the employee retired, there was a program in his place that could solve nearly all of the company's sterilization problems.

computer will take over decision-making from middle-managers and below within a short period of time.

That also means that those who develop software technology to improve the performance of companies, will have opportunities galore for proposals. They will be able to approach companies in competitive industries with proposals for everything from pricing information based upon economic trends, to the success of a new product based upon consumer spending patterns and preferences.

For the software engineer the field can be a bonanza. Computers are going to play a role in the coming paperless office, as well, says Izzo. Laser disk technology, which is similar to a videodisk with storage data, will enable companies to store data as well as pictures at an extremely cheap cost—less expensive than filing cabinets, reams of paper, and endless file folders. It will also enable secretaries and executives to find important information more rapidly than ever. The executive with the half-dozen file folders on his desk and paperwork spread all over his credenza, will have the ability to find what he is looking for at a moment's notice. The time-savings capability alone will be a boom to business.

Those specializing in computers and installation are on the verge of another breakthrough. In the past, it has always been the data processing department that has the information and controls the output, but competition is creating a demand for rapid information. Each department within a company will have its own data processing, and the computers will be tied together through a special network.

This computer integration, where the personal computers of one company are all working as one unit, means that everyone at one personal computer can have access to the database. No longer will there be delays because one department has to request information from another because it does not have access to the information through its own computers.

Those selling and installing computer equipment will be making proposals not to just one department (data processing), but to 10 or 15, depending upon how many exist within a firm. Multiple systems is already a breakthrough that companies in highly competitive industries are anxiously awaiting.

The need for more rapid information is equally as important in high technology industries, where the trend is faster transmission of data with smaller components. Improved electronics, semiconductors, and integrated circuits are going to be elements that every defense contractor will be anxious to see in proposals of the future. These miniaturized or reduced components are also going to require greater control of the environment through improved cooling and refrigeration systems.

Those searching for other opportunities in the defense industry need only look to "Star Wars" (Strategic Defense Initiative) or SDI.

Whereas most associate SDI with a shield that will help protect the United States from missiles, those developing products for the program are already seeing a host of other applications for the technology.

"Spinoff" products and applications will mean that one day laser technology can be used, for example, in the field of medicine. A pinpoint beam can be utilized to kill a potentially deadly virus within a patient. Laser technology also means that dangerous drilling within mines can be taken over by nonhuman elements, and hazardous materials can be manipulated without danger of harming someone.

"Star Wars" has attracted comment and criticism from those within and outside the media who question its viability. One thing, however, that cannot be denied—its technology will be something that dozens of industries, and millions of people, will benefit from.

In a related industry, the crowding of major city airports has already put pressure on aerospace companies to develop short-range aircraft that can feed major airlines and airports from smaller suburban facilities. It is not, however, just a matter of developing these smaller, more economical airplanes. Along with the development comes a demand for more comfort and features that will help feeder airlines attract more passengers.

Thus companies that have—or are developing—technology in the area are going to have a host of proposal and contract-generating opportunities for the future. Even as automobile companies are working on radar systems that will enable motorists to be ensured of accident-free driving, airlines are searching for answers to a myriad of problems—problems that present numerous money-making opportunities for the proposers with companies that can deliver.

Not all the progress and opportunities are in sophisticated high technology fields, however. In the service sector, there are those making proposals who have already found new, unique niches. Just as the need for time saving and convenience services (and products) created drive-in banking, automatic tellers, the plethora of 7-11s, and frozen entrees for every size family, there are new problem/opportunities rapidly emerging.

An erratic tax environment in which employers find themselves paying more taxes for their employees, has created a need for service companies to develop more (and cheaper) methods of enabling employers to reward employees without paying a penalty in greater tax contributions.

As a result, a handful of innovative insurance-related firms have developed the "cafeteria plan." The plan enables an employer to give his employees the option of restructuring their compensation from "all" taxable to "mostly" taxable.

For example, a company may decide to reward a deserving employee with a raise. A portion of that raise is eaten away by taxes, and the company also finds itself paying additional taxes through its required social security contribution for the raise.

There *is* an alternative. A few select companies have gone to employers with the so-called "cafeteria plan." The plan enables an employee to select a benefit (in lieu of a raise) that is paid for with pre-tax dollars.

For instance, employee X has been selected for a $200 monthly raise. The tax structure means that the employee will only take home $100. The company approaches employee X and says "you pay $200 for major medical insurance for your family. Those dollars you pay with are after tax. In other words you have already been taxed on the $200 before you pay the medical. In lieu of your $200 raise, we will pay your major medical. How's that?"

The employee benefits and so does the company. The employee is not taxed on the $200, but he gets the benefit. The company does not have to contribute the extra social security taxes, yet it has given the employee a benefit.

These benefits do not have to be limited to major medical insurance. There are a host of other possible employee benefits that can be developed by innovative companies and sold to companies that are anxious to save tax dollars and satisfy employees at the same time.

Even in the public and educational sector, where many think nothing new is happening, there are creative ideas being proposed that can lead to more revenue and opportunities for colleges and other educational-related institutions.

The most significant trend is the tie between the public and private sectors. For instance, a major company may need more computer repair specialists for its workforce. The company has the option of advertising and screening applicants, going to an employment agency, or perhaps finding a school that is training specialists.

Ideally, companies would prefer finding the right people and training them internally on computers. This has never been cost-effective since the company generally does not have trainers on staff, nor extra computers. There is also the problem of compensating someone while they are being trained. Not many companies can afford to pay wages to a potential employee who is going through training and is still nonproductive.

Thus the tie-in between public/private sectors has become a booming industry. What happens is the public sector (a college perhaps) may approach a private company and say "we know you are in need of computer repair specialists. We suggest you submit a proposal to the government in which you hire the people to train, we supply the computers and training, and the entire project will be underwritten by the government."

Through a grant or proposal, the program is funded. The college is paid partially by the private company and partially by the government. The computers and trainers are placed inside the company by the college. The exact proportion of funds and where they come from will vary, but in the end the private and public sectors enter into a joint venture with government backing.

The government sees the venture as a way to not only decrease unemployment, but to put those who are unemployable (the unskilled) in positions where they have a future. These are the types of innovative programs that have replaced the "war on poverty" approach in which the government simply hired unskilled, unemployed people to work on federal, state, or local projects for a limited time.

Interestingly, most of these programs are not originated by the government. They usually come from someone or an institution in the private sector that sees a need and approaches the government (or another private company) with a possible solution.

Case in point: The Hispanic population in the United States has a high rate of dropout from high school. This increases the growing pool of unskilled, unemployed young adults.

There is a clear need to develop programs that will encourage Hispanics (as well as other minorities) to stay in school. Some educators see the cause of the problem as being the youngsters' inability to see the need for education. They see no reason to stay in school to learn to read and write, because many feel there will be no opportunity for college because of a lack of family funds.

Several years ago, a number of community colleges within one area saw the need and made a proposal to a national foundation. The program consisted of recognizing minority youngsters as early as the 9th grade. They were high risk, with a high probability of dropout before they ever graduated high school. They were told that as they went through high school they would be "given" money for every "A" and "B" they earned in a class. These funds would be set aside and made available to them if they went on to college.

The program lasted four years, and in that time the retention among these students in high school jumped to 83 percent. Nearly 70 percent went on to college.

Why? There are numerous theories that include the motivation being partly money, partly that they could see there was opportunity, and the proper incentive—one they could relate to—was put in place.

Whatever the reason, it worked. As a result, the government and foundations are looking for similar programs and proposals. This is certainly not the first time that the government has become involved in a project that was brought to them by those in the private or public sector.

Governmental tie-ins go beyond the education area. One of the most rapidly growing segments for proposals involves private companies contracting with local, state, and federal agencies for services.

With tighter budgets, every level of government is seeking ways to reduce costs. At the local level, it may be a city eliminating its trash department, and contracting with an independent garbage firm to pick up resident's trash.

Or it could be for building maintenance, parks and recreation, private library services, or even providing drivers to operate government-owned vehicles to transport senior citizens. The bottom line is the city does not have to come up with funds for payroll and employee benefits. Tie-ins between the private and governmental sectors are the wave of the future.

What is next? Where are the needs? For every new technological advancement, one method of doing things may become outdated but a half-dozen new opportunities may be created.

The computer is rapidly making the typewriter a vanishing species. At the same time, the computer has created new opportunities for those who not only design systems, but for furniture and disk manufacturers as well as innovative software companies and a dozen other related industries.

The cassette tape has cut deeply into the sales of long-playing records, but it has created new marketing opportunities with everything from books on tape to recording important lectures.

Where is your industry going, and what will it need in order to get there? Can you foresee the need and propose the solution? If so, you could be writing the winning proposal.

INDEX